The Best Of
2007

TRAVEL +LEISURE

The Best Of
2007

THE WORLD'S GREATEST HOTELS RESORTS +SPAS

TRAVEL +LEISURE
BOOKS

AMERICAN EXPRESS PUBLISHING CORPORATION
NEW YORK

TRAVEL + LEISURE THE BEST OF 2007
THE WORLD'S GREATEST HOTELS, RESORTS, AND SPAS
2007 EDITION

Editors Laura Begley, Nina Willdorf
Project Editor Karen Lehrman
Art Director Howard Greenberg
Photo Editor Robyn Lange
Contributing Editors Andrea Bennett, Melinda Page
Copy Editors Mike Iveson, Ed Karam, Steve Levine,
Margaret Nussey, Shazdeh Omari, Ronni Radner, Kathy Roberson
Assistant Editor Xander Kaplan
Assistant Book Editor Bree Sposato
Reporters Sarah Forrest, Jaime Gross, Amy Gunderson,
Jessica Merrill, Shane Mitchell, Meredith Muegge, Stephanie Putter,
Horacio Silva, Fan Winston
Researchers Robert Alford, Angela Fleury, Jennifer Flowers,
Adam Markovitz, Suzanne Mozes, Mary Staub
Proofreader Susan Groarke
Production Editor David Richey
Editorial Assistants Christine Ajudua, Stirling Kelso,
Caroline Patience

TRAVEL + LEISURE

Editor-in-Chief Nancy Novogrod
Creative Director Nora Sheehan
Executive Editor Jennifer Barr
Managing Editor Michael S. Cain
Associate Managing Editor Jeffrey Bauman
Research Editor Mario R. Mercado
Copy Chief Jane Halsey
Photo Editor Katie Dunn
Production Manager Ayad Sinawi
Editorial Business Associate Andrew G. Forester

AMERICAN EXPRESS PUBLISHING CORPORATION

President and Chief Executive Officer Ed Kelly
Senior Vice President, Chief Marketing Officer Mark V. Stanich
Vice President, Books and Products Marshall Corey
Senior Marketing Manager Bruce Spanier
Assistant Marketing Manager Sarah Ross
Production Director Rosalie Abatemarco Samat
Corporate Production Manager Stuart Handelman
Senior Operations Manager Phil Black
Business Manager Tom Noonan

ISBN 978-1-932624-17-5
ISSN 1559-0372

Published by American Express Publishing Corporation
1120 Avenue of the Americas, New York, New York 10036

Distributed by DK Publishing, Inc.
375 Hudson Street, New York, New York 10014

Manufactured in the United States of America

Cover design by Howard Greenberg

Opposite: A beach *palapa* at the Maroma Resort & Spa, Riviera Maya,
Mexico; photographed by Martin Morrell.
Front Cover: The Reefs, Southampton, Bermuda; photographed by
Annie Schlechter.
Back cover, from left: A room at Mollies Boutique Hotel in Auckland,
New Zealand; photographed by Kieran Scott. A beach *palapa* at the
Maroma Resort & Spa in Riviera Maya, Mexico; photographed by Martin
Morrell. Mirror-steel flourishes on the Hotel Marqués de Riscal in
Elciego, Spain; photographed by Javier Salas.

CONTENTS

KEY TO THE PRICE ICONS $ UNDER $250 $$ $250-$499 $$$ $500-$749 $$$$ $750-$999 $$$$$ $1,000 AND UP

KEY TO THE PRICE ICONS $ UNDER $250 $$ $250–$499 $$$ $500–$749 $$$$ $750–$999 $$$$$ $1,000 AND UP

Como Shambhala Estate at Begawan Giri, in Ubud, Bali.

INTRODUCTION

"Where have you been lately?" This is an endlessly interesting question that the editors at *Travel + Leisure* and I love to field. Many of our answers may be found in *The Best of 2007*, the second in an annual series of books that celebrates the hotels, resorts, and spas we consider the most intriguing right now. We have included a wide range of properties across the globe: some are brand-new, while others are classics that retain—or have recently polished—their luster.

Given the tempting worldwide possibilities, choosing the distinctive destinations on the following pages required the editors of *Travel + Leisure* to review the latest hospitality trends that are defining, or even changing, our times. We celebrate the growing emphasis on authenticity, as so many new properties harness local resources and reflect appropriate regional styles. We are also glad to see that craftsmanship is being held in high regard, and designers, artists, and chefs increasingly recognized for the importance of their contributions. A new kind of service is emerging, more personal and less by the book, making us feel recognized as individuals and at home.

Our quest for innovation has led us to a classic property in London, which has undergone a dignified but cozy reinvention, and the fanciful collaboration of a hotel impresario and an artist in Manhattan. Cities everywhere—from Miami to Istanbul and from Buenos Aires to Hong Kong—call out to us with their vibrant new crop of places to stay. And in Spain's Rioja wine region, we've admired the dazzling results of a renowned architect's first hotel commission. Even in our favorite enduring hill towns of Italy, we've found new *alberghi* we love. We've traveled to the far corners of the world—to Fiji and sub-Saharan Africa—and journeyed back to enjoy the simple pleasures of white-sand beaches and a glass of wine at sunset in Mexico and the Caribbean.

All of the properties you are about to discover have been covered in *Travel + Leisure* during the past year. Throughout, we've flagged the World's Best Award winners—the hotels and resorts that received the highest scores in our most recent annual readers' poll. The rankings are based on the properties' consistent level of quality in categories such as food, décor, and service. You'll find the rankings, plus a directory of our readers' top hotel choices, at the back of the book.

As you explore these hotels, we hope you'll be as inspired as we were and will be able to use this book as your own tool to answer the question, "Where have *you* been lately?"

NANCY NOVOGROD, EDITOR-IN-CHIEF

UNITED STATES + CANADA

The infinity pool of the Mandarin Oriental, in Miami.

THE
BEST
OF
2007

UNITED
STATES
+
CANADA

Teddy Bears Picnic, by artist and designer Julian Schnabel, in the Rose Bar at the Gramercy Park Hotel, above. Above right: A guest room. Opposite: Owner Ian Schrager (seated) and Schnabel in the Jade Bar, shortly before the hotel's opening.

Gramercy Park Hotel

NEW YORK, NEW YORK

As boutique hotels have begun to lose their novelty, fashion arbiters have been wondering what will come next. Leave it to Ian Schrager, the man responsible for Morgans, the Royalton, and the Mondrian, to be one of the first to turn the page. In his $210 million renovation of the venerable Gramercy Park Hotel, Schrager stepped away from the ironic modernism of his longtime design partner, Philippe Starck. Instead, he turned to artist Julian Schnabel, who imbued the property with his signature flamboyance. In the 185 rooms, velvet-upholstered beds mix with long-armed black-metal lamps. And in the lobby, a Venetian glass chandelier is suspended above an elaborate Aubusson carpet, surrounded by monumentally scaled artwork by Cy Twombly and—no surprise—Schnabel himself.

2 Lexington Ave., New York, N.Y.; 866/784-1300 or 212/920-3300; www.gramercyparkhotel.com; doubles from $$$

THE
BEST
OF
2007

UNITED
STATES
+
CANADA

Julian Schnabel's *Blue Japanese Painting No. 3,* in the Jade Bar at the Gramercy Park Hotel.

Nine Zero

BOSTON, MASSACHUSETTS

Count Nine Zero as one of the design-oriented hotels able to successfully balance cool details with a genuinely inviting ambience. The guest rooms, with soothing butter-yellow walls and ebony-stained furnishings, are at once sultry and functional. You get a five-foot-wide hefty maple desk instead of the usual boutique-hotel wedge of fiberglass, plus free Wi-Fi access, Ethernet ports, a halogen lamp, and a fully adjustable, ergonomic, leather-upholstered Humanscale Freedom desk chair. From your room, you can gaze upon either the soaring white steeple of the Park Street Church or the lichen-cloaked headstones of the Granary Burying Ground, the resting place of Paul Revere and John Hancock. On the second floor is the well-reviewed in-house restaurant, Spire, which combines influences from France, Italy, Spain, and Portugal with seasonal New England ingredients.

90 Tremont St., Boston, Mass.; 866/646-3937 or 617/772-5800; www.ninezero.com; doubles from $$$

+ FOUR MORE NEW BOSTON HOTELS

JURYS BOSTON HOTEL

Set in one of the city's last Italian Renaissance Revival buildings, Jurys has an ultra-modern lobby and 225 subdued guest rooms. *350 Stuart St., Boston, Mass.; 866/534-6835 or 617/266-7200; www.jurys-boston-hotels.com; doubles from $*

RITZ-CARLTON, BOSTON COMMON

Sleeping in this glass-and-steel high-rise is like collapsing onto a big pile of money, from the feather beds to the butler who will draw your bath. *10 Avery St., Boston, Mass.; 800/241-3333 or 617/574-7100; www.ritzcarlton.com; doubles from $$$*

ONYX HOTEL

At this 112-room Kimpton, in lieu of a chocolate on the pillow, you may be issued an Atomic Fireball. Modestly sized rooms are done up in urban-bordello chic. *155 Portland St., Boston, Mass.; 866/660-6699 or 617/557-9955; www.onyxhotel.com; doubles from $$*

HOTEL COMMONWEALTH

Stay at this mansard-roofed McChâteau for the amenities: Mascioni robes, L'Occitane bath products, Voss bottled water. *500 Commonwealth Ave., Boston, Mass.; 866/784-4000 or 617/933-5000; www.hotelcommonwealth.com; doubles from $$*

The entrance to the Jurys Boston Hotel, in Back Bay. Opposite, from left: The living area of the Cloud Nine Suite in Nine Zero; a leather headboard, found in all rooms.

THE
BEST
OF
2007

UNITED
STATES
+
CANADA

The Garden Room in the
Mayflower's Spa House.

Mayflower Inn & Spa

WASHINGTON, CONNECTICUT

Facing an oak-shaded pond in rural Connecticut, the
stately Mayflower Inn's recently added Spa House
is a back-to-nature, 20,000-square-foot sanctuary
where you can get in touch with your inner Thoreau.
Manhattan-based designer Randy Ridless (who
masterminded the redesign of Burberry's flagship
boutiques) collaborated with the owners to create a
lavish yet serene interior: a Willem de Kooning abstract
hangs in the sun-filled Garden Room, and hand-painted
frescoes by local artist Matt Wood illuminate the sea-
green hallways. Eight treatment rooms are available for
sweet-violet facials and wild-lime shiatsu massages.
Daily activities range from the rigorous (hikes in nearby
Steeprock Reserve, aquatic Pilates) to the informative
(Reiki, yoga, tree-specimen lectures). Balancing all that
physical activity are cocooning watercolor classes and
knitting circles. And then there's the conscientious
cuisine (think carrot-cardamom couscous with Pacific
halibut), presented in a celestial-blue loggia.

118 Woodbury Rd., Washington, Conn.; 860/868-9466;
www.mayflowerinn.com; doubles from $$

Guest suite 103 at the
Woodlands Resort & Inn,
above. Above right:
The living room in a
guest cottage. Opposite:
The exterior of the
neo-Georgian hotel.

Woodlands Resort & Inn

SUMMERVILLE, SOUTH CAROLINA

If the walls at Woodlands weren't so discreet, they'd
tell a tale of antebellum grandeur, party-giving as civic
duty, and romantic skullduggery. This 1906
neo-Georgian mansion with a whiff of Tara was
commissioned by Pennsylvania railroad baron Robert
Parsons as a winter getaway in Summerville,
24 miles outside Charleston. In Parsons's time,
Summerville was a destination for people who had a
deep desire to be considered fashionable. One hundred
years later, it remains a hot spot, thanks to Woodlands'
second act as a 19-room hotel in a setting of forests
and formal gardens. At check-in, the tack-sharp
concierge serves guests peach-infused iced tea, with
orange slices and simple syrup on the side. And every
time you turn around, someone is offering you a biscuit.

125 Parsons Rd., Summerville, S.C.; 800/774-9999 or 843/875-
2600; www.woodlandsinn.com; doubles from $$

THE
BEST
OF
2007

UNITED
STATES
+
CANADA

The Fearrington
House's columned
porch, above. Above
right: Room 9.

Fearrington House Country Inn

PITTSBORO, NORTH CAROLINA

WORLD'S BEST Some hotels should come with a warning label. Fearrington's would read "Includes massive retail and residential components." Eight miles from Chapel Hill, the 33-room inn is part of a purpose-built "village," complete with shops and a 1,300-acre subdivision, but guests can easily avoid the larger complex if they desire. Fearrington's own grounds encompass five gardens, but its soul is in its restaurant, which is folded into a 1927 farmhouse. British chef Graham Fox goes for broke, reinterpreting regional fare with a French twist (praline mousse with marshmallow ice cream). The rooms, which display original Southern artwork, have recently been renovated in a happy and unpretentious mix of checks and toiles.

2000 Fearrington Village, Pittsboro, N.C.; 800/277-0130 or 919/542-2121; www.fearrington.com; doubles from $

Blackberry Farm

WALLAND, TENNESSEE

WORLD'S BEST About 25 minutes from Knoxville, Blackberry is like a south of the Mason-Dixon Line edition of a Currier & Ives print: ribbons of white fences, a pond stocked with catfish, and houses constructed from Tennessee fieldstone. Set on 4,200 acres in the Great Smoky Mountains, Blackberry's 51 rooms—spread throughout the main house, three guesthouses, and 20 cottages—are done in a plush Anglo-American idiom, complete with fringed swags and decorative pillows in fancy fabrics. Regulation rockers are soldiered onto the front lawn for the day's Big Moment: sundown with tumblers of Hirsch 20-year-old bourbon.

1471 W. Millers Cove Rd., Walland, Tenn.; 800/273-6004 or 865/984-8166; www.blackberryfarm.com; doubles from $$$, including meals

A view of Old Walland Pond and the boathouse at Blackberry Farm.

THE
BEST
OF
2007

UNITED
STATES
+
CANADA

21c Museum Hotel

LOUISVILLE, KENTUCKY

Louisville's newly opened 21c ranks as a bona fide cultural institution in the making, not just a hotel with art. Designed by New York architect Deborah Berke, the 91-room property houses a $10 million collection of paintings, sculptures, photos, and video installations by living artists (hence the hotel's name, a reference to the 21st century). Most of the art comes from the personal collection of owner and philanthropist Steve Wilson and his wife, Laura Lee Brown. (Upon check-in, guests receive iPods preloaded with customized music or a narrated tour of the collection.) Occupying five 19th-century brick buildings, 21c showcases Berke's spare-but-polished industrial style of exposed-brick walls and bead-board ceilings. Old poplar floorboards were turned into bar fronts, and recycled carpet backing became the bar's floor.

700 W. Main St., Louisville, Ky.; 877/217-6400 or 502/217-6300; www.21cmuseumhotel.com; doubles from $

21c Museum Hotel's Room 425, with photos by Carlee Fernandez. Opposite, clockwise from top left: The hotel's Atrium Gallery, with *Red Penguins* by Cracking Art and *Don't Touch Me (Front and Back)* by Sam Taylor-Wood; the hotel restaurant, Proof on Main; Room 315, with a portrait of artist Lucas Samaras by Chuck Close.

THE
BEST
OF
2007

UNITED
STATES
+
CANADA

Stairway to 21c's
Atrium Gallery, with a
series of Thomas
Weisskopf photos
(right) and a Gottfried
Helnwein painting,
Untitled (Modern Sleep).

+ FIVE MORE AMERICAN HOTELS WITH NOTEWORTHY ART COLLECTIONS

Chambers
MINNEAPOLIS, MINNESOTA
Opened in September 2006, the hotel spans two landmark-revival buildings with David Rockwell-designed interiors. Art Highlight: Damien Hirst's *Judas Iscariot*, a bull's head suspended in a formaldehyde-filled glass case, above, part of the artist's Twelve Disciples series.
901 Hennepin Ave., Minneapolis, Minn.; 877/767-6990 or 612/767-6900; www.chambers minneapolis.com

Four Seasons
EAST PALO ALTO, CALIFORNIA
The 10-story Silicon Valley hotel has unobstructed views of the Santa Cruz Mountains and San Francisco Bay. Art Highlight: A silk-screen print from Josef Albers's 1972 series *Formulation; Articulation*, above.
2050 University Ave., East Palo Alto, Calif.; 800/332-3442 or 650/566-1200; www.fourseasons.com

Grand Wailea
MAUI, HAWAII
On Maui's southwest shore, a sprawling 40-acre resort with a 2,000-foot lazy-river pool and the largest spa in Hawaii. Art Highlight: Seventeen bronze sculptures by Fernand Léger, one of the largest collections outside the Musée National Fernand Léger, in Biot, France.
3850 Wailea Alanui Dr., Wailea, Maui, Hawaii; 800/888-6100 or 808/875-1234; www.grandwailea.com

Park Hyatt
CHICAGO, ILLINOIS
A 198-room European-style hotel on historic Water Tower Square, looking out on Lake Michigan and the Museum of Contemporary Art. Art Highlight: Gerhard Richter's 27-foot *Piazza del Duomo, Milan*, above.
800 N. Michigan Ave., Chicago, Ill.; 800/233-1234 or 312/335-1234; www.hyatt.com

Sagamore
MIAMI BEACH, FLORIDA
In South Beach's Art Deco district, the sleek oceanside resort has 93 suites and an infinity pool. Art Highlight: Iván Navarro's *Red Ladder,* an eight-foot ladder made of red fluorescent lights.
1671 Collins Ave., Miami Beach, Fla.; 877/242-6673 or 305/535-8088; www.sagamorehotel.com

THE
BEST
OF
2007

UNITED
STATES
+
CANADA

Mandarin Oriental, Miami

MIAMI, FLORIDA

WORLD'S BEST A modern classic, the Mandarin Oriental elevates the East-meets-West ethos to new heights. One of the hotel's defining elements is its 15,000-square-foot trilevel spa. You will feel immediately calmed by the organic beauty of exotic bamboo, rice paper, and natural linens. If the endless choice of treatments—drawn from Chinese, Ayurvedic, European, Balinese, and Thai traditions—proves too stressful, choose the "Time Ritual" option: you tell the staff how long you wish to be pampered, and a menu will be created to suit your schedule. The spa's Ayurvedic treatments cleanse and balance with fragrant warm oils, Oshadi-clay body wraps, and hot-stone massage. The signature Kundalini Journey combines advanced massage techniques with a sequence of aromatherapy, color and gemstone work, and soothing sound treatments.

500 Brickell Key Dr., Miami, Fla.; 800/526-6566 or 305/913-8383; www.mandarinoriental.com/miami; doubles from $$$

One of three oceanfront pools at Acqualina. Opposite, from left: The Mandarin Oriental's infinity pool, overlooking Biscayne Bay; the hotel's lobby.

Acqualina, A Rosewood Resort

SUNNY ISLES BEACH, FLORIDA

Sunny Isles is North Miami's rapidly developing answer to South Beach, and Rosewood Hotels & Resorts has stepped into the skyscraping fray with Acqualina, a grand 51-story Mediterranean-inspired tower that mixes touches of Collins Avenue grooviness with old-world nostalgia. Baroque fountains and marble-and-gold leaf columns in the public areas evoke an opulent Venetian palace. In the 97 rooms and suites, all is white-and-earth-toned simplicity, with hipster accents, such as refrigerators stocked with Red Bull and welcome trays of hors d'oeuvres served on banana leaves.

17875 Collins Ave., Sunny Isles Beach, Fla.; 888/767-3966 or 305/918-8000; www.acqualinaresort.com; doubles from $$$

THE
BEST
OF
2007

UNITED
STATES
+
CANADA

Boca Raton Resort
& Club's reception
lounge, above. Above
right: Old Homestead
Steak House.

Boca Raton Resort & Club

BOCA RATON, FLORIDA

In 1926, Palm Beach society architect Addison Mizner ventured to the frontier swamp of Boca Raton and created his Jazz Age masterpiece, the 100-room Cloister Inn. Although the Florida land crash closed the inn after just one season, the property was eventually resurrected as the 1,043-room Boca Raton Resort & Club, which is undergoing an ambitious 21st-century makeover courtesy of LXR Luxury Resorts and an all-star ambience team. Thierry Despont (who put his stamp on the bar at the Dorchester, in London) lightened the Spanish-revival promenades with epic Florida à go-go murals. Alexandra Champalimaud (of New York's Carlyle Hotel) created a series of Boca Bungalows. Guests will find outposts of New York's La Goulue and the Old Homestead Steak House, as well as the Monkey Bar, a nod to Mizner's penchant for sashaying about town with his pet monkey.

501 E. Camino Real, Boca Raton, Fla.; 877/597-9896 or 561/395-3000; www.bocaresort.com; doubles from $$

Naples Grande Resort & Club

NAPLES, FLORIDA

South Beach gestalt has come to conservative Naples with the multimillion-dollar renovation of the former Registry Resort & Club. L.A. interior designer Robert Barry, who did the Four Seasons Hotel Los Angeles, gave the 474-room oceanfront resort a clean-lined lobby and lounge, with unfussy plantation-style guest rooms. The most noteworthy upgrade: the addition of 50 bungalow suites. Showcasing custom-designed furniture by Vaughan Benz and the Fong Brothers Company, the suites are a study in organic minimalism—headboards of whitewashed oak, a chunk of coral in a blue glass bowl atop a Vaughan Benz dining table, a sofa bed with ivory cushions. All told, the suites reflect the quiet (and casual) side of modernism, a rarity in these parts.

475 Seagate Dr., Naples, Fla.; 800/247-9810 or 239/597-3232; www.naplesgranderesort.com; doubles from $$

The living room of a new bungalow suite at Naples Grande Resort & Club, above. Above left: The suite's bedroom.

The James

CHICAGO, ILLINOIS

Stephen Hanson's first James hotel, in Scottsdale, blended the cheeky tone and smart looks of design hotels with the user-friendliness and affordability of midlevel chains. (It has since become a Mondrian.) The restaurateur-hotelier then shook things up in the Windy City with a new James. The 297 guest rooms are exercises in mid-aughties minimalism—platform beds, leather cube stools, and slate-tiled bathrooms with brushed-chrome-and-marble sinks. Located among the tony galleries of River North, the James has become a popular spot for art lovers: the lobby, restaurant, bar, and guest rooms double as exhibition spaces. And since this is Chicago, be sure to check out the hotel's requisite steak joint, David Burke's Primehouse, where chef Jason Miller serves choice cuts of dry-aged beef from Kentucky's renowned Creekstone Farms.

55 E. Ontario St., Chicago, Ill.; 877/526-3755; www.jameshotels. com; doubles from $$$

A 650-square-foot suite at the James. Opposite: In the lobby, an installation by Chicago-based artist Joel Russ entitled *Room 28* and a mural by Andrea Mantin and Linn Edwards.

JULIAN SCHNABEL

THE
BEST
OF
2007

UNITED
STATES
+
CANADA

The recently renovated lobby of The Phoenician, above. Above left: A poolside sunset.

The Phoenician

SCOTTSDALE, ARIZONA

WORLD'S BEST After a three-year, $20 million makeover, The Phoenician—Scottsdale's grande dame resort—has reemerged triumphant. The 647-room complex's aesthetic now fuses France of the late 1930's with a dash of Southwestern flair. Grandmotherly furnishings have been banished from the main lobby; the rooms and suites have been "un-done" in muted earth tones; and guests staying in the secluded, 60-room Canyon Suites have access to an S550 Mercedes Benz and driver. With the hotel's 2-to-1 staff-to-guest ratio, you can easily forget that you're sharing three golf courses, nine pools, 12 tennis courts, and six restaurants with 1,800 other guests. Chef Bradford Thompson, formerly of Manhattan's Daniel, maintains the award-winning status of Mary Elaine's (French with a modern twist), while the Jamaican-themed poolside menu works well for lunch.

6000 E. Camelback Rd., Scottsdale, Ariz.; 800/888-8234 or 480/941-8200; www.thephoenician.com; doubles from $$$

A Hotel Valley Ho guest room with an oversize bathtub, above. Above right: Striped lounge chairs, decorating each terrace.

Hotel Valley Ho

SCOTTSDALE, ARIZONA

Anchoring a revival of Scottsdale's historic, gallery-rich downtown is the legendary Hotel Valley Ho, newly saddled up after a four-year, $80 million restoration by the team behind the nearby Sanctuary on Camelback Mountain. Built in 1956 by a disciple of Frank Lloyd Wright, the former two-story motor lodge has had the cast-concrete relief panels on its aerodynamic exterior buffed up in hopes of returning it to its Hollywood-era splendor, when newlyweds Natalie Wood and Robert Wagner stayed here. The retro-chic guest rooms now have sliding glass doors, terraces overlooking Camelback Mountain, and oversize tubs. Chef Charles Wiley has reinvented 1950's comfort food (tuna casserole, anyone?) at Café ZuZu, and old-school Trader Vic's pu-pu platters pair perfectly with mai tais.

6850 E. Main St., Scottsdale, Ariz.; 866/882-4484 or 480/248-2000; www.hotelvalleyho.com; doubles from $$

A suite at the Sunset Tower, above. Above right: Original brass details on the stairway. Opposite: The exterior of the 1928 hotel, an Art Deco landmark.

Sunset Tower Hotel

WEST HOLLYWOOD, CALIFORNIA

Hospitality historians might point to the Sunset Tower's recent resurrection as a pivotal moment. "I want to create places for people who want something more sophisticated than a nightclub in the lobby," says Jeff Klein, the New York hotelier behind the City Club who spent $25 million acquiring and rehabilitating this 1928 West Hollywood Art Deco landmark. In its salad days, the 40-room hotel was home to the likes of Frank Sinatra and Howard Hughes. After changing hands in the 80's and 90's, it was left with a new name—the Argyle—and an over-the-top design that obscured its iconic architecture. Klein restored its name and hired Paul Fortune, who had designed the former L.A. nightspot Les Deux Cafés, to bring back the glamour factor. At night, the lobby lounge softly swings to live piano music or Sinatra recordings from the 40's and 50's.

8358 Sunset Blvd., West Hollywood, Calif.; 800/225-2637 or 323/654-7100; www.sunsettowerhotel.com; doubles from $$

THE
BEST
OF
2007

UNITED
STATES
+
CANADA

The Sunset Tower's Tower Bar.

BEST OF L.A. HOTEL BARS

CLUB BAR
PENINSULA BEVERLY HILLS
Dimly lit, so no one can see whose client you're signing— or whose cheek you're stroking. *9882 S. Santa Monica Blvd., Beverly Hills, Calif.; 310/ 551-2888; www.beverlyhills. peninsula.com*

POLO LOUNGE
BEVERLY HILLS HOTEL
Still as voluptuous as a 50's starlet, still filled with tycoons, still a vision in pink and green. *9641 Sunset Blvd., Beverly Hills, Calif.; 310/276-2251; www.beverlyhillshotel.com*

SIDEBAR
BEVERLY WILSHIRE
The new, mod, Richard Meier-designed space, with appetizers from Wolfgang Puck. *9500 Wilshire Blvd., Beverly Hills, Calif.; 310/275-5200; www.fourseasons.com/ beverlywilshire*

TRADER VIC'S
BEVERLY HILTON
Rattan walls, dugout canoes, totem poles, drinks on fire: L.A.'s most famous tiki bar has never been better. *9876 Wilshire Blvd., Beverly Hills, Calif.; 310/276-6345; www.tradervics.com*

WRITER'S BAR
RAFFLES L'ERMITAGE BEVERLY HILLS
Screenplays are traded like currency over $22 cocktails at this clubby, refined oasis. *9291 Burton Way, Beverly Hills, Calif.; 310/278-3344; www.beverlyhills.raffles.com*

BAR MARMONT
CHATEAU MARMONT
West Hollywood's coolest, most seductive boîte has reopened after an extensive polishing. *8221 Sunset Blvd., West Hollywood, Calif.; 323/656-1010; www.chateaumarmont.com*

LOUNGE AT THE STANDARD
STANDARD HOLLYWOOD
The Skybar's funkier rival, with similar views, plus AstroTurf, inflatable rafts, and Ping-Pong. *8300 Sunset Blvd., West Hollywood, Calif.; 323/650-9090; www.standardhotel.com*

SKYBAR
MONDRIAN LOS ANGELES
Sexiness incarnate, on a pavilion that overlooks the endless city. *8440 Sunset Blvd., West Hollywood, Calif.; 323/650-8999; www.mondrianhotel.com*

TOWER BAR
SUNSET TOWER HOTEL
Art Deco glamour in Bugsy Siegel's old apartment, with jazz piano and a fireplace. *8358 Sunset Blvd., West Hollywood, Calif.; 323/654-7100; www.sunsettowerhotel.com*

CAMEO BAR
VICEROY SANTA MONICA
A beachy riff on Regency style. Porcelain hounds guard the doors. *1819 Ocean Ave., Santa Monica, Calif.; 310/260-7515; www. viceroysantamonica.com*

THE BAR
HOTEL BEL-AIR
Brandy snifters, a roaring hearth, and mahogany paneling. *701 Stone Canyon Rd., Los Angeles, Calif.; 310/472-1211; www.hotelbelair.com*

ROOFTOP BAR
STANDARD DOWNTOWN L.A.
Where the beau monde goes to observe the skyline (and one another) on quasi-private waterbeds. *550 S. Flower St., Los Angeles, Calif.; 213/892-8080; www.standardhotel.com*

WHISKEY BLUE
W LOS ANGELES WESTWOOD
The moody bar plays host to Westwood's young and beautiful. *930 Hilgard Ave., Los Angeles, Calif.; 310/208-8765; www.whotels.com*

A private outdoor soaking tub at Rancho Valencia Resort & Spa. Opposite: Bold simplicity at 17, the Alden-Houston's restaurant.

Rancho Valencia Resort & Spa

RANCHO SANTA FE, CALIFORNIA

WORLD'S BEST Located in a bougainvillea-and-hibiscus-filled canyon 25 miles north of San Diego, the recently opened 10,000-square-foot spa at the 18-year-old Rancho Valencia Resort has only one goal: pure pampering. Designed in partnership with Auberge Resorts, the spa has 10 treatment suites housed in a hacienda-style building that overlooks a courtyard with a serenity fountain. Snack on the chef's fresh-baked zucchini bread and citrus-infused iced tea before heading in for a signature scrub or facial—with just-picked ingredients (avocados, lemons, and tangerines) from the spa's own trees. Couples can partake of a variety of treatments, including aromatic baths and terra-cotta clay bakes. Spend time sweating it out in the fitness room—or kick back, banana smoothie in hand, on your treatment room's private outdoor patio.

5921 Valencia Circle, Rancho Santa Fe, Calif.; 800/548-3664 or 858/756-1123; www.ranchovalencia.com; doubles from $$

THE
BEST
OF
2007

UNITED
STATES
+
CANADA

Alden-Houston

HOUSTON, TEXAS

Downtown Houston is undergoing a deep revitalization, and the new Alden-Houston has played a role in the process. Formerly the Sam Houston Hotel, this 1920's 10-story tower now has comfortable interiors, with grand leather headboards and 400-thread-count sheets, and luxe amenities, such as complimentary car service. The Alden-Houston's lobby is dominated by a pulsing, 30-foot-long David Lander light sculpture, and the 97 rooms have Texas-size showers crafted of Russian granite. In the restaurant, executive chef Ryan Pera (formerly the *chef poissonnier* at New York's Le Cirque) serves grass-fed filet mignon with wild mushrooms and buttermilk onion rings.

1117 Prairie St., Houston, Tex.; 877/348-8800 or 832/200-8800; www.aldenhotels.com; doubles from $$

The exterior of Hotel Gault, on Rue Ste.-Hélène, right. Below right: Pierre Paulin's Orange Slice chairs in the lobby's dining area. Opposite: The hotel's lobby, with original ceiling and pillars.

Hotel Gault

MONTREAL, CANADA

On the quietly hip southern fringe of Old Montreal, the Hotel Gault is sure to attract anyone who chooses a place to stay based on the provenance of the furniture. Beyond the ornate Beaux Arts façade of a former textile warehouse, the Gault's interior is a highly polished showcase of brand-name Modernism. Pierre Paulin's Orange Slice chairs add whimsy to the monumental lobby, and most of the 30 individually designed, loftlike rooms are decorated with Eileen Gray side tables, Artemide lamps, and Arne Jacobsen faucets. The design inspires guests to get creative; some of the rooms have movable fabric partitions—thin floor-to-ceiling fabric runners—so you can add your own touch to the layout.

449 Rue Ste.-Hélène, Montreal, Quebec, Canada; 866/904-1616 or 514/904-1616; www.hotelgault.com; doubles from $

THE
BEST
OF
2007

UNITED
STATES
+
CANADA

The Aerie's Villa Cielo, overlooking the San Juan Islands.

The Aerie

VANCOUVER ISLAND, CANADA

WORLD'S BEST Set 1,500 feet above the ocean, in the hills of southern Vancouver Island, the 35-room Aerie has commanded some of the best views of the San Juan Islands since its opening in 1991. With the recent unveiling of Villa Cielo—an arched Mediterranean-style building 300 feet above the main property—the resort is reaching even greater heights. The Villa, which is open from March through October (the road leading up to it can get icy during the winter), harbors six sprawling suites with Brazilian cherrywood floors, silk carpets, and gas fireplaces; the showers and the deep-soaking tubs are made for two. If you decide to actually leave your room, you can go on a mushroom hunt with a local monk or arrange a private cooking class—incorporating the famed produce of the surrounding Cowichan Valley.

600 Ebedora Lane, Malahat, British Columbia, Canada; 800/518-1933 or 250/743-7115; www.aerie.bc.ca; doubles from $$

Diamond Head, reflected in the mirror above the bed at the Halekulani's Vera Wang Suite.

THE
BEST
OF
2007

─────

UNITED
STATES
+
CANADA

Halekulani

HONOLULU, HAWAII

WORLD'S BEST Nineteen years ago, on a golf trip to the Big Island, Vera Wang got engaged in Kukuihaele, a small plantation town on the Hamakua Coast of Oahu. Her latest reason for returning: to create the Vera Wang Suite at the 100-year-old Halekulani, on the southeast coast. Wang infused her namesake one-bedroom suite–the crown jewel among the hotel's 455 rooms—with a highly personal union of Asian and Hawaiian decorative references. The predawn palette of lavender, persimmon, and celadon is punctuated with Thai porcelain, ebony-stained canoe paddles, and hemp rugs on the wenge-wood floors. The suite is also a showcase for all things Vera Wang–from crystal to candles–most of it sold in the new Vera Wang boutique downstairs.

2199 Kalia Rd., Honolulu, Hawaii; www.halekulani.com; 800/367-2343 or 808/923-2311; doubles from $$

49

Four Seasons Resort, Hualalai

KAUPULEHU-KONA, HAWAII

WORLD'S BEST You come to the Big Island to see Hawaii, not a high-rise hotel. The Four Seasons Resort, Hualalai, knows that and blends in with sea and sky so well it seems barely there. Like a coastal *kauhale,* or hamlet, the 243 rooms–clustered in four crescents– are practically invisible from offshore. The roofline of the staggered two-story bungalows creates its own wave pattern as it undulates through the fronds of transplanted palms. In the resort's spa, high walls of stacked volcanic rock create spaces that are both open-air and private: you can get an energizing lomilomi massage in an outdoor thatched *hale.* The Four Seasons is rightfully proud of its Hawaiian Interpretive Center, where full-time curators help guests dig deeper into local culture.

100 Kaupulehu Dr., Kaupulehu-kona, Hawaii; 888/340-5662 or 808/325-8000; www.fourseasons.com; doubles from $$$

One of five pools
at the Four Seasons
Resort, Hualalai,
on the Kona Coast.

MEXICO +
CENTRAL +
SOUTH
AMERICA

One & Only Palmilla,
in Los Cabos, Mexico.

THE
BEST
OF
2007

MEXICO
+
CENTRAL
+
SOUTH
AMERICA

Hotel Básico's rooftop lounge pools, above. Above right: A chalkboard lists the daily lunch specials at the restaurant.

Hotel Básico

PLAYA DEL CARMEN, MEXICO

Only a couple of decades ago, the corridor that starts below Cancún and extends south to the ancient Mayan ruins of Tulum was a sleepy stretch of Caribbean coastline. Today, what's known as the Riviera Maya has reinvented itself as a first-rate destination. One of the more interesting places to stay is the Básico, the latest venture from the hip Micha brothers, who were behind the popular Hotel Deseo, also in bustling Playa del Carmen. This 15-room hideaway, just a block from the beach, forgoes the Deseo's streamlined aesthetic for a rougher, more industrial look. Rooms tend to be on the small side, but what they lack in size they make up for in style: exposed support beams, walls made of cement and local sand, and floors covered with recycled tires.

Avda. Quinta, Playa del Carmen, Quintana Roo, Mexico; 866/978-4897 or 52-984/879-4448; www.hotelbasico.com; doubles from $

Maroma Resort & Spa

RIVIERA MAYA, MEXICO

This renowned resort between Cancún and Tulum recently reopened its doors after an extensive floor-to-ceiling renovation. The result: nine new *Sian Nah* (Mayan for "house of heaven") Suites, each with its own massage space, gym, and plunge pool; a self-serve bar at the 7,000-square-foot, Mayan-inspired Kinan Spa; El Sol restaurant, where chef Guillermo Gomez turns out modern Mayan-Creole dishes; and a fleet of waterfront beds, a picturesque perch for sipping mango-and-cilantro margaritas. The 65 original, thatched-roof bungalows have also been spruced up with luxe linens, painted Mexican tiles with century-old designs, and handwoven hammocks and rugs. The charming staff—from the women who scatter bougainvillea blossoms on your bed at turndown to the waiters who prepare guacamole tableside—elevate the experience from mundane to genuinely personal.

Km 51, Carr. 307, Riviera Maya, Quintana Roo, Mexico; 866/454-9351 or 52-998/872-8200; www.maromahotel.com; doubles from $$, including breakfast

A beach *palapa*, at the Maroma Resort & Spa.

biblioteca

Azúcar's outdoor library. Opposite: Stone paths connect 20 thatched bungalows.

THE
BEST
OF
2007

MEXICO
+
CENTRAL
+
SOUTH
AMERICA

Azúcar

MONTE GORDO, MEXICO

Acclaimed hotelier Carlos Couturier—part of the team who helped create Mexico's Habita and Deseo hotels—is breaking new ground with Azúcar, a three-hour drive from Veracruz. Named for the area's sugar factories, the resort's 20 whitewashed, thatched bungalows (just off a bustling main road) all have private terraces with hammocks. Individually selected driftwood and reproductions of furnishings from Couturier's grandparents' ranch lend local flavor, while brightly colored poolside beanbags and rose-hued pillows accent the spare design. By day, relax beachside with a hot-stone massage, or drive through vanilla plantations and citrus groves to El Tajín (the ninth-century ruins 30 minutes to the north). Then let the chef prepare the catch of the day—such as grilled freshwater langoustines with spicy chipotle sauce—and watch the sun set.

Km 83.5, Carr. Federal Nautla-Poza Rica, Monte Gordo, Veracruz, Mexico; 800/728-9098 or 52-232/321-0678; www.hotelazucar. com; doubles from $

57

THE
BEST
OF
2007

MEXICO
+
CENTRAL
+
SOUTH
AMERICA

The Vista Pool at
One & Only Palmilla,
with views of San
José Bay and the
Sierra de la Laguna.

One & Only Palmilla

SAN JOSÉ DEL CABO, MEXICO

WORLD'S BEST The hotel scene changed radically in Los Cabos when the classic Palmilla resort reopened its doors three years ago as a One & Only property. So what does a $90 million makeover from legendary hotelier Sol Kerzner get you? Adam D. Tihany designing Charlie Trotter's C Restaurant, a blue-glass fantasy where the star chef reinterprets traditional Mexican dishes, as with his seared yellowfin tuna with *huitlacoche* farfalle. A Jack Nicklaus–designed golf course. And 172 hotel rooms serviced by a staff of doting butlers. Kerzner also tempted away Edward Steiner, the managing director who helped put the nearby Las Ventanas resort on every Hollywood Palm Pilot.

Km 7.5, Carr. Transpeninsular, San José del Cabo, Baja, Mexico; 866/829-2977 or 52-624/146-7000; www.oneandonlyresorts. com; doubles from $$$

THE
BEST
OF
2007
―――
MEXICO
+
CENTRAL
+
SOUTH
AMERICA

The pool outside
Betseyville, left. Below left:
The colorful living room.
Opposite: The designer and
her dog, Lucy.

Betseyville

BARRA DE POTOSÍ, MEXICO

With its open-air rooms and flashy décor, Betsey
Johnson's rough-around-the-edges rental villa isn't for
everyone—but it's perfect if you like the idea of stepping
into a Frida Kahlo-meets-Carmen Miranda world.
Betseyville is a compound of five thatched bungalows in
the fishing village of Barra de Potosí (population 500),
south of Zihuatanejo. Set in an oasis of hibiscus, poppies,
and palms, the villa's *palapa*-style cottages splash on the
kitsch—colorful chandeliers, printed chiffon curtains,
funky antiques, claw-foot tubs. And for those who would
like to reproduce the retreat's whimsical sensibility,
Johnson has launched a Betseyville-inspired line of
home accessories.

Frac. 1-A, Playa Blanca, Camino a Barra de Potosí, Guerrero,
Mexico; 800/387-2726; www.lacurevillas.com; from $$$$$ for
nine people, including breakfast

60

THE
BEST
OF
2007

MEXICO
+
CENTRAL
+
SOUTH
AMERICA

The Francis Ford Coppola Villa's private pool, at Blancaneaux Lodge. Below left: The path leading to the Coppola Villa. Opposite: Outside the Coppola Villa.

Blancaneaux Lodge

CAYO DISTRICT, BELIZE

WORLD'S BEST Francis Ford Coppola came to Belize in search of an Apocalypse Now–style jungle paradise. He found just what he was looking for in the secluded Mountain Pine Ridge Forest Reserve: an abandoned lodge called Blancaneaux. Accessible only by a two-and-a-half-hour bumpy drive on Pine Ridge Road (or via private plane), the lodge is set on 80 acres and consists of an array of thatched villas and cabanas—some with open-air living areas and all decorated with Central American furniture and hand-woven textiles that were chosen by Coppola and his wife, Eleanor. The restaurant, Montagna, serves homemade pizza, specialties of Belize, and Coppola-label wine. You can swim in the river, hike in the nature reserve, or tour the extensive Mayan ruins nearby—and then hit the spa for a Thai massage.

Mountain Pine Ridge Forest Reserve, Cayo District, Belize; 800/746-3743 or 011-501/824-3878; www.blancaneaux.com; doubles from $$, including breakfast

THE
BEST
OF
2007

MEXICO
+
CENTRAL
+
SOUTH
AMERICA

Inn at Coyote Mountain

SAN RAMÓN, COSTA RICA

Traditionally, Costa Rica hasn't been known for its fine cuisine. With the 2004 opening of the Inn at Coyote Mountain, a 90-minute drive west of San José near San Ramón, the country's reputation has been redeemed. On a remote hilltop near the Monteverde Cloud Forest, Charles Leary and Vaughn Perret, the chef-owners of Trout Point Lodge in Nova Scotia, have created an intimate retreat where aspiring chefs— professional or not—can sign up for three-day courses on Latin-Creole cooking (think tropical jambalaya). Built in the Mudejar style of Spanish architecture, the four-room inn has romantic, mosquito netting-draped beds, glass-tile tubs, and a spectacular observatory with its own spiral staircase.

Calle La Tabla, San Ramón, Costa Rica; 800/980-0713 or 506/383-0544; www.cerrocoyote.com; doubles from $$$$$ for a three-night stay, including meals

The Hacienda, the main building of the Inn at Coyote Mountain, with a Morisco-style fountain.

A balcony decorated with Guatemalan textiles and ceramics at Quinta Maconda, above. Above right: The interior courtyard.

Quinta Maconda

ANTIGUA, GUATEMALA

Named after a town from Gabriel García Márquez's *One Hundred Years of Solitude,* this former private home in a colonial city in Guatemala marries old-world charm with high-tech convenience. Each of the four spacious rooms blends colonial antiques and textiles with modern amenities, such as wireless Internet connections. Three of the rooms have functioning fireplaces, and the master bedroom opens onto a private terrace overlooking the gardens. Meals, which incorporate regional recipes and the organic greens grown on the property, are served in the formal dining room or in the guest rooms, and breakfast on the bougainvillea-covered patio is a special treat—don't miss the scrambled eggs with ginger.

11 5A Avda. Norte, Antigua, Guatemala; 866/621-4032 or 502/5309-1423; www.quintamaconda.com; doubles from $, including breakfast

Hotel Unique

São Paulo has few hotels futuristic enough to match its modern vibe; the Unique is one of them. Designed by Niemeyer protégé Ruy Ohtake, Hotel Unique rises up like a matte gray semicircle festooned with porthole windows. The ground-floor glass façade illuminates the marble-slabbed lobby and its bar, with a backlit wall of bottles that soars to the glass-bottomed swimming pool above. Adjacent is the hotel library, stocked with 300 titles on art, design, and architecture. The same surprising juxtapositions are found in each of the 85 rooms and 10 suites. A window separates the bed from the bath, and the exterior rooms curve with the building's arc. But the rooftop is where you're going to want to spend your time. Reached via a panoramic elevator, the enclosed restaurant specializes in Brazilian and Japanese cuisine, while DJ's spin against the backdrop of the São Paulo skyline.

4700 Avda. Brigadeiro Luís Antônio, São Paulo, Brazil; 800/770-8771 or 55-11/3055-4710; www.hotelunique.com.br; doubles from $$

The Hotel Unique's lobby, complete with library, bar, and floor-to-ceiling views of São Paulo.

THE
BEST
OF
2007

MEXICO
+
CENTRAL
+
SOUTH
AMERICA

Pousada Teju-Açu

PERNAMBUCO, BRAZIL

There are more spinner dolphins and sea turtles than humans on Fernando de Noronha, 340 miles off the coast of Recife. The Brazilian environmental protection agency limits visitors at the mountainous archipelago and national marine park to 700 people a day, so its immaculate beaches, set between craggy sea cliffs and volcanic rock formations, are virtually deserted. The new Pousada Teju-Açu is an ideal base for soaking up the solitude. Its six eucalyptus- and ipe-wood bungalows, each with two apartments, resemble tree houses, with hammocks slung across outdoor verandas. The open-air restaurant prepares regional dishes like *goiabada e requeijão* (guava marmalade and cheese), a dessert known in Brazil as *Romeu e Julieta* for its flirtatious pairing of flavors.

Estrada da Alamoa, Boldró, Pernambuco, Brazil; 55-81/3619-1277; www.pousadateju.com.br; doubles from $$

The restaurant at Pousada Teju-Açu, below. Below right: A guest room. Opposite: The restaurant and pool.

THE
BEST
OF
2007

MEXICO
+
CENTRAL
+
SOUTH
AMERICA

Spotlight:
Buenos Aires

Marble floors and crystal chandeliers in the Salón Baccarat at the Palacio Duhau–Park Hyatt, right. Below right: A Park Suite in the new Posadas building. Opposite: The terrace of the main building.

Palacio Duhau–Park Hyatt

BUENOS AIRES, ARGENTINA

This just-opened Park Hyatt redefines luxury in the Argentine capital. Originally built in 1934 by French architect León Dourge for the Duhau family, the hotel's ironwork, crystal chandeliers, and gardens recall the Belle Époque. An underground walkway and gallery connect the Palacio and its 23 guest rooms to the newly built 142-room Posadas building. Ask for a room that overlooks the full-sensory garden, which changes colors, fragrances, and sounds with the seasons. Before dinner at the Duhau Restaurant, stop at the hotel's Vinoteca. The sommelier and *maître fromager* will pair wines from among 3,500 bottles of Argentine vintages with the best regional cheeses. And in the indoor heated pool at the Ahín Spa, which takes its name from the language of the ancient Mapuche tribe of southern Argentina, 750 colored bulbs simulate the changing of light from dawn to dusk.

1661 Avda. Alvear, Buenos Aires, Argentina; 800/233-1234 or 54-11/5171-1234; www.buenosaires.park.hyatt.com; doubles from $$

THE
BEST
OF
2007

MEXICO
+
CENTRAL
+
SOUTH
AMERICA

Spotlight:
Buenos Aires

Home Hotel

BUENOS AIRES, ARGENTINA

With its Scandinavian design, vintage French wallpaper, and handmade thyme-and-verbena soaps, Home Hotel feels like the home you wish you had. British music producer Tom Rixton and his wife, former publicist Patricia O'Shea, decided to create the hotel during their 2002 wedding in the hip Palermo Viejo neighborhood when they couldn't find suitable accommodations for all their guests. The result: 14 rooms, three spacious suites, and one loft apartment that fuse understated Saarinen reproductions with brushed concrete and flower-filled window boxes. The showstopper is the secluded, freestanding Garden Suite—its plunge pool and rooftop terrace are ideal for hosting a private party.

5860 Calle Honduras, Buenos Aires, Argentina; 54-11/4778-1008; www.homebuenosaires.com; doubles from $, including breakfast

Esplendor de Buenos Aires

BUENOS AIRES, ARGENTINA

Located in a Neoclassical building near the Borges Cultural Center, Esplendor has the vibe of a modern-art museum—note the floating staircase, crisp white walls, and massive portraits of Argentine icons (Che Guevara, Eva Perón) made of such unorthodox materials as cookies, bullets, and thread. The 51 rooms are done in seven different pastel colors and have Bertoia steel-mesh chairs; French doors open out onto Evita-worthy balconies. If street noise bothers you, request a room facing the unadorned but quiet inner patio. Natural light pours into the Esplendor Restaurant & Bar, where moldings and vintage mirrors have been perfectly restored.

780 Calle San Martín, Buenos Aires, Argentina; 54-11/5256-8800; www.esplendorbuenosaires.com; doubles from $

Cetrino restaurant,
at 725 Continental Hotel,
above. Above right: A guest
room. Opposite, from left:
Framed vintage floral
wallpaper in Home Hotel's
lobby; the Esplendor
Restaurant & Bar.

725 Continental Hotel

BUENOS AIRES, ARGENTINA

On one of B.A.'s busiest streets, this beautiful 1927
Art Deco hexagonal building could stand in for a Design
Within Reach showroom, complete with Eames,
Mies van der Rohe, and Le Corbusier pieces scattered
about. The 192 rooms have been updated with
hardwood floors, mood lighting, flat-screen TV's, and
floor-to-ceiling silk curtains. Bathrooms are designed
using travertine or Carrara marble and Philippe Starck
fittings. Because of the hotel's proximity to the theater
district, its sleek rooftop bar, with an outdoor heated
swimming pool, has become a popular spot for martini
lunches and pre-show cocktails.

725 Avda. Roque Saenz Peña, Buenos Aires, Argentina;
54-11/4131-8000; www.725continental.com; doubles from $$,
including breakfast

THE
BEST
OF
2007

MEXICO
+
CENTRAL
+
SOUTH
AMERICA

Viñas de Cafayate Wine Resort

CAFAYATE, ARGENTINA

Hidden by vines and ringed by mountains, this Spanish colonial-inspired inn sits a mile outside the village of Cafayate, a two-hour flight from Buenos Aires. A fireplace crackles in the living room, and the twelve rustic guest rooms have private bathrooms and views of the vineyards and distant peaks. A celebrated chef from Salta has designed a sophisticated (yet inexpensive) menu—try the veal lomo-style (tenderloin) in a Malbec reduction—spiked with organic vegetables from the restaurant's own garden. Pair the meal with the famous local varietal, Torrontés de Cafayate, a dry and crisp white.

25 De Mayo Camino al Divisadero, Cafayate, Argentina; 54-11/4522-7754; www.tenriverstenlakes.com; doubles from $, including breakfast

The pool at the Viñas de Cafayate. Opposite: A deck overlooking the vineyards.

75

Eolo, which borders the southern Patagonian ice field. Opposite, from left: Tomás Demaría, an Eolo guide; Oveja Room.

THE
BEST
OF
2007
—
MEXICO
+
CENTRAL
+
SOUTH
AMERICA

Spotlight:
Patagonia

Eolo

EL CALAFATE, ARGENTINA

While Patagonia—the 304,000 square miles of electric-blue lakes, endless steppes, and spiky peaks that span lower South America—remains largely unspoiled, the region is undergoing a full-scale development boom. Built in an austere style inspired by gabled estancias, Eolo sits on the isolated Patagonian steppe, 552 miles above the tip of the continent. Inside, armchairs upholstered in corduroy mingle with an English Empire table and 18th-century Spanish chairs. The overall effect is sophisticated yet homey—the kind of place where you don't worry about kicking off your muddy boots when you return from a hike. Guest rooms have a similarly relaxed feel: beds are made with crisp white sheets and big fluffy duvets, wall-to-wall sisal carpets are overlaid with vibrantly colored woven-wool rugs; cream-colored walls are hung with sepia photographs of local flora and fauna.

Km 23, Ruta Provincial 11, El Calafate, Argentina; 54-114/700-0075; www.eolo.com.ar; doubles from $$$$$ for a three-night stay, all-inclusive

77

THE
BEST
OF
2007

MEXICO
+
CENTRAL
+
SOUTH
AMERICA

Spotlight:
Patagonia

Los Cerros

EL CHALTÉN, ARGENTINA

El Chaltén, a dusty speck of a town situated in an unusually beautiful spot beneath the granite spires of Cerro Fitz Roy and Cerro Torre, has hardscrabble charm: until recently, there were few lodging options for those not willing to camp out or share a bathroom. Los Cerros opened in 2004, and what it lacks in luxury it makes up for in comfort: the 44 rooms are generally small and fairly basic, with nondescript functional furniture, cheerful striped duvets, geometric-print curtains, and a picture window with a stunning view of snowcapped mountains. Come for the outdoor activities, including some of the best hiking in the region.

San Martín, El Chaltén, Argentina; 54-114/814-3934; www. loscerrosdelchalten.com; doubles from $$$$$ for a three-night stay, all-inclusive

A hall that leads to the guest rooms at Altiplánico Sur, above. Above right: The starkly decorated lounge. Opposite: A sitting room at Los Cerros.

Altiplánico Sur

PUERTO NATALES, CHILE

A further testament to the pace of development in the area is Altiplánico Sur—a bunker hotel set into a hillside, its roof covered in grass and dandelions, and its façade faced in bricks of turf. The 22 smallish rooms are heavy on concrete (walls, bed platforms, nightstands) and metal (wrought-iron chairs, steel-and-glass tables), softened here and there with a sheepskin rug or a driftwood lamp. All have good views, but those closest to the property's central hall offer slightly better ones. If you don't already have an agenda, the small but friendly staff can point you toward the many operators in nearby Puerto Natales for guidance. This being Patagonia, it's unlikely you'll go wrong.

Huerto Familiar 282, Puerto Natales, Chile; 56-61/412-525; www.altiplanico.cl; doubles from $, including breakfast

THE
BEST
OF
2007

MEXICO
+
CENTRAL
+
SOUTH
AMERICA

Spotlight:
Patagonia

The pool at Remota, left. Below left: The resort's relaxation room, called La Playa. Opposite: A walkway to the bank of the Seno de Ultima Esperanza (Last Hope Sound).

Remota

PUERTO NATALES, CHILE

One of the more stylish new bases in Patagonia for exploration is Remota, an upscale lodge designed by the great Chilean architect Germán del Sol (creator of the Explora hotel-adventure company). While the exterior is severe, angular, and clad in black asphalt, the interior is a study in del Sol's brand of inventive modernism: consciously rusticated elements combined with *pizarra* (slate) floors, heavy modular furniture, and museum-quality Chilean artifacts. The hotel can arrange an array of trips into the Patagonian countryside, including a visit to an organic vegetable farm; a hike up the nearby Cerro Benitez for an astonishing 360-degree view; and a walk along a stream littered with fossils in the Sierra Baguales, followed by lunch with a cowboy who has lived alone in the valley for 20 years.

Km 1.6, Ruta 9 Norte, Puerto Natales, Chile; 56-2/387-1500; www. remota.cl; doubles from $$$$$ for a three-night stay, all-inclusive

Serena Hotel

PUNTA DEL ESTE, URUGUAY

Punta del Este, the South American jet-set playground once favored by the likes of Brigitte Bardot and the Rat Pack, is getting its glamorous groove back, and the Serena Hotel is hastening the recovery. Located on the *playa mansa*, or mild beach, side of the peninsula, the 32-room Serena is a chic and intimate alternative to its Goliath-size neighbors. The lobby looks like a trendy but friendly art gallery, and the mainly white rooms are austere without being aggressively uncomfortable. But you're not going to want to be indoors anyway: the daybed-flanked infinity pool has waiter service and an unobstructed view of the marina, and the nearly private beach has some of the best people-watching in town.

Rambla Williman, Parada 24, Punta del Este, Uruguay; 598-42/233-441; www.serenahotel.com.uy; sea-view doubles from $, including breakfast

The infinity pool at the Serena Hotel. Opposite: Daybeds at the hotel.

THE CARIBBEAN+ BERMUDA

Cabana 55, at 9 Beaches in Bermuda.

The main reflecting pool at Amanyara, with the library on the left.

Amanyara

PROVIDENCIALES, TURKS AND CAICOS

Despite a mini-wave of hotel openings in the past decade, the Turks and Caicos (the 40 islands and cays southeast of the Bahamas) remain largely under the radar—the ideal setting, in other words, for a luxe hideaway. Eight years in the making, Amanyara is the first West Indian outpost from Singapore-based Amanresorts and the group's largest property yet, with 40 guest pavilions, 33 multi-bedroom villas, and an Asian-inspired spa. You'd be hard-pressed to find any coconut palms or drinks with umbrellas here. Rather, architect Jean-Michel Gathy, who has designed other Aman properties as well as the Setai hotel in Miami Beach, created a Zen oasis that complements the landscape's subtle beauty. Low-slung pavilions, situated either beside the ocean or inland along a network of tranquil ponds, are constructed out of teak, kapur, and *balau* woods. In the colonnaded lobby, there's no proper reception desk—just a phalanx of telepathically attentive staff.

Northwest Point, Providenciales, Turks and Caicos; 866/941-8133 or 649/941-8133; www.amanresorts.com; doubles from $$$$$

THE
BEST
OF
2007

THE
CARIBBEAN
+
BERMUDA

A bedroom at Amanyara. Opposite, clockwise from top left: A daybed, between the infinity pool and the Atlantic Ocean; one of the 40 glass-walled guest rooms; the *balau* and kapur wood ceiling at the hotel bar; the circular bar.

The Sivory Punta
Cana's infinity pool.

THE
BEST
OF
2007

THE
CARIBBEAN
+
BERMUDA

Sivory Punta Cana

PUNTA CANA, DOMINICAN REPUBLIC

A new breed of boutique hotel is sprouting up along the
Dominican Republic's Caribbean coast. Typical of the
trend is the Sivory Punta Cana, a serene and secluded
resort on a long stretch of beach about an hour's drive
from the Punta Cana International Airport. Sivory's
grounds are dotted with sea grape trees and two-story
terra-cotta villas, which house 55 handsomely
furnished suites. Since neighboring resorts are more
buffet than soufflé, the hotel's emphasis on food and
cocktails is a welcome change. You can choose from
among three restaurants—Asian fusion, Mediterranean,
or nouvelle French—and three lounges (including
a cigar bar). The wine cellar is stocked with more than
8,000 bottles, full-size highlights of which reside in
a small refrigerator in every room.

Sivory Beach, Punta Cana, Dominican Republic; 809/552-0500;
www.sivorypuntacana.com; doubles from $$

91

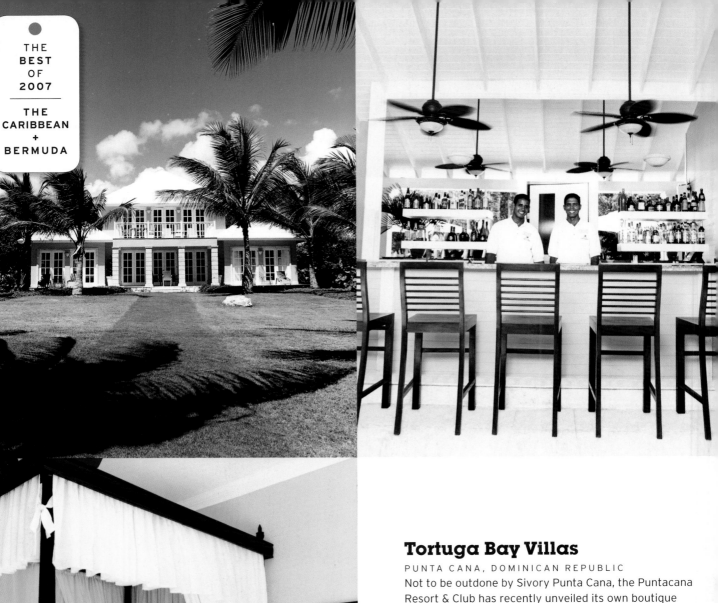

THE
BEST
OF
2007

THE
CARIBBEAN
+
BERMUDA

Tortuga Bay Villas

PUNTA CANA, DOMINICAN REPUBLIC

Not to be outdone by Sivory Punta Cana, the Puntacana Resort & Club has recently unveiled its own boutique offshoot, Tortuga Bay Villas. Designed by Puntacana Resort partner and sometime resident Oscar de la Renta, Tortuga Bay's airy suites, in 15 freestanding villas, create an isolated oasis within the 15,000-acre resort. Its powder-white beach, pool area, and on-site restaurant are open only to villa guests. Your sole contact with the outside world is a satellite-TV hookup and a cell phone connection to your villa manager, but should you want to commune with the larger complex, there are any number of places to do so: a golf course, nine restaurants, five bars, and a spa run by Six Senses, where holistic remedies such as the hot- and cold-stone facial and lomilomi massage are administered by masterful therapists.

Punta Cana, Dominican Republic; 809/959-2262; www.puntacana. com; doubles from $$$, including breakfast

The view from a beachfront villa at Tortuga Bay Villas. Opposite, clockwise from top left: A villa overlooking the golf course; the Manantial bar; a classic villa bedroom.

Hôtel Guanahani's
L'Indigo restaurant.

Hôtel Guanahani & Spa

GRAND CUL-DE-SAC, ST. BART'S

If you like low-key, you'll love Guanahani. It will never win a personality contest, but then personality is hardly the point here. The hotel contents itself with offering a traditional destination-resort experience, like Little Dix Bay on Virgin Gorda or Caneel Bay on St. John's. Guanahani is just not interested in buzz. Several dozen gaily painted West Indian cottages, garnished with lacy gingerbread trim, occupy a 16-acre peninsula. Each of the Creole-style bungalows, in brilliant fuchsia, turquoise, and tangerine, has a terrace, and most overlook the hotel's two private beaches. Being a card-carrying resort means that guests can check in and never once leave the hotel, if they are not of a mind to do so.

Grand Cul-de-Sac, St. Bart's; 800/223-6800 or 590-590/276-660; www.leguanahani.com; doubles from $$$$$, including breakfast

THE
BEST
OF
2007

THE
CARIBBEAN
+
BERMUDA

A Christian Liaigre-designed guest room, at Le Sereno, above. Above right: Dipping into the resort's freshwater swimming pool.

Le Sereno

GRAND CUL-DE-SAC, ST. BART'S

Ever since Christian Liaigre signed his name to Club Med Bora Bora about a decade ago, style-obsessed hotel junkies have dared to hope that the French designer might bring his handsome and spare sensibility to another beach resort. The wait is over. On a small but exquisite stretch of sand on the east end of St. Bart's, Le Sereno's 37 oceanfront rooms are done up in a modern colonial style: whitewashed walls, teak floors, beds draped in mosquito netting. Each has an outdoor shower and sliding glass doors that open onto a private terrace and garden, should you prefer sunbathing in solitude. Otherwise join the glitterati and claim a chaise longue beside the freshwater infinity pool.

Grand Cul-de-Sac, St. Bart's; 590-590/298-300; www.lesereno.com; doubles from $$$

95

THE
BEST
OF
2007

THE
CARIBBEAN
+
BERMUDA

The bar at Kú, set between the pool and the Atlantic Ocean.

Kú

SHOAL BAY EAST, ANGUILLA

From the hotel group behind celebrity favorite Cap Juluca comes Kú, which means "sacred place" in the Arawak Indian language. The name is appropriate, given that the hotel sits on the white-sand beach of Shoal Bay East near Fountain Cave, one of the tribe's ceremonial sites. The urbane newcomer provides luxury for less, with South Beach–chic suites—white and pale-aqua walls, white-tiled floors, blond furnishings and fabrics. The suites are as airy as they are minimalist, with living/dining rooms, full kitchens, and ocean-view balconies. Kú's spa and pool may be on the small side, but its 75-foot beachfront bar is the longest on the island. At the adjoining French-Caribbean restaurant, live music sets a laid-back vibe for barefoot dancing on the beach.

Shoal Bay East, Anguilla; 800/869-5827 or 264/497-2011; www.ku-anguilla.com; doubles from $$

A one-bedroom house at Petit Bacaye Cottage Hotel, right. Below right: Mosquito nets adorn a bamboo four-poster bed.

Petit Bacaye Cottage Hotel

WESTERHALL, GRENADA

Far removed from the tourist crush of Grand Anse, Grenada's main beach, lies Petit Bacaye, a beachfront country-cottage hotel in rural St. David's parish. Its five thatched-roof cabanas and two larger houses, hidden among banana trees and giant flowering ginger, have bamboo or mahogany beds and private verandas. While there isn't a radio or television to be found, a resident masseuse stands by with coconut and nutmeg oils. Local fishermen keep the seaside restaurant supplied with fresh lobster, snapper, and grouper, and the hotel's trees provide bananas, pawpaw, and guava. At sundown, guests are encouraged to take rum punch and baskets of chilled lobster salad to the water's edge and watch the egrets come home to roost.

Westerhall, Grenada; 473/443-2902 or 44-1794/323-227; www.petitbacaye.com; doubles from $

THE
BEST
OF
2007

THE
CARIBBEAN
+
BERMUDA

The bar at Little Dix Bay, left. Below left: Spa pools.

Little Dix Bay, A Rosewood Resort

VIRGIN GORDA, BRITISH VIRGIN ISLANDS

WORLD'S BEST — When Laurance Rockefeller founded Little Dix Bay in 1964 as a haven for well-to-do travelers, he had the foresight to choose an island that would dodge the wrath of rampant development, which has spoiled so many pristine Caribbean locales. Some four decades later, Little Dix continues to pamper the rich and demanding, even more so now, after a recent $25 million overhaul by oil heiress Caroline Rose Hunt's Rosewood group. And the resort's new Asia-meets-the-tropics style—indigenous woods, handcrafted furniture, Italian linens—was worth every million. In response to the growing demand, there are now three sprawling hilltop villas, each with its own private plunge pool, decked-out kitchen, and outdoor stone showers.

Virgin Gorda, British Virgin Islands; 888/767-3966 or 284/495-5555; www.littledixbay.com; doubles from $$$

98

Peter Island Resort

PETER ISLAND, BRITISH VIRGIN ISLANDS

WORLD'S BEST — A 30-minute ferry ride from Tortola, Peter Island Resort is the ultimate hideaway: a private, 1,800-acre, 52-room, white sand-ringed retreat. For guests of the three hilltop villas, the price tag is steep ($4,000 to $12,000 a night), but perks include a personal staff and help customizing the accommodations before you arrive—from the villa director. And then there's the sprawling new spa, on a secluded windswept beach. Its couples' suites can be rented by the day; side-by-side treatments are influenced by the region, from the Fresh Coconut Rub to the Tropical Lime and Ginger Buff, which incorporates salt harvested from a neighboring island.

Peter Island, British Virgin Islands; 800/346-4451 or 284/495-2000; www.peterisland.com; doubles from $$$, including meals

A masseuse arranging
fresh flowers in
Peter Island's spa.

THE
BEST
OF
2007

THE
CARIBBEAN
+
BERMUDA

Marin Bay, which surrounds Club Med Buccaneer's Creek. Opposite, from left: One of the resort's 293 guest rooms; palm trees and pastel buildings line the resort's winding walkways.

Club Med Buccaneer's Creek

MARIN BAY, MARTINIQUE

The company that invented the all-inclusive resort in the 1950's is now reinventing it. With a $60 million overhaul of Buccaneer's Creek, Club Med is shedding its "sun, sand, sex" image in favor of a more polished, health-conscious one. The 293 guest quarters, with colorful West Indian–inspired fabrics and tiled floors, now have mini-fridges, flat-screen TV's, and rain-shower baths. Dining has also been upgraded, with three new restaurants: a French-Caribbean fusion menu in the heart of a coconut grove; a traditional buffet; and a poolside grill. A 5,000-square-foot infinity pool is also a first, as is the Club Med Spa and Club Med Gym. Perhaps the biggest change is the attitude: the disco shuts down before dawn, and the gourmet cheese table is often more crowded than the bar.

Marin Bay, Martinique; 888/932-2582; www.clubmed.com; $$$$$ per person for seven nights, all-inclusive

THE
BEST
OF
2007

THE
CARIBBEAN
+
BERMUDA

The oceanfront pool at the Ritz-Carlton, Grand Cayman, above. Above right: The Silver Palm Lounge, named for the silver thatch palm, the national tree of the Cayman Islands.

Ritz-Carlton, Grand Cayman

SEVEN MILE BEACH, GRAND CAYMAN

Forty years ago, the island of Grand Cayman was transformed into a world-class financial center—the Switzerland of the Caribbean. Today, the big luxury-hotel chains are betting that the island's ultra-efficient infrastructure, great sailing and diving, and one-hour flight time from Miami will also make it the next big destination. With its new 365-room beachfront hotel, the Ritz-Carlton has gotten a jump on the competition. The 144-acre high-end playground introduces a who's who of branded amenities: Jean-Michel Cousteau nature tours, a Greg Norman–designed golf course, Nick Bollettieri tennis pros, a La Prairie spa, and five restaurants, including two run by acclaimed chef Eric Ripert.

Seven Mile Beach, Grand Cayman; 800/241-3333 or 345/943-9000; www.ritzcarlton.com; doubles from $$$

The Reefs'
private beach.

The Reefs

SOUTHAMPTON, BERMUDA

WORLD'S BEST A classic on Bermuda's rocky south shore (celebrating its 60th anniversary this year), the Reefs has well earned its reputation for exceptional service and repeat visitors. Built on limestone cliffs and surrounding a swath of private pink sand, the resort's salmon-stone walls, sloping white roofs, and ocean-view moon gate (couples make wishes beneath its arch) embody the quintessential Bermuda experience.

Each of the 65 lanais and suites overlooks the beach; the walk to the water, lined with palm trees and sea grape, wraps around the hotel and lets out at the water's edge. Snorkelers will find a stretch of low-lying reef, 30 yards out, abundant with fluorescent parrot fish and sergeant majors.

56 South Shore Rd., Southampton, Bermuda; 800/742-2008 or 441/238-0222; www.thereefs.com; doubles from $$$, including breakfast, tea, and dinner

THE
BEST
OF
2007

THE
CARIBBEAN
+
BERMUDA

9 Beaches

SANDYS, BERMUDA

You no longer have to travel halfway across the globe to sleep in an overwater villa. 9 Beaches brings these chic and simple bungalows to Bermuda (for a third of the price of those found in Polynesia). The 84 cabanas are really tent-cabin hybrids, constructed out of vinyl and canvas on aluminum frames. The sea-blue-and-white décor is charming, and the all-important basics are there: hot water, cold mini-fridge, electricity, air-conditioning, and a complimentary cell phone. You can rent one of the villas situated either hillside or oceanfront, but the overwater ones are clearly the most appealing. There's a special Plexiglas fish-viewing panel set into the floor, and each night you fall asleep lulled by the quiet rhythm of gentle waves.

4 Daniels Head Lane, Sandys, Bermuda; 866/841-9009 or 441/239-2999; www.9beaches.com; doubles from $$, including breakfast

One of 84 bungalows
at 9 Beaches, on Bermuda.

EUROPE

Vinoteca, the bar at Hotel Marqués de Riscal in Elciego, Spain.

Bovey Castle's
expansive grounds,
above. Above right:
A member of the
castle's activities
team with the
catch of the day.

Bovey Castle

NORTH BOVEY, DEVON, ENGLAND

A touch forbidding, in the best Mary Shelley tradition, this Jacobean-style castle on 368 acres within Dartmoor National Park recently received a $50 million revamping by the former owner of Scotland's legendary Skibo Castle. The 64-room hotel has a façade of local granite, two stories of mullioned windows, and Gothic flourishes throughout. Inside, plaster tracery is in the breathy manner of John Adam, and triple-width staircases are ballroom-ready. Outside, an 18-hole golf course, two trout lakes, and an archery field keep guests busy. Sign up for a hawk walk or potholing—exploring the underground caves that dot the area.

Dartmoor National Park, North Bovey, Devon, England; 44-1647/445-016; www.boveycastle.com; doubles from $$, including breakfast

A carefully
restored Regency-
style guest room
at Hotel Endsleigh.

Hotel Endsleigh

DEVON, ENGLAND

Built in 1812, this stone manor embodied the popular
rustic cottage orné style of the times: a grotto-like shell
house, a Marie Antoinette-ish marble dairy, and a terrace
paved with sheep's knuckles. These elements remain
deliciously intact, but now powering the Endsleigh is
Olga Polizzi, design director of Sir Rocco Forte's hotel
group (Hotel Savoy in Florence, the Hotel de Russie in
Rome). Half of the 16 guest rooms overlook the Tamar
River, but each has individual details, like original rolltop
tubs and hand-painted wallpaper of birds nibbling plums.
The leading architect of the day, Sir Humphry Repton,
created the 108-acre grounds in a style that hewed
rapturously to the picturesque.

Milton Abbot, Tavistock, Devon, England; 44-1822/870-000;
www.hotelendsleigh.com; doubles from $$, including breakfast

Brown's Hotel

LONDON, ENGLAND

Coaxing a beloved hotel into the 21st century is a
delicate matter, particularly when the hotel in question
is Brown's, an elegant array of 11 town houses known
since 1837 for its ultra-private atmosphere and storied
roster of pedigreed guests (Teddy Roosevelt, Winston
Churchill). But new owner Sir Rocco Forte and, once
again, designer Olga Polizzi managed to preserve the
hotel's higgledy-piggledy style even as they brought
edgy modern art into the 117 suites and lobby. The
restaurant—in muted seashell colors and with 1930's
FontanaArte lighting fixtures—satisfies the old guard,
while the Terrence Donovan bar—where the walls are
plastered with black-and-white fashion photographs—
seduces the younger set with champagne cocktails.

33 Albemarle St., Mayfair, London, England; 800/223-6800 or
44-20/7493-6020; www.brownshotel.com; doubles from $$$

Inside the lounge and
English tearoom at
Brown's Hotel, below.
Below left: The main
staircase. Opposite:
The hotel's entrance.

Inverlochy Castle,
in the foothills of
Scotland's Ben
Nevis mountain.

Inverlochy Castle

FORT WILLIAM, SCOTLAND

WORLD'S BEST Built as a private estate in 1863 and converted into a hotel a century later, this turreted Highland castle at the base of Ben Nevis mountain has carefully preserved the features that made it a favorite of Queen Victoria. Crystal chandeliers hang over the two-story, frescoed Great Hall. Each of the 18 rooms, with their floral wallcoverings and canopies, looks toward the mountain (Britain's highest), the castle's own loch, or its walled garden. Take part in the same activities as Inverlochy's original inhabitants: snooker, clay-pigeon shooting, and trout fishing (the kitchen will prepare your catch). Diners eat traditional dishes such as saddle of rabbit with linnhe prawns, seated on the same furniture the King of Norway gave to the estate's first owners.

Torlundy, Fort William, Scotland; 888/424-0106 or 44-1397/702-177; www.inverlochycastlehotel.com; doubles from $$$

More than 300 bubble lights, designed by Tom Dixon, cascade from the ceiling in the G Hotel's Grand Salon.

G Hotel

GALWAY CITY, IRELAND

While Galway has been gaining attention as a seaside bolt-hole for euro-flush Dubliners, the new G Hotel is about to permanently alter notions about Irish style. Designed by the celebrated milliner Philip Treacy— famous for his fanciful collaborations with Karl Lagerfeld and Alexander McQueen—the steel-and-glass complex uses provocative and witty visual references, such as Versailles, the Ziegfeld Follies, and Andy Warhol. A long public gallery is punctuated by a catwalk carpet in raspberry red; the silver-toned Grand Salon is Treacy's own Hall of Mirrors; and the Pink Salon is defined by hot-pink camouflage-print sofas. The 101 bedrooms, adorned with sketches by fashion illustrator David Downton, include a suite named after supermodel Linda Evangelista.

Galway City, Ireland; 800/525-4800 or 353/9186-5200; www.theghotel.ie; doubles from $$$

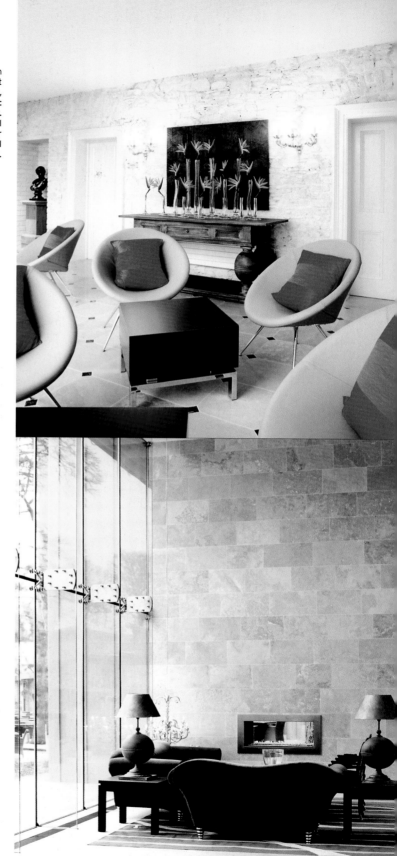

A relaxation lounge in Monart Destination Spa, right. Below right: The hotel's lobby. Opposite: A natural springwater hydrotherapy pool in the spa.

Monart Destination Spa

COUNTY WEXFORD, IRELAND

The 18th-century former Jameson whiskey family estate—known as the Still—could hardly have anticipated its latest incarnation. Glass corridors now link the stone manse with a polished new spa. Guests can detoxify in the salt grotto and Swedish log sauna or have a caviar facial. Chic, natural-hued guest rooms have modern touches like plasma televisions, but the antique four-poster beds and freestanding tubs in the two suites in the original building will appeal to traditionalists.

The Still, County Wexford, Ireland; 353-53/923-8999; www.monart.ie; doubles from $$$, including breakfast

Light sculptures by German designer Ingo Maurer in the courtyard of the Kruisherenhotel.

Kruisherenhotel

MAASTRICHT, THE NETHERLANDS

In the realm of unlikely trends: ancient monasteries are being reinvented as luxury hotels with rigorously chic interiors. Among the most stylish—and least remote—is Kruisherenhotel, carved out of a 15th-century church complex near Maastricht's main shopping district. Hotelier Camille Oostwegel, known for smartly repurposing crumbling Low Country châteaux as luxury accommodations, assembled the new 60-room hotel inside the church's exoskeleton. A cardinal-red runner suspended in the nave and choir leads to a dining loft that resembles an erector-set project. Ingo Maurer's quirky "flying saucer" chandeliers hover from the vaulted ceilings, and the chancel houses a wine bar with tufted-velvet banquettes. In the bedrooms, massive support beams emerge at curious angles from the wall.

19–23 Kruiserengang, Maastricht, the Netherlands; 800/337-4685 or 31-43/329-2020; www.chateauhotels.nl; doubles from $$

The Kruisherenhotel's lobby. Above: A sculpture in the bar. Opposite: The Kruisherenhotel's dining room, with chandeliers by designer Ingo Maurer.

+ THREE MORE MONASTERY HOTELS

Abbaye de la Bussière

ABBAYE DE LA BUSSIÈRE
DIJON, FRANCE

Surrounded by Côte d'Or vineyards and stately barge canals, this 12th-century abbey has been revitalized with exquisite ornamental details: limestone arches supported by laughing gargoyles, heraldic frescoes, stained-glass refectory windows, and a marble spiral staircase to the adjacent château.
La Bussière-sur-Ouche, Dijon, France; 800/735-2478 or 33-3/80-49-02-29; www.abbayedelabussiere.fr; doubles from $$

POUSADA SANTA MARIA DO BOURO
AMARES, PORTUGAL

This 12th-century monastery turned inn, attached to a tiny church in a village of northern Portugal's Gerês Mountains, retains its formidable Romanesque demeanor—right down to the stylishly austere bedrooms (former monk's cells) and their extremely firm mattresses.
Lugar do Terreiro, Santa Maria do Bouro, Amares, Portugal; 800/337-4685 or 351-2/5337-1970; www.pousadas.pt; doubles from $, including breakfast

RELAIS SAN MAURIZIO
SANTO STEFANO BELBO, ITALY

Presiding over a cedar- and grapevine-studded hilltop in Italy's Piedmont region, this monastery hotel has a Caudalie Vinothérapie spa and a restaurant with an exceptional wine cellar, stocked with Barolos and Barbarescos.
39 Località San Maurizio, Santo Stefano Belbo, Italy; 800/735-2478 or 39-0141/841-900; www. relaissanmaurizio.it; doubles from $$

The lounge bar
at Kube Rooms.

Kube Rooms & Bars

PARIS, FRANCE

It's no surprise that the Kube, in Paris's up-and-coming La Goutte d'Or neighborhood, fully celebrates the cube, "the most modern of shapes," according to the general director, Jérôme Foucaud. The shape plays a part throughout, from the Louvre-inspired glass box that functions as the reception area to the 41 rooms, where rectangular beds are lit from below (and appear to levitate). Clever gimmicks aren't confined to shapes alone: there's also an Ice Kube bar made of, yes, ice; electronic fingerprint readers instead of room keys; a sound system concealed within red ceiling fixtures; and a modern version of the lava lamp, with fluid images projected onto plasma screens.

1–5 Passage Ruelle, 18th Arr., Paris, France; 33-1/42-05-20-00; www.kubehotel.com; doubles from $$

The ancient brick-vaulted drawing room of the Château de Cassis.

Château de Cassis

CASSIS, FRANCE

A former 13th-century stone fortress may not seem like the most welcoming structure for a bed-and-breakfast, but Château de Cassis feels at once intimate and modern. It hovers 250 feet above the Mediterranean, in Cassis, which is quietly becoming an insider's alternative to St.-Tropez. Carved from a citadel that dates back to the Roman presence in Provence, the inn is steeped in history. Bricks salvaged from the fortress's ancient ovens line the towering vaulted public spaces. In the five suites—each with a private garden—rigorously edited furnishings are a breezy cocktail of high and low: ebony four-poster beds, pierced Moroccan wall lights, woven-plastic floor mats, and terra-cotta olive-oil jars.

Traverse du Château, Cassis, France; 33-6/25-37-51-80; www.chateaudecassis.com; doubles from $$

The courtyard pool at Pastis Hôtel-St. Tropez, above. Above right: A French bergère and black-and-white photos by Nic Tucker, in Room 1.

Pastis Hôtel-St. Tropez

ST.-TROPEZ, FRANCE

Like the property in the similarly titled 1994 book *Hotel Pastis* (whose author, Peter Mayle, drops by on occasion), Pastis's owners are transplanted Brits—and there's no shortage of Anglo style on display to prove it. With their eclectic Provence-by-way-of-London aesthetic, retail designers John and Pauline Larkin aim to make guests feel as if they are staying in a private house. Mies daybeds mix with Indian rugs, Chinese armoires, and beds dressed in traditional Provençal *boutis* spreads. Off-white walls showcase Hockney and Lichtenstein prints, as well as framed Sex Pistols and Rolling Stones album covers that date back to the Larkins' courtship. The furniture was scored at area flea markets or, in the case of the pewter bar in the lobby, custom-made.

61 Ave. du Général Leclerc, St.-Tropez, France; 33-4/98-12-56-50; www.pastis-st-tropez.com; doubles from $$

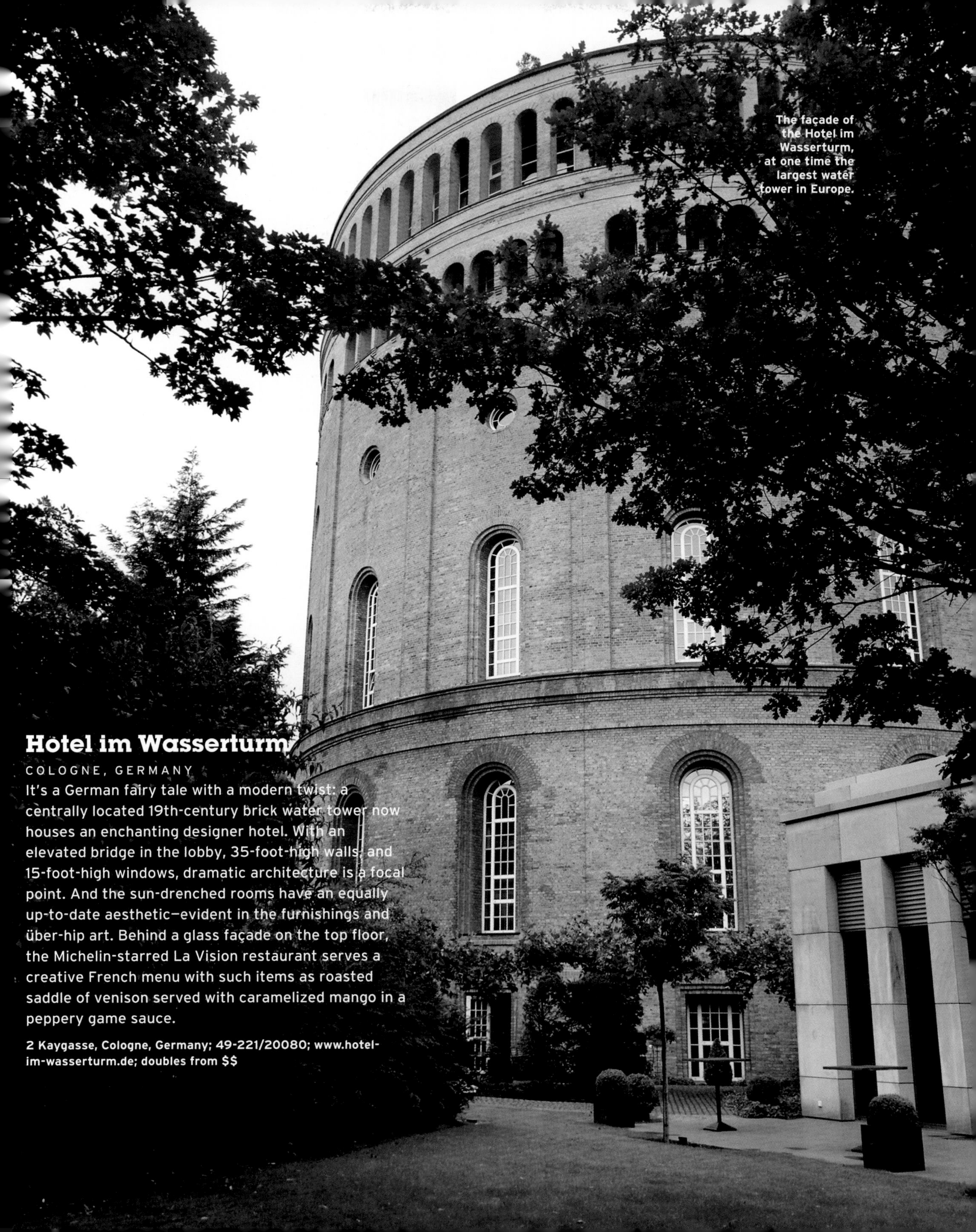

The façade of the Hotel im Wasserturm, at one time the largest water tower in Europe.

Hotel im Wasserturm

COLOGNE, GERMANY

It's a German fairy tale with a modern twist: a centrally located 19th-century brick water tower now houses an enchanting designer hotel. With an elevated bridge in the lobby, 35-foot-high walls, and 15-foot-high windows, dramatic architecture is a focal point. And the sun-drenched rooms have an equally up-to-date aesthetic—evident in the furnishings and über-hip art. Behind a glass façade on the top floor, the Michelin-starred La Vision restaurant serves a creative French menu with such items as roasted saddle of venison served with caramelized mango in a peppery game sauce.

2 Kaygasse, Cologne, Germany; 49-221/20080; www.hotel-im-wasserturm.de; doubles from $$

Radisson SAS Hotel, Frankfurt

FRANKFURT, GERMANY

Forty-seven years after Arne Jacobsen created Radisson SAS's first hotel, in Copenhagen, the fast-growing group continues its tradition of tapping A-list designers. At its latest property, Adam D. Tihany has created public spaces in a style he calls Industrial Luxe: glimmering décor and functional objets d'art (such as an iconic suspended wine tower) contrast with the exposed concrete of the structure itself. The futuristic blue glass–and–metal skyscraper– which floats between the autobahn and Frankfurt's exposition grounds–provides a surprising bit of whimsy in an otherwise buttoned-up city. Italian architect Matteo Thun painted the 16 floors in reds, pinks, and white, then gave each of the 428 rooms a distinct style, following one of four themes—Chic, Fresh, Fashion, At Home.

65 Franklinstrasse, Frankfurt, Germany; 800/333-3333 or 49-69/770-1550; www.frankfurt.radissonsas.com; doubles from $

The Radisson SAS Hotel's library, in the lobby.

Mavida Balance Hotel & Spa

ZELL AM SEE, AUSTRIA

Amid the lakes, mountains, and glaciers of a small Austrian village, architect Niki Szilagyi provides a new image of holistic hospitality at the Mavida Balance Hotel & Spa. In the 47 rooms and suites, Italian and German design play yin and yang: egg-shaped lamps by Flos shed warm light on chairs and beds by Casamilano, while slate-sided bathrooms come with edgy Hansgrohe fixtures and angular Dornbracht sinks. Elsewhere, nature takes center stage—in custom furniture made from native woods like elm and larch, artwork by Jutta de Bock (which uses actual sand from Lake Zell), and giant driftwood sculptures. In the open kitchen, cooks prepare healthful dinners using local produce seasoned with tarragon, thyme, and sage, all picked from Mavida's rooftop garden. Guests can seek inner harmony in the basement spa through sessions in the Blue Box—an oval room outfitted with two vibrating fiberglass recliners—and the saltwater Floatarium, where sensory deprivation is the ultimate experience of decadence.

11 Kirchenweg, Zell am See, Austria; 43-6/542-5410; www.mavida.at; doubles from $$, including breakfast

A view of the Hohe Tauern mountains from a suite at the Mavida Balance Hotel & Spa.

The 18th-century garden at the Villa Olmi Resort.

Villa Olmi Resort

FLORENCE, ITALY

Staying in the 18th-century Villa Olmi Resort—surrounded by expansive green acres just 10 minutes from Florence's Duomo—means not having to choose between city and country. Recently restored by a prominent Florentine family, the patrician retreat has just 50 guest rooms, all with original details: vaulted ceilings, marble bathrooms, antique furnishings, floral frescoes. Wander the formal gardens or bike the hills of Bagno a Ripoli. In the afternoon, a chauffeur-driven car can make the quick trip to the Duomo and the Uffizi—and be back in time for dinner in the estate's former stable.

4-8 Via degli Olmi, Bagno a Ripoli, Florence, Italy; 39-055/637-710; www.villaolmiresort.com; doubles from $$

Albergo Diffuso Santo Stefano di Sessanio

SANTO STEFANO DI SESSANIO, ITALY

The town of Santo Stefano di Sessanio (population 116), in the mountainous central Italian region of Abruzzi, may seem an unlikely place to find a boutique hotel. But as part of a $6.5 million overhaul, Italian-Swedish philosopher and preservationist Daniele Elow Kihlgren recently turned a handful of 15th-century buildings into a rustic-chic 44-room inn, complete with a weaver's atelier and an herbalist. In a nod to the area's traditions, the emphasis throughout the Albergo is on local craftsmanship, from the olive-oil soaps in the bathrooms to the hand-woven bedcovers colored with native plant dyes. In creating the inn's restaurant, "town elders" and an anthropologist were consulted for historical—and gastronomical—accuracy.

Santo Stefano di Sessanio, Italy; 39-085/497-2324; www.sextantio.it; doubles from $

The ancient stone buildings that surround the Albergo Diffuso Santo Stefano di Sessanio, above. Above left: A guest room.

Hotel Emilia

ANCONA, ITALY

Far from Capri's crush and Tuscany's throngs lie the untrammeled Adriatic beaches and austere hill towns of Le Marche. Hotel Emilia, a quietly grand villa set into a green plain overlooking a dizzying drop to the sea, captures the unadorned beauty of the area. The 1970's structures look like they might have been built by a disciple of Le Corbusier (but were in fact designed by Paola Salmoni, an architect from Ancona). Spare interiors are punctuated by Achille Castiglioni lights. The restaurant prepares simple but fabulous food such as spaghetti with *cozze* (mussels) using recipes from the Marche region, many handed down to the family-owners by their grandma Emilia. Eat by the pool reclining on a chaise while absentmindedly following the movements of couples playing Ping-Pong. Then stroll down to the beautiful white- and black-pebbled beach of Portonovo.

Poggio di Portonovo, Ancona, Italy; 39-071/801-145; www.hotelemilia.com; doubles from $$

The pool at Hotel
Emilia, overlooking the
Adriatic Sea. Opposite:
The main lawn.

H=110 cm   H=110 cm

The interior
courtyard of
the Buonanotte
Garibaldi, above.
Above right: The
inn's living room.

Buonanotte Garibaldi

ROME, ITALY

Furniture and fashion designer Luisa Longo has
transformed her family's 1960's villa into an intimate
three-bedroom guesthouse, located in Rome's artsy
Trastevere quarter. Longo has filled the inn's color-
themed rooms (Orange, Blue, Green) with family
heirlooms and her own Matisse- and Kandinsky-inspired
designs (bright silk bedspreads, lamps with abstract
swirls), all of which are for sale, conveniently, in the
adjoining studio. A palm-filled courtyard, ideal for
lounging after a long day of wandering the district's
labyrinthine streets, adds to the B&B's charm.

83 Via Garibaldi, Rome, Italy; 39-06/5833-0733; www.buonanotte
garibaldi.com; doubles from $$

The lobby at Byblos Art Hotel, right. Below right: *VB 43* (2002) by Vanessa Beecroft, hanging in the lobby.

Byblos Art Hotel Villa Amistà

CORRUBBIO DI NEGARINE, ITALY

Amid Valpolicella vineyards outside Romeo and Juliet's hometown of Verona, this classical Venetian-style villa appears ripe for an old-world romance. If the star-crossed lovers were to step through the arched doorway today, they would be in for a surprise. Proprietor Dino Facchini (who also owns the fashion line Byblos) has updated the estate with a frescoed ballroom tarted up with photographs of red-haired nudes by Vanessa Beecroft. The 60 rooms have whimsical details like harlequin patterns, fridges with painted faces, and asymmetrical mirrors. But the hotel is more than a house of fun. Couples can wind down in the Roman-style pool, detox in the spa, or head to the restaurant for sea bass sweetened with rose petals.

78 Via Cedrare, Corrubbio di Negarine, Italy; 39-045/685-5555; www.villaamista.com; doubles from $$

Castello del Nero's back patio and pool. Right: One of the hotel's six frescoed suites.

Castello del Nero

TAVARNELLE VAL DI PESA, ITALY

This 50-room boutique hotel, designed by Alain Mertens (interior designer to Madonna and Sting), is another reinvention of the classic Tuscan villa. The 12th-century former nobleman's residence on 990 hilly acres finds Philippe Starck Ghost chairs set beneath family crests and frescoes, and ancient stone-framed windows hung with bold curtains. Most of the rooms have wood-beamed ceilings, flat-screen TV's, and marble bathrooms, not to mention stunning views of the property's olive groves and vineyards. But be sure to venture out of your room for an aromatic massage at the spa or a meal of organic Tuscan dishes such as rice-and-spelt risotto served with porcini mushrooms and chestnuts at the hotel's stable turned restaurant. Also on the estate: a historic, frescoed chapel and adjoining Florentine rose garden—ideal for reenacting scenes from your favorite E. M. Forster novel.

7 Strada Spicciano, Tavarnelle Val di Pesa, Italy; 800/223-6800 or 39-055/806-470; www.castellodelnero.com; doubles from $$$$

Mirror-steel
flourishes on the
Frank Gehry-
designed Hotel
Marqués de Riscal.

Hotel Marqués de Riscal

ELCIEGO, SPAIN

Depending on whom you talk to, the architecture critic
at *El País* or the Elciego shopkeeper, Frank Gehry's hotel
at the Herederos del Marqués de Riscal winery erupts
with sublime grace or horrific violence. Reminiscent of
the Guggenheim Bilbao, with its restless whorls of
deconstructed metal, the main building of the hotel
(which is being managed by Starwood) is composed of
rectilinear sandstone elements buried in a knot of
curvilinear titanium and mirror-finish stainless steel. The
in-house restaurant specializes in soul-stirring Riojan
dishes like *croquetas bechamel*, and 14 meta-sleek guest
rooms quote the exterior's snaking forms in wall lights
and extravagant burnt-caramel leather headboards that
climb 15 feet to the ceiling. The remaining 29 rooms and
a Caudalie Vinotherapie spa–where guests can try a Red
Vine Bath–are in a stucco annex.

1 Calle Torrea, Elciego, Spain; 800/325-3589 or 34/945-
180-880; www.luxurycollection.com; doubles from $$$$$,
including breakfast

The corridor connecting the main building to the Hotel Marqués de Riscal's annex. Clockwise from bottom left: Tempranillo vines; a guest room with Gehry's signature windows; the rooftop lounge terrace.

The relaxation area next to the indoor pool at the hotel's Caudalie spa.

A Mudejar-style salon at the Gran Hotel Son Julia, above. Above right: A junior suite. Opposite: One of the hotel's pools.

Gran Hotel Son Julia

LLUCMAJOR, MAJORCA

At the end of a lavender-and-cypress-lined drive in Majorca's southeastern countryside, the Gran Hotel Son Julia presides over a landscape of orange and almond groves with an air of noblesse oblige. Once home to the aristocratic Julia family, the 15th-century stone estate is flanked by stucco terraces, jasmine-filled gardens, and two pools. The interiors are equally fit for royalty: abstract paintings by Majorcan artist Miquel Mesquida Sansó hang beneath vaulted ceilings; radiant handmade glass sconces light the terrazzo-floored hallways; and many of the 24 guest rooms are outfitted with four-poster beds. There's even a tiny Gothic chapel and a Mudejar-style salon inspired by the Alhambra.

Carr. S'Arenal a Llucmajor, Llucmajor, Majorca; 34/971-669-700; www.sonjulia.com; doubles from $$

The entrance to the Hospes Palau de la Mar.

Hospes Palau de la Mar

VALENCIA, SPAIN

A decade ago, Spain's third-largest city was known for its oranges and paella; it hardly felt like a major destination. Today, Valencia's population is booming, the skyline has been refashioned by the likes of Santiago Calatrava, and a spate of upmarket designer hotels is signaling the city's change in fortune. Among the most notable is the 66-room Palau de la Mar. A Hospes design team reconceived two adjoining 19th-century mansions near the Turia River, balancing original details—ornate carved doors, a marble double staircase in the lobby—with contemporary touches like modern art and a glass-and-steel patio.

14 Navarro Reverter, Valencia, Spain; 34/96-316-2884; www.hospes.es; doubles from $$

Hotel Neptuno

VALENCIA, SPAIN

When Valencia won the bid to host the 2007 America's Cup, there wasn't a single hotel on the waterfront near where the races are to be held. Since then, developers have scrambled to build ocean-side accommodations to suit the city's new profile. One property has emerged from the frenzy as the clear standout: Hotel Neptuno. With its cool retro signage and rooftop Jacuzzi, Neptuno's exterior is evocative of Modernist Miami. The inside, meanwhile, is pure Spain, with a dramatic glass elevator surrounded by a cascading waterfall and paintings by Valencian artists. Thirteen of the 47 rooms face the beach, and while they're not the most spacious, they make the most of what they have, with rectangles of chocolate-colored wood serving as headboard, nightstand, and light fixtures.

2 Passeig de Neptuno, Valencia, Spain; 34/96-356-7777; www.hotelneptunovalencia.com; doubles from $$

The lobby bar at
Hotel Neptuno.

The indoor lap pool at the Four Seasons Hotel Ritz, Lisbon. Left: The Almada Negreiros lounge.

Four Seasons Hotel Ritz, Lisbon

LISBON, PORTUGAL

The Portuguese capital has emerged as a city whose creative energy coexists harmoniously with its old-world charms. A prime example is the Four Seasons Hotel Ritz, Lisbon. Commissioned by Salazar in 1953, the 282-room gilt-edged sanctuary—with museum-quality sculptures and tapestries—is set on one of Lisbon's seven hills, overlooking the Eduardo VII Park. In 2003 the hotel added an appropriately luxurious pool and 16,000-square-foot spa, with tall panels of polished dark wood, high ceilings, and Zen-like relaxation rooms. The restaurant, Varanda, which serves light nouvelle-Portuguese cuisine (predictably strong on seafood), continues to attract Lisbon's captains of industry and society doyennes.

88 Rua Rodrigo da Fonseca, Lisbon, Portugal; 800/332-3442 or 351-21/381-1400; www.fourseasons.com; doubles from $$

145

Argentikon

CHIOS, GREECE

The Argentikon is not a typical unadorned, whitewashed Mediterranean villa. Built by an aristocratic Italian family named Argenti during the Genoese occupation of the island of Chios, the five restored 16th-century buildings ensure guests the same level of privacy that originally drew ministers and royalty. Each of the eight suites is majestically decorated (heavy wood, period furniture, frescoed ceilings, damask curtains), and two suites can be converted into a sprawling apartment, with five bedrooms, three bathrooms, and two living rooms. Throughout, history reigns, with ornate stonework, a timeless rose garden, and a *manganos* (horse-drawn waterwheel), the oldest in Chios.

Chios, Greece; 30-227/103-3111; www.argentikon.gr; doubles from $$$$

The Castello Suite at the Argentikon, below. Below right: The villa's swimming pool.

Sumahan on the Water

ÇENGELKÖY, TURKEY

To convert a 19th-century Istanbul distillery into a boutique hotel, owner-architects Mark and Nedret Butler looked to the Bosporus for inspiration. At their 18-room Sumahan on the Water, the most compelling element is the view of palaces, skyscrapers, Hagia Sophia, and, of course, that sparkling strait. European starlets keep a low profile in the residential-style lobby, with its steel crossbeams, high ceilings, and fireplace. Sea and sky, framed by picture windows, blend into the blues and grays of the guest suites. Aboard the hotel's yacht, *Sumahan I*, you can float along the Bosporus to the sound of the evening call to prayers.

51 Kuleli Caddesi, Çengelköy, Turkey; 90-216/422-8000; www.sumahan.com; doubles from $$

The Sumahan's indoor-outdoor dining room, overlooking the Bosporus.

The Grand Hotel Europe's lobby bar.

Grand Hotel Europe

ST. PETERSBURG, RUSSIA

After a two-year, $30 million makeover from new owners Orient-Express, this Neoclassical grand dame, which has played host to Queen Elizabeth II and former president Bill Clinton and is one of St. Petersburg's most stately landmarks, looks better than ever. Since its opening in 1830, the hotel has gone by various names (Kuolon, Evropeyskaya) and also served as an orphanage during the Revolution and a hospital during World War II. French designer Michel Jouannet (responsible for the face-lift of the Cipriani Hotel in Venice) has primped the 301 rooms to plush perfection. Specialties of the hotel's famed Caviar Bar—Caspian caviar, blini, chilled Tsarskaya Gold vodka—will make you feel as though you're dining with czars.

1/7 Nevsky Prospekt, St. Petersburg, Russia; 800/237-1236 or 7-812/329-6000; www.grandhoteleurope.com; doubles from $$$

148

The exterior of Hotel Yasmin, in the center of Prague, above. Above right: Noodles, the hotel's café and bar.

Hotel Yasmin

PRAGUE, CZECH REPUBLIC

Design junkies traveling to Prague, take note: even if you don't stay at the over-the-top Hotel Yasmin, it's worth it to stop in for a peek. The 198-room property, housed in a former office building near Wenceslas Square, gleefully thumbs its nose at the city's baroque leanings. Silver orbs dangle from the ceiling in the hotel restaurant, Noodles; sculptures covered in red faux fur stand like sentinels in public spaces; and bathrooms are clad in black tile. This is definitely not the Prague of its backpacker heyday.

12/913 Politickych Veznu, Prague, Czech Republic; 420-2/3410-0100; www.hotel-yasmin.cz; doubles from $$

AFRICA+
THE MIDDLE EAST

Singita Grumeti Reserves, in Surengeti National Park, Tanzania.

THE
BEST
OF
2007

AFRICA
+
THE
MIDDLE
EAST

A covered *sala*, or
veranda, at Faru
Faru, in Singita
Grumeti Reserves.

Singita Grumeti Reserves

GRUMETI RESERVES, TANZANIA

South Africa's pioneering Singita tourism group
revamped a pair of lavish lodges and a tented camp in
the Grumeti Reserves of Serengeti National Park. You
almost expect to see Teddy Roosevelt behind the wheel
of one of the two vintage Chevrolets parked at the
entrance to Sabora, a safari camp accessorized with
antique mahogany chests, worn-leather folding chairs,
and thick Persian rugs. Faru Faru, with six chalets
overlooking the Grumeti River, channels a Swahili beach
resort; a swimming pool curves in front of an open-air
lounge, where guests sip sunset cocktails as elephants
gather at the watering hole below. The reserve's flagship
is Sasakwa, an East African ranch house set on a plateau
with panoramic views of the plains. The lodge's wood-
paneled libraries have an English country club feel, and
there are seven cottage residences, each with a garden
and plunge pool. Tennis courts, a spa, and a yoga center
occupy guests between twice-daily game drives, where
sightings include wildebeest, zebras, and gazelles.

Grumeti Reserves, Tanzania; 800/735-2478 or 770/947-7049;
www.grumetireserves.com. $$$$, all-inclusive, per person for
Sabora and Faru Faru, $$$$$ for Sasakwa

THE
BEST
OF
2007

AFRICA
+
THE
MIDDLE
EAST

Marataba

LIMPOPO, SOUTH AFRICA

Marataba is the newest golden-era safari experience from the Hunter Hotels group, responsible for bringing crystal-decanter, high-thread-count wilderness chic to coastal South Africa. Prouvé-style furniture that would look at home in a SoHo loft adorns the 15 tented suites, three with river views. Architectural lighting hangs from roughly hewn beams in the main lodge, and chaises line the outer edges of the 40-foot plunge pool. Suite No. 1, reached by a walking bridge that spans a small gorge (and is high enough for an elephant to pass below), is the most secluded. Its vast picture window has views of the Waterberg Mountains to the north. Marataba's biggest asset is its location, in Marakele National Park, which holds large numbers of the Big Five (lion, elephant, buffalo, leopard, and black rhinoceros) and is a sanctuary for rare antelope, like roan and sable, and 400 kinds of birds, including the endangered Cape vulture.

Limpopo, South Africa; 800/735-2478 or 27-44/532-7818; www.hunterhotels.com; doubles from $$$$, all-inclusive

Marataba, in South Africa's 131,000-acre Marakele National Park.

Spotlight:
Cape Town

A guest room at An African Villa, above. Above right: Zulu wedding hats on a headboard. Opposite: The library, with an illuminated papier-mâché kudu head guarding the fireplace.

An African Villa

CAPE TOWN, SOUTH AFRICA

Three terraced Victorian houses in the sunny hills of Cape Town's Tamboerskloof district make up this 12-room boutique hotel. Distinctly African, the floors are covered with antelope-skin rugs, and halls are lit by onyx lamps crafted by local members of the Xhosa tribe. Every piece of furniture was commissioned specifically for the hotel, and most of it is for sale—from the papier-mâché lampshade in the shape of a kudu head over the fireplace to the red Zulu hats mounted on a headboard. Owners Jimmy van Tonder and Louis Nel like to give guests a personal introduction to the city at the hotel's candlelit pool, glasses of Pinotage in hand.

19 Carstens St., Tamboerskloof, Cape Town, South Africa; 27-21/423-2162; www.capetowncity.co.za/villa; doubles from $, including breakfast

THE
BEST
OF
2007

AFRICA
+
THE
MIDDLE
EAST

Spotlight:
Cape Town

Cape Grace

CAPE TOWN, SOUTH AFRICA

WORLD'S BEST The luxe 122-room Cape Grace, on a private quay on the Victoria & Alfred Waterfront, is best known for its top-notch service. The large and comfortable quarters are handsomely outfitted with mahogany furniture, cream-colored linens, botanical prints, and brass light fixtures. The view of Table Mountain from the top-floor spa is the best in town. The marina-side whiskey bar, Bascule, stocks 460 single-malts and blends; watch the international yachts drift into port from an outside table. At informal evening discussions in the library, sip a glass of Shiraz from nearby Franschhoek while brushing up on South African history. For an eye on contemporary culture, the hotel's personal shopper runs tours of area boutiques and art studios.

West Quay, Victoria & Alfred Waterfront, Cape Town, South Africa; 800/223-6800 or 27-21/410-7100; www.capegrace.com; doubles from $$$

Daddy Long Legs

CAPE TOWN, SOUTH AFRICA

Thirteen artists were each given the same budget to decorate the rooms at Daddy Long Legs. Guests are taken on a tour of the unoccupied "exhibitions" and then invited to select their favorite. Among the options: Open Room, with wallpaper picturing Cape Town sunsets, and You Are Here, a serene space with maps pinpointing this prime spot on one of the city's oldest and most vibrant streets. On weekends, ad hoc Drama Night parties (with open-mike sessions and free concerts) are held in the lounge. Every couple of months, the contemporary art in the hallways is changed—creating another excuse for a party. A tip: if you're sensitive to noise, pick a room at the rear of the building, far from the lounge and the street.

134 Long St., Cape Town, South Africa; 27-21/422-3074; www.daddylonglegs.co.za; doubles from $

The entrance to the Victorian Cape Cadogan, above. Opposite, from left: Corrugated-iron ceiling and jarrah-wood chairs at the Bascule Whisky Bar at Cape Grace; the Open Room at Daddy Long Legs.

Cape Cadogan Boutique Hotel

CAPE TOWN, SOUTH AFRICA

Once a dark Victorian house, this national monument is now flooded with light, thanks to a renovation by its English and South African owners, who tore down walls and retrofitted period windows and doors. In the 12-room hotel, Italian crystal chandeliers and framed pastel prints complement the cheery whites and golds of the walls, curtains, and bed coverings, and beaded screens add a little flair. Bedrooms have travertine-tiled bathrooms that open onto a private courtyard. A basket of fresh fruit and a decanter of wine greet guests upon arrival; after a night out, port and chocolates await by the fireplace in the lounge.

5 Upper Union St., Tamboerskloof, Cape Town, South Africa; 27-21/480-8080; www.capecadogan.com; doubles from $

THE
BEST
OF
2007

AFRICA
+
THE
MIDDLE
EAST

Spotlight:
Cape Town

The heated outdoor pool at the Vineyard Hotel & Spa fronts the glass-enclosed fitness center.

Vineyard Hotel & Spa

CAPE TOWN, SOUTH AFRICA

The Vineyard, built around a 200-year-old homestead in the tranquil and leafy suburb of Newlands, has just emerged from a significant face-lift. A majority of its 173 bedrooms have been redone, and the work is most successful in the 10 Riverside rooms—with natural colors, Mozambican wood floors, stone-tiled bathrooms, and private gardens. In addition to a state-of-the-art gym, the hotel now has an Angsana Spa, where the signature massage blends Thai, Swedish, and Balinese techniques. Vineyard's Au Jardin restaurant also brings international influences; for example, French chef Alex Coupy prepares such dishes as Mozambican black tiger prawn curry. When you've had your fill of relaxation, the city center is just 15 minutes away.

Colinton Rd., Newlands, Cape Town, South Africa; 27-21/657-4500; www.vineyard.co.za; doubles from $

Mount Nelson Hotel's
Planet Champagne Bar,
above. Above right:
The hotel lounge.

Mount Nelson Hotel

CAPE TOWN, SOUTH AFRICA

WORLD'S BEST This pink hotel—also known as the Nellie—has been a Cape Town favorite for more than 100 years. Guests continue to come for the old-world elegance, the elaborate afternoon tea, and the sweeping nine-acre gardens with two pools and tennis courts. New executive chef Ian Mancais, who created the Rangali Hilton's undersea restaurant in the Maldives, has added flash to the menu with Southeast Asian flavors. And a recent refurbishment of the Oasis wing has restored the grande dame's classic style, with gleaming mirrors, four-poster beds, and historic prints of South Africa. In the terraced Victorian cottages, the Garden Suites are a secret hideaway for visiting celebrities seeking sanctuary.

76 Orange St., Gardens, Cape Town, South Africa; 800/237-1236 or 27-21/483-1000; www.mountnelson.co.za; doubles from $$$, including breakfast

THE
BEST
OF
2007

AFRICA
+
THE
MIDDLE
EAST

A path leading to
a Karoo cottage at
Samara Private Game
Reserve, above. Above
right: The lodge's main
dining room. Opposite:
The Kobbe Suite at
Dar Seffarine.

Samara Private Game Reserve

GRAAFF-REINET, SOUTH AFRICA

It's easy to forget that a world beyond the horizon exists at Samara, one of the Eastern Cape's largest private game reserves. The six suites are decorated in indigenous Cape style (reed ceilings, tin roofs, yellowwood and stinkwood furniture), and picture windows look out on big skies and purple mountains. Animals such as springbok, eland, oryx, and the endangered Cape mountain zebra roam the property. For total privacy (and more luxury), splurge on one of the three freestanding Karoo cottages: they have sitting areas, fireplaces, and outdoor showers and are located steps from the main lodge. Game drives are spent tracking rare cheetah. In the evenings, everyone heads to a *boma* (rural fortress) to dine on springbok loin, venison carpaccio, and Karoo lamb *koftas* (meatballs) served in ostrich eggs.

Graaff-Reinet, South Africa; 27-49/891-0880; www.samara.co.za; doubles from $$$, all-inclusive

Dar Seffarine

FEZ, MOROCCO

As tourists and builders take over Marrakesh, the former capital of Morocco, Fez, is becoming its spiritual center. Europeans and Americans, charmed by the city's rich history, are snapping up still-affordable *dars* and *riads* to open bed-and-breakfasts, replete with extravagant tile work and lacy iron grilles. One of the more atmospheric new inns is Dar Seffarine, a 16th-century palace in Fez's ancient medina, with six exactingly appointed rooms and a tranquil, beautifully tiled courtyard. Just beyond its high walls is Place Seffarine—a whirl of sights, sounds, and scents where silver merchants hawk their wares.

14 Derb Sbaa Louyate, Fez, Morocco; 212-71/113-528; www.darseffarine.com; doubles from $, including breakfast

THE
BEST
OF
2007

AFRICA
+
THE
MIDDLE
EAST

Hotel Le Mirage

TANGIER, MOROCCO

After decades of neglect, Tangier is metamorphosing into a North African St.-Tropez, and several hotels are rising to the occasion. At the posh Le Mirage resort, a complex of 25 pristine white-tiled bungalows are built on cliffs that tumble down into the Atlantic. Bold paisleys and English plaids cover tufted chairs and ottomans (and the walls), and dark Moorish-style lattice woodwork outlines archways. Not much separates you from the sea, save for the simple white balustrades on the oversize balconies. A seafood-inspired menu in the main restaurant includes saffron-flavored *soupe de poisson,* garlicky grilled prawns, and, the signature dish, oven-baked fish crusted in sea salt.

Cap Spartel, Tangier, Morocco; 212-39/333-332; www.lemirage-tanger.com; doubles from $$

Cliffside bungalows overlooking the Atlantic, at Hotel Le Mirage.

A ring of tents at Pansea Ksar Ghilane, right. Below right: The VIP bedroom. Opposite: The resort's swimming pool.

Pansea Ksar Ghilane

KSAR GHILANE, TUNISIA

With travel frontiers dwindling, the Tunisian desert still holds the promise of a true pioneer experience. Those willing to endure a rugged four-hour drive over unpaved Saharan roads and through blinding salt flats will be rewarded with Ksar Ghilane, an otherworldly camp on 25 acres of olive, pomegranate, and tamarisk trees. The 60 private, 300-square-foot canvas tents are improbably equipped with full bathrooms, heating, and even air conditioning. Climb the five-story observation tower for a look beyond the mirage-like, sultry pool. Unlike conventional camps, Ksar Ghilane won't harangue guests with a long menu of activities. The most anyone suggests you do is visit the ruins of a second-century A.D. Roman fort or try a bedouin dinner of *gargoulette* (a type of lamb stew), served in low-slung wool tents.

Ksar Ghilane, Tunisia; 216-75/621-870; www.pansea.com; doubles from $

THE
BEST
OF
2007

AFRICA
+
THE
MIDDLE
EAST

Left, from top: A
corridor in the Burj
Al Arab's Assawan
Spa & Health Club;
the hotel's Al Mahara
restaurant; a view of
the Sahn Eddar room,
at the base of the
world's tallest atrium.
Opposite: The hotel's
interior atrium.

Burj Al Arab

JUMEIRAH, DUBAI, UNITED ARAB EMIRATES
For a prime example of Dubai's extravagance, look no
further than the 1,000-foot, $2,000-a-night, self-
proclaimed "seven-star" Burj Al Arab. The furniture in
each of the 202 duplex suites is idiosyncratic, oversize,
and color-saturated, as if designed by the love child of
Salvador Dalí and Antonio Gaudí. Your own personal
butler will unpack for you (there is a special hidden-away
area just for luggage storage) and arrange for an
aromatherapy bath in the comfort of your own whirlpool.
Moving among the giant chairs to reach for pistachio-and-
honey sweets on the coffee table, you'll feel like a tiny
Alice in an Arabian Wonderland. One hotel restaurant, Al
Muntaha, extends over the ocean and can be reached only
by a panoramic elevator; the other, Al Mahara, features a
large seawater aquarium and is accessed via a three-
minute "simulated submarine voyage."

Jumeirah, Dubai, United Arab Emirates; 877/854-8051 or 971-
4/301-7777; www.burj-al-arab.com; doubles from $$$$$

ASIA

THE
BEST
OF
2007

ASIA

Spotlight:
Bali

Bulgari Resort, Bali

ULUWATU, BALI

Italian refinement meets Asian hospitality at Bulgari's first resort, on a 500-foot-high headland on the southern shore of Bali. The 59 freestanding villas are built of ylang-ylang thatch, volcanic stone, and dark tropical woods, while the spa's main pavilion is an antique, hand-carved *joglo* house, relocated from the island of Java. The Milanese style of designer Antonio Citterio (who also created the Bulgari Hotel in Milan) is apparent in the chocolate tones of the cliff-top bar, the geometry of the bamboo-beamed ceilings, and the clean lines of the black terrazzo bathrooms. A helicopter and vintage Harley-Davidsons are available for use, but the hotel's best feature is the untouched beach, worthy of Robinson Crusoe.

Jalan Goa Lempeh, Banjar Dinas Kangin, Uluwatu, Bali; 800/628-5427 or 62-361/847-1000; www.bulgarihotels.com; doubles from $$$$

172

A villa pool at Ubud Hanging Gardens. Left: The master bedroom in Como Shambhala's Tejasuara villa.

Como Shambhala Estate at Begawan Giri

UBUD, BALI

Travelers seeking an off-the-radar retreat in Bali can find it in the Como Shambhala Estate at Begawan Giri, a new spa from hotelier Christina Ong (Parrot Cay, the Metropolitan). Added on to the original Begawan Giri—where each of the five villas has its own infinity pool—are 13 treatment rooms, an open-air yoga studio, several lounging pavilions, and two restaurants with exotic menus that are tailored to any dietary whim (try the sea vegetable and avocado salad, with or without daikon). Both visiting masters (Robert Thurman has led Buddhist seminars) and holistic specialists in residence are on-site to provide a range of experiences to enrich body and mind.

Ubud, Bali; 62-361/978-888; www.comoshambhala.bz; doubles from $$

Ubud Hanging Gardens

PAYANGAN, BALI

Overlooking the dramatic Ayung River gorge, this recently opened 38-villa resort is a botanical masterpiece. Landscape architects William Warren (author of *Balinese Gardens*) and John Pettigrew planted birds-of-paradise and orchids, plus cocoa, coffee, durian, lychee, and rambutan trees, throughout the terraced grounds. Each villa has been decorated in a simple but luxurious Balinese style and comes with a private plunge pool, open-air shower, and *bale*, a traditional pavilion for relaxing. A funicular (yes, the property is that steep) transports guests from the rooms to the hillside below, where there's a two-level, free-form infinity pool; two Balinese-French restaurants; and the spa, which has three pavilions with thatched alang-alang roofs.

Payangan, Bali; 800/237-1236 or 62-361/982-2700; www. ubudhanginggardens.com; doubles from $$

Outside the main
building at the Four
Seasons Resort Bali
at Sayan. Above right:
The resort's Ayung
Terrace restaurant.

Four Seasons Resort Bali at Sayan

UBUD, BALI

WORLD'S BEST When it opened its second property on Bali in 1998, the Four Seasons gambled on an audacious design concept for the resort, which is hidden in the highlands outside the artists' town of Ubud. The main building resembles a flying saucer practically hanging over the sacred Ayung River, where villagers come to perform their daily ablutions. But the idea worked, and over the last decade the resort has drawn a loyal following for its unparalleled service as well as its plush accommodations. From inside one of the villas located deep in the valley—amid rice paddies, heliconias, and coconut palms—the steep walls of the valley look like a green waterfall tumbling down. And the echoing bird cries can reach symphonic proportions.

Sayan, Ubud, Bali; 800/332-3442 or 62-361/977-577; www.fourseasons.com; doubles from $$

THE
BEST
OF
2007

ASIA

Spotlight:
Bali

Water gardens ring
the Padi restaurant
at Ritz-Carlton
Bali Resort & Spa.

Ritz-Carlton Bali Resort & Spa

JIMBARAN, BALI

WORLD'S BEST All the luxuries (silk drapes, marble baths) that the Ritz is known for have been transported to this choice island location, a private jetty that juts out into the Indian Ocean off Bali's southern coast. Wardrobes made of Indonesian woods (sonokeling, anygre, or nyatoh) accent the 375 rooms. Elaborately carved stone gates lead to the even more exclusive villas, where a flower-petal bath in a windowed, two-person soaking tub is drawn up on arrival. There are 12 restaurants, but the best dining option is on a private pier, with the ocean below, surrounded only by candlelight and fringed Balinese umbrellas.

Jimbaran, Bali; 800/241-3333 or 62-361/702-222; www.ritzcarlton.com; doubles from $$

A pool at one of the Four Seasons Resort Bali at Jimbaran Bay's nine estates.

Four Seasons Resort Bali at Jimbaran Bay

DENPASAR, BALI

WORLD'S BEST The winding lanes running through the island's first Four Seasons Resort replicate the feel of a traditional Balinese village, complete with tiny rice offerings to the gods tucked in doorways. The 147 villas—lavish versions of thatched-roof houses with brightly painted wood doors, marble floors, and teak furnishings—surround private plunge pools attended by gargoylesque stone fountains. For more local flavor, follow a trip to the food market with a class at the resort's cooking school, where you can learn to make dishes like banana-leaf-wrapped red snapper.

Jimbaran, Denpasar, Bali; 800/332-3442 or 62-361/701-010; www.fourseasons.com; doubles from $$$

D2 Hotel

CHIANG MAI, THAILAND

Design aficionados heading to Thailand's cultural capital now have a 21st-century destination to visit between tours of ancient temples. A mango's toss from Chiang Mai's Night Bazaar, the 131-room D2 Hotel combines natural Thai materials with high-style spunk. Softening the lobby's bold, futuristic strokes are handmade carpets and raw-silk pillows. In the guest rooms, you'll find fresh sugi conifers (pine-tree plants) and daybeds strewn with bright-saffron, ball-shaped silk cushions. The Mix Bar is framed in frosted glass and lit by raindrop pendants. At the airy Moxie restaurant, artists, writers, and members of Bangkok society sample watermelon mojitos and penne tossed with fried holy basil. Chiang Mai's chestnut-colored Ping River, open-air bars, and vivid flower markets are all within a 10-minute walk.

100 Chang Klan Rd., Chiang Mai, Thailand; 800/525-4800 or 66-53/999-999; www.d2hotels.com; doubles from $

The lobby of the D2 Hotel.

Dream Bangkok

BANGKOK, THAILAND

The latest from hipster hotelier Vikram Chatwal, who created New York's Dream Hotel, is the 100-room Dream Bangkok, on cosmopolitan Sukhumvit Road. A winding staircase leads from the sofa-filled lobby to the Flava Restaurant + Lounge, where the menu, created by expat Australian chef David Hamilton, melds Thai and Western culinary traditions in dishes like banana-flower salad with fresh green coconut and chile paste. Soft lights guide guests through the inky darkness of indigo-blue corridors. By day the rooms are all white and chrome, but with the addition of nighttime mood lighting, things become surreal: the whites resemble the neon of the streets, and the platform beds—lit from below—appear to float.

10 Sukhumvit Soi 15, Klongtoey Nua, Wattana, Bangkok, Thailand; 877/474-7500 or 66-2/254-8500; www.dreambkk.com; doubles from $

Dream Bangkok's Flava Restaurant + Lounge, above. Above left: The hotel lobby.

Aleenta Resort & Spa Phuket-Phangnga

PHANGNGA, THAILAND

There's not a thatched roof or pagoda in sight at Aleenta's newest resort and spa, set on a pristine stretch of private beach an hour north of Phuket. A follow-up to the Aleenta in Hua Hin, the famed beach town 140 miles south of Bangkok, the hotel retains much of what has made its sister property so popular, from its intimate size (only 30 suites and villas) to its integration of indoor and outdoor space (some walls are made almost entirely of glass). Clean lines define the white, cream, and brown rooms, which have teak and oak detailing. The hotel is crisscrossed by wooden walkways that meet at right angles and divide the suites' private plunge pools. The result is a striking silhouette—a series of pale rectangles rising from the sand.

Khao Pilai Beach, Kok Kloy, Phangnga, Thailand; 800/525-4800 or 66-2/508-5333; www.aleenta.com; doubles from $$

A beachfront villa facing the Andaman Sea, at the Aleenta Resort & Spa.

Poolside sun loungers at the Four Seasons Tented Camp, right. Below right: The Textile Tent. Opposite: Looking out over the Ruak River from the Silver Tent.

Four Seasons Tented Camp Golden Triangle

CHIANG RAI, THAILAND

The mountains of northern Thailand—where Burma, Thailand, and Laos meet—now harbor one of the world's most luxurious campsites. Fifteen open-air tents with polished-teak floors and hand-wrought, copper-clad bathtubs take the edge off of roughing it. Though not completely: to reach the spa, restaurant, and two bars, you walk beneath bamboo trees and jungle ferns and brave a 60-foot-high suspension bridge. Days can be spent exploring local villages, riding one of the six pachyderms in residence (they have their own tent and pool), or floating down the Mekong. Gourmet picnics, including linen napkins, a folding table, and stools, are supplied for your excursions. Not to miss: a Thai massage on your private sundeck at dusk, listening to a chorus of frogs and birds along the Ruak River.

Chiang Rai, Golden Triangle, Thailand; 800/332-3442 or 66-53/931-200; www.fourseasons.com; doubles from $$$$$, two-night minimum, all-inclusive

183

Lotus flowers in Chiva-Som's reflecting pool, left. Below left: A Thai pavilion *sala*, or outdoor living room. Opposite: Poolside, near the beach.

Chiva-Som International Health Resort

HUA HIN, THAILAND

WORLD'S BEST Given that its setting is near the King of Thailand's summer palace, it's only fitting that this destination spa—hidden within seven acres of banyan- and frangipani-filled gardens on the beach of Hua Hin—makes you feel like royalty. After a welcoming lemongrass tea, a personal adviser will help you plan your program of classes, lectures, and treatments, which include holistic approaches from around the world, such as a detoxifying Chi Nei Tsang abdominal organ massage and Australian bush flower stress-relief elixirs. With a 7-to-1 staff-to-guest ratio, as many ultramodern treatment rooms as there are guest rooms (57), and butlers, Chiva-Som takes service seriously.

Hua Hin, Thailand; 66-3/253-6536; www.chivasom.com; doubles from $$$$, three-night minimum, all inclusive

Carcosa Seri Negara,
a former British
government residence.

Carcosa Seri Negara

KUALA LUMPUR, MALAYSIA

Getting a handle on Malaysia's rapid growth is as simple as looking at the soaring skyline of Kuala Lumpur. One welcome reminder of the city's colonial past is the Carcosa Seri Negara, a rambling two-story mansion that functioned as the residence of the colonial governor of the Malay States in the early 1900's, and as host to visiting British royals in the years since. An old-school formality still imbues the 13-suite hotel, filled with Victorian-era furniture, gold-plated sink basins, and French windows that open out to tropical gardens. A butler attends to guests around the clock, and the bar serves those trying to recapture the era of Somerset Maugham, when colonial officers in remote jungle outposts still dressed up for dinner.

Taman Tasik Perdana, Kuala Lumpur, Malaysia; 60-3/2295-0888; www.carcosa.com.my; suites from $$

One Hotel Angkor

SIEM REAP, CAMBODIA

Siem Reap is no stranger to luxury. But the new One Hotel Angkor is putting a modern spin on the concept with something the town has never seen before: a one-room hotel. Think of One Hotel, located on the Passage, a pedestrian-only lane in the heart of the former colonial quarter, as your own stylish pied-à-terre, a row house with a thatched roof and wooden jalousies that's straight out of a Graham Greene novel. A curvaceous, king-size platform bed dominates the master bedroom. In the bathroom, everything is built for two: a doorless, three-foot-wide shower; a seven-foot-long step-in tub; and an ingenious vanity with deep twin sinks. A bamboo lamp, hand-loomed silk pillows, and lemongrass soap add indigenous touches. Guests are issued a complimentary mobile phone while in residence; order from any area restaurant, and a staffer will fetch your meal for you. An alfresco massage? Done. A private car and guide to the ruins? No problem. The best caipirinha in town? Coming right up the stairs.

Siem Reap, Cambodia; 415/992-5431 or 855-12/246-912; www.theonehotelangkor.com; $$

One Hotel Angkor's lobby and cafe. Above, from left: The entire hotel; an open-air whirlpool and daybed screened by yellow palms.

Heritance Kandalama

DAMBULLA, SRI LANKA

Few hotels are more sensitively fitted to their setting than the Kandalama, a luxury eco-lodge (certified by the U.S. Green Building Council) set against a cliff and roofed with sod, in the center of Sri Lanka's Cultural Triangle, an area filled with ancient Buddhist temples and monuments. Airy and large, the 152 rooms are furnished with local mahogany and dense-grained padauk beds, tables, and chairs. More than 165 species of birds make their home in the surrounding forest. Linger on the terrace, watching hawks kiting in thermals above the lake or herons, their wings unfurling with the creaky mechanics of umbrella spokes.

Sigiriya, Dambulla, Sri Lanka; 94-11/230-8408; www.heritance hotels.com; doubles from $

Heritance Kandalama, with a night-lit infinity pool

SwaSwara's pavilion
suites, facing
the Arabian Sea.

SwaSwara

GOKARNA, KARNATAKA, INDIA

India's ancient healing tradition of Ayurveda is sweeping the spa world. To experience it at its purest, head to the source: Karnataka, India's holistic heartland. Named after the Sanskrit words for *self* and *sound,* the 34-acre SwaSwara, a new 24-villa yoga retreat, sits on a cliff dotted with rice paddies, overlooking a beach that's appropriately named Om. The hotel's Ayurvedic therapists customize total-health stays that include yoga, massage, and meditation. Tailor your meals to match your strict regimen. Or not: the regular menu items (fresh fish, locally grown produce, tangy *kokum* juice) are also good for your health. All villas have air-conditioning, tiled roofs, and a private path to the beach.

Gokarna, Karnataka, India; 91-484/266-8221; www.swaswara.com; doubles from $$, including breakfast

Lori-Avan Dzoraget Hotel

LORI PROVINCE, ARMENIA

A tourism boom has come to Armenia, and a network of stylish places are replacing stoic Soviet hotels. The Lori-Avan Dzoraget Hotel—one of the three Heritage Hotels owned by James Tufenkian, the New York-based founder of Tufenkian Artisan Carpets—epitomizes the country's entry into luxury-level hospitality. The three-floor, 34-room mountain retreat rests on the cusp of the Debed River in the northern region of Armenia, rimmed by imposing rock formations and a maze of rivers and forests. The medieval castle-like hotel in many ways exemplifies the colorful clash of the old and new currently found in central Asia: the interior is furnished with contemporary pieces and Armenian rugs from Tufenkian's extensive supply, but you can still step outside and watch shepherds herding their flocks just beyond the driveway.

Lori Province, Armenia; 374-10/547-888; www.tufenkianheritage.com; doubles from $

The Lori-Avan Dzoraget Hotel, in the Armenian countryside.

THE
BEST
OF
2007

ASIA

Spotlight:
Hong Kong

The Four Seasons Hong Kong's Caprice restaurant, right. Below right: An executive suite. Opposite: Two waterfront swimming pools.

Four Seasons Hotel Hong Kong

CENTRAL, HONG KONG

WORLD'S BEST In a city as confining as Hong Kong, light is a remarkably rare commodity. Reflecting the industrial style of Cesar Pelli's glass-sheathed skyscraper next door, the new Four Seasons is flooded with sun, whether you're in the 22,000-square-foot spa or sitting on a velvet banquette in the marble lobby. The crowd ranges from foreign diplomats to Hong Kong socialites, and the two types of rooms—Chinese and Western—reflect the changing clientele of the city. The Chinese option is outfitted with shiny lacquer, gold leaf, and dark teaks, while the Western is clubbier, accented with neutral tones and leather. Spin Design Studio from Tokyo is responsible for the lit-from-below catwalk and stingray-skin cupboards of Caprice, which has already become one of Asia's top French dining rooms. Its chef, fresh from the Michelin-three-starred Le Cinq in Paris, turns out haute Gallic dishes such as langoustine tartare with watercress mousse and Iranian caviar.

8 Finance St., Central, Hong Kong; 800/819-5053 or 852/3196-8888; www.fourseasons.com; doubles from $$

InterContinental Hong Kong

KOWLOON, HONG KONG

WORLD'S BEST The infinity pool on the terrace of the new $11,200-a-night Presidential Suite at the InterContinental appears to share water with Victoria Harbour. (If only the pool had regular edges, you could rest your scotch on one of them as you gazed through the mist at those luminous skyscrapers.) The 7,000-square-foot suite comes with two 24-hour butlers, a gymnasium, and high-tech toilet seats that rise automatically when you enter the room. This over-the-top lair is just one of the impressive additions to the property, which has undergone an overhaul to stay competitive in the city's heated hotel market. There's also a fleet of butlers for guests in the 495 spiffed-up rooms (with iPod docks and Bose surround sound), and outposts of Nobu and Alain Ducasse's Spoon. One thing didn't require improvement: the hotel's unrivaled views of Hong Kong.

18 Salisbury Rd., Kowloon, Hong Kong; 800/327-0200 or 852/2721-1211; www.intercontinental.com; doubles from $$

A suite at the InterContinental, above. Above left: Hong Kong's harbor and skyline, seen from the Presidential Suite.

The Langham Place
Hotel's rooftop lap
pool, above. Above
right: The Chuan spa.

Langham Place Hotel Hong Kong

KOWLOON, HONG KONG

This 665-room glass-and-steel retreat manages to meld business, pleasure, and even art seamlessly. The fun begins at arrival: walking in from the frenetic foot traffic of the Mongkok neighborhood, guests are greeted by a pair of enormous, cartoonish sculptures of Mao's Red Guards, just one of the hotel's 1,700 pieces of Chinese art. Forty stories up, relaxation takes center stage at Chuan, a Chinese-style spa occupying the top three floors of the hotel, offering more than 60 treatments, a gym with teak floors, and a sun-drenched rooftop pool.

555 Shanghai St., Kowloon, Hong Kong; 800/223-5652 or 852/3552-3388; www.langhamhotels.com; doubles from $$

The Windsor Hotel Toya Resort & Spa

HOKKAIDO, JAPAN

With its wide-open spaces, sprawling cattle ranches, and pioneer spirit, the island of Hokkaido is where people from this highly stratified society go to experience raw, untamed beauty. Designed to take full advantage of its mountaintop location, the hotel resembles a colossal, gleaming cruise ship docked on the shores of the volcano-carved Lake Toya. While the exterior reflects Hokkaido's unconventional nature, the interior feels distinctly Western, with beds dressed in crisp white, formal chairs, and rolled-arm sofas. A handful of Japanese-style suites have tatami flooring, cypress bathtubs, and tables that hover near the floor. Guests can take in the surrounding Shikotsu Toya National Park on horseback or mountain bike. Or head to nearby ski areas Niseko and Rusutsu, then return for a soak in the hotel's *onsen,* or Japanese hot spring.

Shimizu, Hokkaido, Japan; 800/745-8883 or 81-142/731-111; www.windsor-hotels.co.jp; doubles from $$

The lobby of the Windsor Hotel, with Lake Toya in the distance.

AUSTRALIA + NEW ZEALAND + THE SOUTH PACIFIC

A luxury suite
on Bedarra Island,
in Australia.

THE
BEST
OF
2007
—
AUSTRALIA
+
NEW
ZEALAND
+
THE SOUTH
PACIFIC

The Byron at Byron Resort & Spa's airy reception area, left. Below left: A bedroom, with jacaranda-fiber sculptures. Opposite: The resort's 80-foot pool.

The Byron at Byron Resort & Spa

BYRON BAY, AUSTRALIA

About 75 minutes by air from Sydney, Byron Bay has long been known for its pristine sands and stunning headlands. Now, with this posh new Balinese-style eco-resort, the laid-back beach town has a hotel that's worthy of the setting. Set within a 45-acre rain forest, Byron at Byron Resort & Spa was designed by local architect Ed Haysom to blend into the natural canopy. The open plan of the main building flows between indoors and out: wide, covered verandas are furnished with cane lounges and slow-turning ceiling fans. The alfresco restaurant serves mod Oz delicacies with a refined twist. Take a 10-minute tour through the rain forest to the unspoiled Tallow Beach, or just sit back at Byron's infinity pool and poolside sauna and soak in the natural setting.

77-97 Broken Head Rd., Byron Bay, Australia; 61-2/6639-2000; www.thebyronatbyron.com.au; doubles from $$

THE
BEST
OF
2007

AUSTRALIA
+
NEW
ZEALAND
+
THE SOUTH
PACIFIC

Buckland Studio Retreat

BUCKLAND VALLEY, AUSTRALIA

The attending wombats, king parrots, echidnas, and wallabies provide a constant reminder that this romantic country escape is set in one of the world's most varied natural habitats. At the foot of Mount Buffalo, the four stone-and-corrugated-iron studios stand in stylish contrast (taupe walls and duvets, overstuffed club furniture, a fully equipped kitchen) to the surrounding farmland. Each studio has two decks, to better take in views of vineyards, olive groves, and distant mountains. A casual café serves a nouvelle Australian breakfast, such as crispy pancetta, mushrooms, and poached eggs on toasted sourdough with homemade baked beans.

McCormack's Lane, Buckland Valley, Australia; 61-3/5755-2280; www.thebuckland.com.au; studios from $, including breakfast

A Queensland walnut bed in one of four private studios at Buckland Studio Retreat, above. Above left: A studio deck, with views of Mount Buffalo.

202

Huski

FALLS CREEK, AUSTRALIA

Hip hotels are slowly trumping the staid in the ski community of Falls Creek, about four and a half hours by car from Melbourne. Consider Huski, a Cubist riot of timber and glass, to be the edgiest entry. Just below Falls Creek's highest slope, the resort's vistas extend to the peak of Mount Spion Kopje. The Produce Store, on the ground floor, serves as both a café and a reception area. After a day on the slopes, the communal table and open fireplace—along with warming menu items like spicy pumpkin soup and hot chocolate—provide a welcome respite. Inside the 14 suites, you'll find cozy touches like in-floor heating and hand-knit throws, plus custom-designed furniture and pixilated photographs by Melbourne artist Peter Bennetts.

3 Sitzmark St., Falls Creek, Australia; 61-1300/652-260; www.huski.com.au; studios from $$$ for two-night minimum

Huski, a modernist ski lodge.

The Islington Hotel

TASMANIA, AUSTRALIA

On an island full of pastoral inns, the Islington stands out like a bold Rothko painting in a gallery of Norman Rockwells. The 11-room Regency-era building is filled with art and antiques from the private collection of the husband-and-wife owners, Amy and Nicholas Parkinson-Bates: sketches by Picasso and Australian artist Brett Whiteley, a chaise longue swathed in leopard-print Thai silk, Persian carpets, and lacquered Japanese furniture. Islington's centerpiece is a glass-enclosed conservatory, where guests can dine while contemplating mist-shrouded Mount Wellington. The innkeepers act more like hosts than managers: they'll arrange a chauffeured tour of the nearby Cole River Valley vineyards and share a brandy with you in the drawing room when you return.

321 Davey St., Hobart, Tasmania, Australia; 61-3/6220-2123; www.islingtonhotel.com; doubles from $$

Mount Wellington, as seen from the Islington's conservatory.

The deck at the
Avalon Coastal
Retreat, on Great
Oyster Bay, above.
Above left: A lounge,
with views of
Freycinet Peninsula
and National Park.

THE
BEST
OF
2007

AUSTRALIA
+
NEW
ZEALAND
+
THE SOUTH
PACIFIC

Avalon Coastal Retreat

TASMANIA, AUSTRALIA

The east coast of Tasmania has been a well-kept Aussie secret for some time—and for good reason. Thanks to sheltering hills and warm offshore currents, it's the antipodean alternative to the Mediterranean, with one of the country's best year-round climates. A onetime farmhouse off the Tasman Highway, the Avalon Coastal Retreat has been transformed by local architect Craig Rosevear into a three-bedroom Modernist glass house, with a pine soaking tub and locally made oak beds. The B&B doesn't have a restaurant, but guests have access to a kitchen stocked with chicken and herb sausages from the Wursthaus Kitchen, a top food purveyor in Tasmania.

Great Oyster Bay, Tasmania, Australia; 61-1/3003-61136; www.avaloncoastalretreat.com.au; doubles from $$

THE
BEST
OF
2007
—
AUSTRALIA
+
NEW
ZEALAND
+
THE SOUTH
PACIFIC

Spotlight:
Great Barrier
Reef

A room at Bedarra, with a view of Wedgerock Bay, right. Below right: Bedarra's sunlit deck. Opposite: One of the two private Pavilions.

Voyages Bedarra Island

GREAT BARRIER REEF, AUSTRALIA

If you read tomorrow that George Clooney spent a long weekend at Bedarra applying baby oil to his latest chérie's bottom, you shouldn't be surprised. It's that kind of place: exclusive, private, and very expensive. Forget swimming—you come here to read, nap; eat, nap; drink, nap; and so on. Buttering toast and flicking sand with your toes is as strenuous as it gets. A more languorous experience is impossible to imagine. Except at meals, don't count on running into anyone. People keep to themselves; if they're not out on the reef or curled up on a lounge overlooking Hernandia Bay, they're in one of the 16 freestanding rooms or the pair of cubic, nearly all-glass Pavilions. Sell the farm, pawn your tiara—do whatever it takes to book those two rooms.

Great Barrier Reef, Australia; 800/225-9849 or 61-7/4068-8233; www.bedarraisland.com; doubles from $$$$

THE
BEST
OF
2007

AUSTRALIA
+
NEW
ZEALAND
+
THE SOUTH
PACIFIC

Spotlight:
**Great Barrier
Reef**

Orpheus Island.
Right: One of
Wilson Island's
six rustic tents.

Orpheus Island Resort

GREAT BARRIER REEF, AUSTRALIA

One of the rare privately owned Great Barrier Reef
resorts, Orpheus is an unpretentious, attitude-free place.
All buildings are tucked discreetly below the tree line
and veiled in vegetation. If Orpheus proves one thing, it's
that there's nothing wrong with bromides as long as
they're the right ones: romantic arrival by seaplane,
hammocks strung over the sand between arching
coconut palms, sunset sippies (cocktails) on the beach
while feeding a colony of silvery diamond-scaled mullet,
docile as puppies. The food would be ridiculous if the
chefs who dream it up weren't so earnest. You may have
had preserved-lemon-and-garlic-grilled scampi on a
rosé-and-oyster-scented rice-noodle salad with wok-
tossed enoki mushrooms and slivered asparagus
before—but never in your bare feet. And never while
blacktip sharks cleave the water inches away.

Great Barrier Reef, Australia; 61-7/4777-7377; www.orpheus.
com.au; doubles from $$$$$

Wilson Island

GREAT BARRIER REEF, AUSTRALIA

Wilson is the castaway option on the Reef. The six guest
rooms—or rather, guest tents—are a mere 22 paces from
the shore and have no electricity (only battery-powered
Coleman lamps with charming night-light settings), no
closets, not even mirrors. Closets, in any case, would be
unnecessary, since luggage is restricted to one small bag.
Sadly, this eliminates as potential clients those high-
fashion beachcombers who can't get through the day
without a Goyard trunk full of unguents. Actually,
"resort" is a big word to describe such a small enterprise,
especially given the daunting limitations imposed by the
location. Wilson is superprotected, designed to have
virtually zero impact on the environment. Which means
that everything is micromanaged—even the sand. The
payoff for the happy few who make it to Wilson is the
most natural, unvarnished experience in the region.

Great Barrier Reef, Australia; 800/225-9849 or 61-7/4972-9055;
www.wilsonisland.com; doubles from $$$$

Hayman Island

WORLD'S BEST Hayman is one of the reef's big resorts, with 234 guest rooms, 500 employees, acres of marble flooring, and five dining venues. The once-before-I-die icon has been accepting paying guests since 1935. Back then, the clientele was largely fishermen, and the accommodations were basic cabins. The next year, the American novelist Zane Grey filmed *White Death* on the island. Capitalizing on a sensational crescent of vanilla-sand beach, a luxury resort soon replaced the cabins and flourished for two decades before a 1970 cyclone. After the resort reopened six months later, 650,000 trees and shrubs were introduced to the island; of the 1,000 palms, 22 form a glamorous avenue. Rooms fronting the seven-times-Olympic-size swimming pool—so gigantic it loses 1,500 gallons of water in evaporation and runoff per day—have terraces that jut into the water, so you can jump right in from your bed. Are the pools a little splashy? Yes. Are they fun? Absolutely.

Great Barrier Reef, Australia; 800/223-6800 or 61-2/8272-7000; www.hayman.com.au; doubles from $$

A private plunge pool at Hayman Island.

THE
BEST
OF
2007

AUSTRALIA
+
NEW
ZEALAND
+
THE SOUTH
PACIFIC

The Admiral's Room
at River Birches,
above. Above left:
The drawing room.

River Birches Lodge

NORTH ISLAND, NEW ZEALAND

Turangi, a trout fisherman's town on the banks of New Zealand's Tongariro River, is typically associated with 70's-era lodges, where deer heads adorn pine walls. The remote River Birches aims for a dramatically different aesthetic. Created by Jason and Rebeca Bleibtreu, a globe-trotting couple based in Bangkok, the cedar inn is an East-meets-West collage of Thai silk curtains, Maori weavings, native rimu wood, and Burmese furniture. The three guest rooms are a stone's throw from the river's best angling pools; request the Admiral's Room, which comes with a private outdoor cedar hot tub sheltered by monster ponga ferns. At night, wrap yourself in a wool throw and listen to the sounds of the Tongariro River.

19 Koura St., Turangi, North Island, New Zealand; 64-7/386-0445; www.riverbirches.co.nz; doubles from $, including breakfast

Mollies Boutique Hotel

AUCKLAND, NEW ZEALAND

The brainchild of international opera coach Frances Wilson and her husband, Stephen Fitzgerald, Mollies is filled with the sound of music. Wilson often coaches singers from the Auckland Opera Studio on the premises; on occasion the hotel has been transformed into a residential opera school; and five of the 13 suites have grand pianos. Built in 1880 as the residence of the first mayor of Auckland, the property–which looks out over the city's Waitemata Harbour–is furnished with period pieces collected personally by Wilson, a onetime antiques dealer.

6 Tweed St., St. Mary's Bay, Auckland, New Zealand; 800/525-4800 or 64-9/376-3489; www.mollies.co.nz; doubles from $$

A premium villa suite at Mollies.

Beachfront at the
Wakaya Club, right.
Below right: Inside a
bure with a bamboo
four-poster bed.
Opposite: A Buddha
sculpture in the hotel's
Breeze Spa.

Wakaya Club

WAKAYA ISLAND, FIJI

It takes long-range vision to transform a 2,200-acre isle,
uninhabited for about 140 years, into an impeccable resort,
but entrepreneur David Gilmour succeeded with the
Wakaya Club. The resort came into being back in 1990,
when Gilmour built some *bures*, or bungalows, and then an
aerie called Vale O on a peninsula. He and his wife, Jill,
now have 10 *bures*, an open-air restaurant, and an orchid
hothouse. The Gilmours' most recent addition is a two-
bedroom *bure* with a lava-rock outdoor shower and its
own plunge pool, where celebrity visitors like Bill Gates can
hole up in privacy. One of the highlights of a stay: a watsu
session at the Breeze Spa. Each time a therapist dips you
in the mosaic-tile pool that has underwater speakers, you'll
hear a cappella hymns sung by a local choir.

Wakaya Island, Fiji; 800/828-3454; www.wakaya.com; doubles
from $$$$$, including meals

THE
BEST
OF
2007

AUSTRALIA
+
NEW
ZEALAND
+
THE SOUTH
PACIFIC

Spotlight:
Fiji

The lower deck of the Royal Davui's Banyan Restaurant, above. Above right: the resort's pool.

Royal Davui Island Resort

UGAGA ISLAND, FIJI

An eight-acre gumdrop of an island has been turned into the Royal Davui Island Resort by the Southwicks, a fifth-generation Fijian family who also operate a commercial fishing fleet in the area—hence, the sashimi of yellowfin tuna on the dinner menu. The resort has 16 mahogany *vales,* or villas, clinging to the cliffs above a marine sanctuary and a shallow reef that ripples turquoise and silver at dusk. Meals are served in a tree house built around a giant banyan. Tropical orchids and bamboo shade steep paths that are perfect for hiking. And don't be afraid of a swim in the reef-protected waters of the Beqa Lagoon: the staff at the resort delights in telling guests about the myth of Masilaca, a god who is said to have taught the local Sawau tribe how to dance across hot coals without getting burned and who protects islanders—and visitors—from sharks.

Ugaga Island, Fiji; 679/336-1624; www.royaldavui.com; doubles from $$$$$, including meals

214

A villa at Nukubati, under the shadow of Delai Balenicagi mountain.

Nukubati Island Resort

NUKUBATI ISLAND, FIJI

On Nukubati Island, Fijian-born hotelier Jenny Leewai Bourke has created an eco-sensitive resort concept that preserves the past. Her seven-room private-island property commands a 50-mile coastline unmarred by power lines. The plantation-style lodge runs on solar power and generators; rainwater is captured in cisterns. In keeping with the green ethos, Bourke hires women from nearby villages to weave floor mats for the public spaces, which are filled with rattan furniture and native art. Three honeymoon bungalows have thatched-roof porches and fan-cooled bedrooms. In addition to the satisfaction of protecting the fragile local environment, guests are rewarded with unadulterated night skies and easy access to the Great Sea Reef, one of the richest dive sites in the South Pacific.

Nukubati Island, Fiji; 800/707-3454, or 011-679/881-3901; www.nukubati.com; doubles from $$$, including meals

THE
BEST
OF
2007

AUSTRALIA
+
NEW
ZEALAND
+
THE SOUTH
PACIFIC

Spotlight:
Fiji

A daybed on
the beach at
Dolphin Island.

Dolphin Island Resort

DOLPHIN ISLAND, FIJI

The 13-acre Dolphin Island is the domain of Alex Van
Heeren, who also owns New Zealand's lavish Huka Lodge.
The rustic-chic Fijian hideaway can host only a single party
of up to four people at a time. These lucky few have full
command of the frangipani-and-jacaranda–shaded main
bungalow, with a wraparound veranda and downy sofas.
The air-conditioned, two-bedroom sleeping pavilion is
decorated with a collection of South Seas artifacts and a
black-and-brown tapa (cloth made from mulberry bark)
mural above the bed. Paddle a kayak around the bay or
hike across the island's steep side to a bluff above Bligh
Water. There, a coconut-frond hut has a fan-cooled daybed
for whiling away the day in seclusion. Back at the resort,
the doting staff prepares coconut shrimp, handmade rotis,
and mud crab in fresh coconut-cream curry for dinner.

Dolphin Island, Fiji; 011-64/7378-5791; www.dolphinislandfiji.co.nz;
doubles from $$$$$ for three-night minimum, all-inclusive

THE
BEST
OF
2007

AUSTRALIA
+
NEW
ZEALAND
+
THE SOUTH
PACIFIC

Thatched overwater
villas at the St. Regis
Resort, Bora Bora.

St. Regis Resort, Bora Bora

BORA-BORA

Bora-Bora—the name alone evokes an exotic paradise that entranced the likes of Marlon Brando in the 1970's and has continued to seduce high-end travelers with the opening of luxe resort after luxe resort. Now a new set of A-listers is discovering the island, thanks to the opening of the 100-room St. Regis, Bora Bora. It's no wonder. With 76 thatched overwater villas, outdoor showers, a fleet of butlers, chef Jean-Georges Vongerichten behind the restaurant, and a spa set on its own island, the resort reaches high levels of indulgence. Thankfully, it also doesn't take itself too seriously. The humorously named Lagoonarium is filled with native fish and is ideal for snorkeling. And for a flashback to the seventies, there's a swim-up bar in the pool.

Bora-Bora; 877/787-3447 or 689/607-888; www.stregis.com; doubles from $$$$

Inside one of the 70 bungalows at Bora Bora Lagoon Resort & Spa.

Bora Bora Lagoon Resort & Spa

MOTU TOOPUA, BORA-BORA

WORLD'S BEST On the private island of Motu Toopua, the Bora Bora Lagoon Resort & Spa makes the most of its location. Every morning, breakfast arrives at each of the 77 Polynesian-style bungalows (50 over water) by outrigger canoe. The hotel's namesake (and very blue) lagoon is only steps away from each room's private deck, and inside, colorful reef-dwellers like orange-striped triggerfish are viewed through vitrines built into the polished yucca-wood floor. In the spa, treatments in open-air rooms are in keeping with the aquatic theme: the "te ua maohi" is a sand-and-seaweed scrub and massage under a shower of warm water. Couples in search of solitude are sent off to an uninhabited island (though they're hardly marooned) with picnic baskets filled with lobster, lamb, and local Hinano beer.

Motu Toopua, Bora-Bora; 800/860-4095 or 689/604-000; www.boraboralagoon.com; bungalows from $$$

221

WORLD'S BEST

In the annual World's Best Awards survey, readers of *Travel + Leisure* are asked to name their favorite hotels and spas around the world based on location, service, food, and value, among other criteria. Each year, the changing list of winners reveals readers' evolving, but always exacting, standards of excellence. In the following World's Best section are the winners' rankings, organized by region on a scale of 0 to 100. In addition, you'll find a comprehensive, easy-to-use directory of World's Best properties, created by T+L's editors and correspondents around the globe, complete with service information and descriptions of each property, from the number of rooms (and which one to book) to the special details that distinguish it from the competition. Think of it as the ultimate guide to the greatest places to visit right now.

Post Ranch Inn,
Big Sur, California.

THE RANKINGS

Le Sirenuse,
in Positano, Italy.

Lebombo Lodge, at Singita
Private Game Reserve, in
Sabi Sands, South Africa.

Top 100 Hotels Worldwide

1 **Singita Private Game Reserve,** Sabi Sands, South Africa **97.56**
2 **Four Seasons Resort Bali at Sayan** **96.11**
3 **Oberoi Udaivilas,** Udaipur, India **94.28**
4 **The Peninsula,** Bangkok **94.03**
5 **Four Seasons Resort Bali at Jimbaran Bay 93.59**
6 **Oberoi Rajvilas,** Jaipur, India **93.50**
7 **Ritz-Carlton Bali Resort & Spa 93.18**
8 **Inverlochy Castle,** Fort William, Scotland **92.86**
9 **The Oriental,** Bangkok **92.40**
10 **Taj Lake Palace,** Udaipur, India **91.79**
11 **Four Seasons Resort,** Chiang Mai, Thailand **91.72**
12 **Four Seasons Resort Hualalai,** Hawaii **91.71**
13 **The Aerie,** Malahat, Vancouver Island **91.67**
14 **Four Seasons Hotel Gresham Palace,** Budapest **91.57**
15 **Sooke Harbour House,** Sooke, Vancouver Island **91.54**
16 **Waterloo House,** Hamilton, Bermuda **91.45**
17 **Charlotte Inn,** Edgartown, Martha's Vineyard **91.25**
18 **Château Les Crayères,** Reims, France **91.23**
19 **Halekulani,** Honolulu, Oahu **91.21**
20 **The Peninsula,** Hong Kong **91.06**
21 **Inn at Little Washington,** Washington, Virginia **90.87**
22 **Wickaninnish Inn,** Tofino, Vancouver Island **90.83**
23 **Chief's Camp,** Moremi Game Reserve, Botswana **90.53**
24 **Mombo Camp,** Moremi Game Reserve, Botswana **90.39**
25 **Ritz-Carlton,** Santiago, Chile **90.37**
26 **Four Seasons Resort,** Carmelo, Uruguay **90.25**
27 **Ladera Resort,** St. Lucia **90.24**
28 **La Casa Que Canta,** Zihuatanejo, Mexico **90.20**
29 **Hotel Villa Cipriani,** Asolo, Italy **90.18**
30 **Alvear Palace Hotel,** Buenos Aires **90.12**
31 **Inn at Montchanin Village,** Montchanin, Delaware **90.00**
32 **MalaMala Game Reserve,** Sabi Sands, South Africa **90.00**
33 **Banyan Tree,** Phuket, Thailand **89.89**
34 **Four Seasons Hotel,** Hong Kong **89.89**
35 **Kichwa Tembo,** Masai Mara, Kenya **89.83**
36 **WaterColor Inn,** Santa Rosa Beach, Florida **89.82**
37 **Four Seasons Resort,** Jackson Hole, Wyoming **89.82**
38 **Huka Lodge,** Taupo, New Zealand **89.78**
39 **Kirawira Camp,** Serengeti National Park, Tanzania **89.74**
40 **Post Ranch Inn,** Big Sur, California **89.67**
41 **Amanpuri,** Phuket, Thailand **89.67**
42 **La Colombe d'Or Hôtel,** St.-Paul-de-Vence, France **89.66**
43 **Four Seasons Hotel,** Prague **89.33**
44 **Lodge at Koele,** Lanai **89.31**
45 **Phinda Private Game Reserve,** KwaZulu-Natal, South Africa **89.25**
46 **Four Seasons Resort Costa Rica at Peninsula Papagayo 89.24**
47 **Bauer Il Palazzo,** Venice **89.23**
48 **Four Seasons Hotel,** Istanbul **89.21**
49 **Buckland Manor Country House Hotel,** Gloucestershire, England **89.14**
50 **The Point,** Saranac Lake, New York **89.09**
51 **Four Seasons Hotel,** Singapore **89.04**

52 **Cape Grace,** Cape Town **89.01**
53 **Grand Hotel a Villa Feltrinelli,** Gargnano, Italy **88.97**
54 **Oberoi Amarvilas,** Agra, India **88.94**
55 **Hotel Monasterio,** Cuzco, Peru **88.81**
56 **Hotel Bel-Air,** Los Angeles **88.81**
57 **The Peninsula,** Beverly Hills **88.75**
58 **Voyages Lizard Island,** Great Barrier Reef, Australia **88.68**
59 **The Peninsula,** Chicago **88.66**
60 **Raffles Hotel,** Singapore **88.62**
61 **Mandarin Oriental,** Hong Kong **88.62**
62 **Chobe Chilwero Lodge,** Chobe National Park, Botswana **88.54**
63 **Four Seasons Hotel,** Chicago **88.48**
64 **St. Regis Hotel,** Beijing **88.39**
65 **Ana Mandara Resort & Six Senses Spa,** Nha Trang, Vietnam **88.33**
66 **Ritz-Carlton, Bachelor Gulch,** Beaver Creek, Colorado **88.26**
67 **Villa Gallici,** Aix-en-Provence, France **88.25**
68 **Villa San Michele,** Fiesole, Italy **88.23**
69 **Four Seasons Hotel George V,** Paris **88.22**
70 **Grand-Hôtel du Cap-Ferrat,** St.-Jean-Cap-Ferrat, France **88.14**
71 **Llao Llao Hotel & Resort,** San Carlos de Bariloche, Argentina **88.13**
72 **Le Vieux Logis,** Trémolat, France **88.06**
73 **Royal Livingstone,** Livingstone, Zambia **88.04**
74 **Tu Tu' Tun Lodge,** Gold Beach, Oregon **88.03**
75 **The Sukhothai,** Bangkok **87.88**
76 **Dromoland Castle,** Newmarket-on-Fergus, Ireland **87.86**
77 **Monmouth Plantation,** Natchez, Mississippi **87.84**
78 **Four Seasons Hotel,** Buenos Aires **87.81**
79 **Little Nell,** Aspen, Colorado **87.78**
80 **Cliff House at Pikes Peak,** Manitou Springs, Colorado **87.71**
81 **Ritz-Carlton,** Naples, Florida **87.67**
82 **Blackberry Farm,** Walland, Tennessee **87.66**
83 **L'Auberge Carmel,** Carmel-by-the-Sea, California **87.62**
84 **Palazzo Sasso,** Ravello, Italy **87.55**
85 **InterContinental,** Hong Kong **87.47**
86 **Ritz-Carlton Orlando, Grande Lakes,** Florida **87.34**
87 **Chateau du Sureau & Spa,** Oakhurst, California **87.33**
88 **Château Eza,** Èze Village, France **87.33**
89 **The Ritz,** Paris **87.27**
90 **Blancaneaux Lodge,** Mountain Pine Ridge, Belize **87.27**
91 **Four Seasons Resort Maui at Wailea 87.24**
92 **Hotel Kämp,** Helsinki **87.17**
93 **Hôtel de Paris,** Monte Carlo **87.17**
94 **Mansion on Turtle Creek, A Rosewood Hotel,** Dallas **87.13**
95 **Ashford Castle,** Cong, Ireland **87.05**
96 **Auberge du Soleil,** Rutherford, California **87.04**
97 **Sabi Sabi Private Game Reserve,** Sabi Sands, South Africa **87.00**
97 **Inn at Thorn Hill & Spa,** Jackson, New Hampshire **87.00**
99 **Ritz-Carlton Lodge, Reynolds Plantation,** Greensboro, Georgia **86.99**
100 **One & Only Palmilla,** Los Cabos, Mexico **86.98**

THE
BEST
OF
2007

UNITED
STATES
+
CANADA

WORLD'S BEST
RANKINGS

Inn at Little Washington,
in Washington, Virginia.

Top 100 Hotels in the United States + Canada

1 **The Aerie,** Malahat, Vancouver Island **91.67**
2 **Sooke Harbour House,** Sooke, Vancouver Island **91.54**
3 **Charlotte Inn,** Edgartown, Martha's Vineyard **91.25**
4 **Inn at Little Washington,** Washington, Virginia **90.87**
5 **Wickaninnish Inn,** Tofino, Vancouver Island **90.83**
6 **Inn at Montchanin Village,** Montchanin, Delaware **90.00**
7 **WaterColor Inn,** Santa Rosa Beach, Florida **89.82**
8 **Four Seasons Resort,** Jackson Hole, Wyoming **89.82**
9 **Post Ranch Inn,** Big Sur, California **89.67**
10 **The Point,** Saranac Lake, New York **89.09**
11 **Hotel Bel-Air,** Los Angeles **88.81**
12 **The Peninsula,** Beverly Hills **88.75**
13 **The Peninsula,** Chicago **88.66**
14 **Four Seasons Hotel,** Chicago **88.48**
15 **Ritz-Carlton, Bachelor Gulch,**
   Beaver Creek, Colorado **88.26**
16 **Tu Tu' Tun Lodge,** Gold Beach, Oregon **88.03**
17 **Monmouth Plantation,** Natchez, Mississippi **87.84**
18 **Little Nell,** Aspen, Colorado **87.78**
19 **Cliff House at Pikes Peak,**
   Manitou Springs, Colorado **87.71**
20 **Ritz-Carlton,** Naples, Florida **87.67**
21 **Blackberry Farm,** Walland, Tennessee **87.66**
22 **L'Auberge Carmel,** Carmel-by-the-Sea, California **87.62**
23 **Ritz-Carlton Orlando, Grande Lakes,** Florida **87.34**
24 **Château du Sureau & Spa,** Oakhurst, California **87.33**
25 **Mansion on Turtle Creek, A Rosewood Hotel,** Dallas **87.13**
26 **Auberge du Soleil,** Rutherford, California **87.04**
27 **Inn at Thorn Hill & Spa,** Jackson, New Hampshire **87.00**
28 **Ritz-Carlton Lodge, Reynolds Plantation,**
   Greensboro, Georgia **86.99**
29 **Fairmont Le Château Montebello,** Quebec **86.82**
30 **Four Seasons Resort,** Palm Beach **86.74**
31 **Sanctuary at Kiawah Island Golf Resort,**
   South Carolina **86.70**
32 **Blantyre,** Lenox, Massachusetts **86.67**
33 **The Lancaster,** Houston **86.66**
34 **Lodge at Pebble Beach,** California **86.62**
35 **Post Hotel & Spa,** Lake Louise, Alberta **86.50**

36 **The Broadmoor,** Colorado Springs **86.49**
37 **Ritz-Carlton, Central Park,** New York City **86.47**
38 **Wheatleigh,** Lenox, Massachusetts **86.36**
39 **Fairmont Château Laurier,** Ottawa **86.35**
40 **Montage Resort & Spa,** Laguna Beach, California **86.31**
41 **Campton Place Hotel,** San Francisco **86.31**
42 **Townsend Hotel,** Birmingham, Michigan **86.26**
43 **Ritz-Carlton, Chicago (A Four Seasons Hotel)** **86.16**
44 **Little Palm Island Resort & Spa,**
   Little Torch Key, Florida **85.94**
45 **Ritz-Carlton, Laguna Niguel,** Dana Point, California **85.93**
46 **Windsor Court Hotel,** New Orleans **85.93**
47 **Regent Beverly Wilshire,** Beverly Hills **85.91**
48 **Bellagio,** Las Vegas **85.89**
49 **Bernardus Lodge,** Carmel Valley, California **85.85**
50 **Ritz-Carlton,** San Francisco **85.83**
51 **Watermark Hotel & Spa,** San Antonio **85.83**
52 **St. Regis Resort,** Aspen, Colorado **85.79**
53 **Inn at the Market,** Seattle **85.77**
54 **Wentworth Mansion,** Charleston, South Carolina **85.75**
55 **Rancho Valencia Resort,** Rancho Santa Fe,
   California **85.68**
56 **Stein Eriksen Lodge,** Park City, Utah **85.64**
57 **The Phoenician,** Scottsdale, Arizona **85.62**
58 **Four Seasons Hotel,** Las Vegas **85.62**
59 **Mandarin Oriental,** Miami **85.61**
60 **Four Seasons Hotel,** San Francisco **85.50**
61 **Boulders Resort & Golden Door Spa,**
   Carefree, Arizona **85.49**
62 **Fearrington House Country Inn & Restaurant,**
   Pittsboro, North Carolina **85.45**
63 **Trump International Hotel & Tower,** New York City **85.45**
64 **Fairmont Chateau Lake Louise,** Alberta **85.44**
65 **The Greenbrier,** White Sulphur Springs,
   West Virginia **85.38**
66 **St. Regis Hotel,** New York City **85.35**
67 **Rimrock Resort Hotel,** Banff, Alberta **85.35**
68 **Hotel Telluride,** Colorado **85.32**
69 **Ventana Inn & Spa,** Big Sur, California **85.28**

THE
BEST
OF
2007

UNITED
STATES
+
CANADA

The Greenbrier, in White Sulphur Springs, West Virginia.

70 **Charleston Place,** Charleston, South Carolina **85.25**
71 **Bellevue Club Hotel,** Bellevue, Washington **85.20**
72 **Inn at Shelburne Farms,** Shelburne, Vermont **85.19**
73 **Madrona Manor,** Healdsburg, California **85.13**
74 **Four Seasons Hotel,** Philadelphia **85.11**
75 **Lowell Hotel,** New York City **85.06**
76 **San Ysidro Ranch, A Rosewood Resort,** Montecito, California **85.04**
77 **Hotel Healdsburg,** California **85.00**
78 **Ritz-Carlton,** Half Moon Bay, California **84.97**
79 **Inn at Spanish Bay,** Pebble Beach, California **84.80**
80 **Four Seasons Resort, The Biltmore,** Santa Barbara, California **84.79**
81 **Mandarin Oriental,** New York City **84.72**
82 **XV Beacon,** Boston **84.72**
83 **Four Seasons Hotel,** New York City **84.72**
84 **Inn on Biltmore Estate,** Asheville, North Carolina **84.72**
85 **Spring Creek Ranch,** Jackson, Wyoming **84.62**
86 **Inn of the Anasazi, A Rosewood Hotel,** Santa Fe **84.53**
87 **Raffles L'Ermitage,** Beverly Hills **84.44**
88 **Hôtel Le Germain,** Montreal **84.40**
89 **Fairmont Banff Springs,** Banff, Alberta **84.39**
90 **Ritz-Carlton Huntington Hotel & Spa,** Pasadena, California **84.38**
91 **Cloister Hotel,** Sea Island, Georgia **84.28**
92 **Wedgewood Hotel & Spa,** Vancouver **84.28**
93 **Rittenhouse Hotel,** Philadelphia **84.26**
94 **Marquesa Hotel,** Key West, Florida **84.24**
95 **The Wauwinet,** Nantucket **84.11**
96 **Hôtel Le St.-James,** Montreal **84.06**
97 **Ritz-Carlton,** Amelia Island, Florida **84.01**
98 **Lake Placid Lodge,** New York **84.00**
99 **Beverly Hills Hotel & Bungalows** **83.99**
100 **American Club,** Kohler, Wisconsin **83.97**

Top 25 Hotel Spas in the United States + Canada

1 **Ritz-Carlton Orlando, Grande Lakes,** Florida **93.36**
2 **Mandarin Oriental,** Miami **90.46**
3 **Park Hyatt,** Toronto **89.80**
4 **Four Seasons Resort,** Jackson Hole, Wyoming **89.58**
5 **Ritz-Carlton, Bachelor Gulch,** Beaver Creek, Colorado **89.58**
6 **Little Palm Island Resort & Spa,** Little Torch Key, Florida **88.99**
7 **Pinehurst Resort,** North Carolina **88.94**
8 **Hyatt Regency Tamaya Resort & Spa,** Santa Ana Pueblo, New Mexico **88.79**
9 **Ritz-Carlton,** Naples, Florida **88.72**

10 **St. Regis Resort, Monarch Beach,** Dana Point, California **88.71**
11 **Sanctuary at Kiawah Island Golf Resort,** South Carolina **88.69**
12 **Grove Park Inn Resort & Spa,** Asheville, North Carolina **88.53**
13 **Mii amo, A Destination Spa at Enchantment,** Sedona, Arizona **88.36**
14 **Four Seasons Hotel,** Las Vegas **88.26**
15 **Auberge du Soleil, Spa du Soleil,** Rutherford, California **88.10**
16 **The Greenbrier,** White Sulphur Springs, West Virginia **88.04**
17 **St. Regis Resort,** Aspen, Colorado **87.76**

18 **American Club,** Kohler, Wisconsin **87.50**
18 **Ojai Valley Inn & Spa,** Ojai, California **87.50**
18 **Houstonian Hotel, Club & Spa,** Houston, Texas **87.50**
18 **Four Seasons Hotel,** Philadelphia **87.50**
22 **The Peninsula,** Chicago **87.28**
23 **Ponte Vedra Inn & Club,** Florida **87.25**
24 **Four Seasons Resort Aviara,** Carlsbad, California **87.16**
25 **Wickaninnish Inn,** Tofino, Vancouver Island **87.04**

Top 25 Hotels in Hawaii

1 **Four Seasons Resort Hualalai,** Hawaii **91.71**
2 **Halekulani,** Honolulu, Oahu **91.21**
3 **Lodge at Koele,** Lanai **89.31**
4 **Four Seasons Resort Maui at Wailea 87.24**
5 **Four Seasons Resort Lanai at Manele Bay 86.34**
6 **Fairmont Kea Lani,** Maui **84.96**
7 **Mauna Lani Bay Hotel & Bungalows,** Hawaii **84.06**
8 **Kahala Hotel & Resort*,** Honolulu, Oahu **83.96**
9 **Grand Hyatt Kauai Resort & Spa 83.44**
10 **Ritz-Carlton, Kapalua,** Maui **82.98**
11 **Princeville Resort,** Kauai **82.92**
12 **Hotel Hana-Maui & Honua Spa,** Maui **82.24**
13 **Hapuna Beach Prince Hotel,** Hawaii **82.14**
14 **JW Marriott Ihilani Resort & Spa,** Oahu **81.77**
15 **Royal Hawaiian,** Honolulu, Oahu **81.23**
16 **Hyatt Regency Maui Resort & Spa 81.20**
17 **Mauna Kea Beach Hotel,** Hawaii **81.01**
18 **Grand Wailea Resort Hotel & Spa,** Maui **80.75**
19 **Fairmont Orchid,** Hawaii **80.67**
20 **Kauai Marriott Resort & Beach Club 80.23**
21 **Hilton Hawaiian Village Beach Resort & Spa,** Honolulu, Oahu **78.78**
22 **Hilton Waikoloa Village,** Hawaii **78.78**
23 **Westin Maui Resort & Spa 78.25**
24 **Kona Village Resort,** Hawaii **78.04**
25 **Sheraton Moana Surfrider,** Honolulu, Oahu **78.03**
   * **Formerly Kahala Mandarin Oriental Hawaii**

Top 10 Hotel Spas in Hawaii

1 **Four Seasons Resort Hualalai,** Hawaii **92.27**
2 **Hotel Hana-Maui & Honua Spa,** Maui **88.44**
3 **Grand Hyatt Kauai Resort & Spa 88.15**
4 **Kahala Hotel & Resort,*** Honolulu, Oahu **87.81**
5 **Hyatt Regency Maui Resort & Spa 87.70**
6 **Grand Wailea Resort Hotel & Spa,** Maui **87.62**
7 **Mauna Lani Bay Hotel & Bungalows,** Hawaii **86.46**
8 **Four Seasons Resort Maui at Wailea 86.31**
9 **Fairmont Orchid,** Hawaii **86.16**
10 **Hyatt Regency Waikiki Resort & Spa,** Honolulu, Oahu **85.86**
   * **Formerly Kahala Mandarin Oriental Hawaii**

Four Seasons Resort
Hualalai, on the
Big Island of Hawaii.

THE
BEST
OF
2007

MEXICO
+
CENTRAL
+
SOUTH
AMERICA

WORLD'S BEST
RANKINGS

La Casa Que Canta,
in Zihuatanejo, Mexico.

Top 25 Hotels in Mexico + Central + South America

1 **Ritz-Carlton,** Santiago **90.37**
2 **Four Seasons Resort,** Carmelo, Uruguay **90.25**
3 **La Casa Que Canta,** Zihuatanejo, Mexico **90.20**
4 **Alvear Palace Hotel,** Buenos Aires **90.12**
5 **Four Seasons Resort Costa Rica at Peninsula Papagayo 89.24**
6 **Hotel Monasterio,** Cuzco, Peru **88.81**
7 **Llao Llao Hotel & Resort,** San Carlos de Bariloche, Argentina **88.13**
8 **Four Seasons Hotel,** Buenos Aires **87.81**
9 **Blancaneaux Lodge,** Mountain Pine Ridge Reserve, Belize **87.27**
10 **One & Only Palmilla,** Los Cabos, Mexico **86.98**
11 **Park Hyatt,** Mendoza, Argentina **86.08**
12 **Ritz-Carlton,** Cancún **85.72**
13 **Las Mañanitas,** Cuernavaca, Mexico **85.67**
14 **Esperanza,** Los Cabos, Mexico **85.57**
15 **Caesar Park,** Buenos Aires **85.43**
16 **Casa Santo Domingo,** Antigua, Guatemala **85.20**
17 **Las Ventanas al Paraíso, A Rosewood Resort,** Los Cabos, Mexico **84.97**
18 **Four Seasons Resort Punta Mita,** Mexico **84.14**
19 **Park Tower,** Buenos Aires **83.95**
20 **Four Seasons Hotel México, D.F.,** Mexico City **82.90**
21 **Machu Picchu Sanctuary Lodge,** Peru **82.64**
22 **JW Marriott Resort & Spa,** Cancún **82.60**
23 **Las Brisas,** Acapulco **82.51**
24 **Royal Hideaway Playacar,** Playa del Carmen, Mexico **82.29**
25 **Casa de Sierra Nevada,** San Miguel de Allende, Mexico **82.02**

Four Seasons Resort Costa Rica at Peninsula Papagayo.

Top 10 Hotel Spas in Mexico + Central + South America

1 **Four Seasons Resort Costa Rica at Peninsula Papagayo 93.01**
2 **One & Only Palmilla,** Los Cabos, Mexico **89.75**
3 **Esperanza,** Los Cabos, Mexico **89.35**
4 **JW Marriott Resort & Spa,** Cancún **86.92**
5 **Las Ventanas al Paraíso, A Rosewood Resort,** Los Cabos, Mexico **86.84**
6 **Ritz-Carlton,** Cancún **86.74**
7 **Four Seasons Resort Punta Mita,** Mexico **86.61**
8 **Four Seasons Hotel,** Buenos Aires **86.36**
9 **Las Brisas,** Acapulco **82.19**
10 **Tabacón Grand Spa & Thermal Resort,** Costa Rica **81.92**

Top 5 Hotel Spas in the Caribbean + Bermuda + the Bahamas

1 **Parrot Cay,** Turks and Caicos **90.63**
2 **One & Only Ocean Club,** Paradise Island, Bahamas **88.79**
3 **Malliouhana Hotel & Spa,** Anguilla **88.49**
4 **Little Dix Bay, A Rosewood Resort,** Virgin Gorda **87.86**
5 **Four Seasons Resort,** Nevis **86.55**

Top 25 Hotels in the Caribbean + Bermuda + the Bahamas

1 **Waterloo House,** Hamilton, Bermuda **91.45**
2 **Ladera,** St. Lucia **90.24**
3 **Cap Juluca,** Anguilla **86.82**
4 **Four Seasons Resort,** Nevis **86.77**
5 **Curtain Bluff Resort,** Antigua **86.67**
5 **Malliouhana Hotel & Spa,** Anguilla **86.67**
7 **Biras Creek Resort,** Virgin Gorda **84.89**
8 **One & Only Ocean Club,** Paradise Island, Bahamas **84.63**
9 **Hôtel Saint-Barth Isle de France,** St. Bart's **84.00**
10 **Sandy Lane Hotel,** St. James, Barbados **83.82**
11 **Couples Swept Away,** Negril, Jamaica **83.79**
12 **Jumby Bay, A Rosewood Resort,** Antigua **83.75**
13 **Four Seasons Resort Great Exuma at Emerald Bay,** Bahamas **83.18**
14 **Eden Rock,** St. Bart's **82.92**
15 **La Samanna,** St. Martin **82.32**
16 **Jamaica Inn,** Ocho Rios, Jamaica **82.22**
17 **Anse Chastanet Resort,** St. Lucia **81.79**
18 **Pink Sands,** Harbour Island, Bahamas **81.73**
19 **Peter Island Resort,** Peter Island **81.52**
20 **Parrot Cay,** Turks and Caicos **81.32**
21 **Grace Bay Club,** Providenciales, Turks and Caicos **81.25**
22 **Couples Sans Souci,** Ocho Rios, Jamaica **81.21**
23 **CuisinArt Resort & Spa,** Anguilla **80.98**
24 **Half Moon,** Rose Hall, Jamaica **80.85**
25 **The Reefs,** Bermuda **80.82**

La Samanna, on St. Martin.
Opposite, top: One & Only
Ocean Club, on Paradise
Island, in the Bahamas.
Bottom: Hôtel Saint-Barth
Isle de France, on St. Bart's.

THE
BEST
OF
2007

THE
CARIBBEAN
+
BERMUDA
+
THE
BAHAMAS

WORLD'S BEST
RANKINGS

WORLD'S BEST
RANKINGS

Le Meurice, in Paris.

Top 50 Hotels in Europe

1 **Inverlochy Castle,** Fort William, Scotland **92.86**
2 **Four Seasons Hotel Gresham Palace,** Budapest **91.57**
3 **Château Les Crayères,** Reims, France **91.23**
4 **Hotel Villa Cipriani,** Asolo, Italy **90.18**
5 **La Colombe d'Or,** St.-Paul-de-Vence, France **89.66**
6 **Four Seasons Hotel,** Prague **89.33**
7 **Bauer Il Palazzo,** Venice **89.23**
8 **Four Seasons Hotel,** Istanbul **89.21**
9 **Buckland Manor Country House Hotel,** Gloucestershire, England **89.14**
10 **Grand Hotel a Villa Feltrinelli,** Gargnano, Italy **88.97**
11 **Villa Gallici,** Aix-en-Provence, France **88.25**
12 **Villa San Michele,** Fiesole, Italy **88.23**
13 **Four Seasons Hotel George V,** Paris **88.22**
14 **Grand-Hôtel du Cap-Ferrat,** St.-Jean-Cap-Ferrat, France **88.14**
15 **Le Vieux Logis,** Trémolat, France **88.06**
16 **Dromoland Castle,** Newmarket-on-Fergus, Ireland **87.86**
17 **Palazzo Sasso,** Ravello, Italy **87.55**
18 **Château Eza,** Èze Village, France **87.33**
19 **The Ritz,** Paris **87.27**
20 **Hotel Kämp,** Helsinki **87.17**
21 **Hôtel de Paris,** Monte Carlo **87.17**
22 **Ashford Castle,** Cong, Ireland **87.05**
23 **La Réserve de Beaulieu,** Beaulieu-sur-Mer, France **86.96**
24 **Brenner's Park-Hotel & Spa,** Baden-Baden, Germany **86.88**
25 **Hôtel Hermitage,** Monte Carlo **86.85**
26 **Domaine des Hauts de Loire,** Onzain, France **86.83**
27 **Villa d'Este,** Cernobbio, Italy **86.81**
28 **Hotel Gritti Palace,** Venice **86.75**
29 **Palace Luzern,** Lucerne, Switzerland **86.68**
30 **Le Sirenuse,** Positano, Italy **86.68**
31 **Beau-Rivage Palace,** Lausanne, Switzerland **86.63**
32 **Hostellerie de Crillon le Brave,** France **86.59**
33 **Baur au Lac,** Zurich **86.54**
34 **Sheen Falls Lodge,** Kenmare, Ireland **86.53**
35 **Grand Hotel Miramare,** Santa Margherita Ligure, Italy **86.52**
36 **Il San Pietro di Positano,** Italy **86.46**
37 **Oustau de Baumanière,** Les-Baux-de-Provence, France **86.38**
38 **The Goring,** London **86.11**
39 **Le Meurice,** Paris **86.10**
40 **Château de la Chèvre d'Or,** Èze Village, France **85.98**
41 **Hôtel de Crillon,** Paris **85.93**
42 **Adare Manor Hotel & Golf Resort,** Adare, Ireland **85.77**
43 **The Lanesborough,** London **85.75**
44 **Hotel Goldener Hirsch,** Salzburg **85.69**
45 **Four Seasons Hotel,** Milan **85.66**
46 **Waterford Castle Hotel & Golf Club,** Waterford, Ireland **85.52**
47 **Hotel Taschenbergpalais Kempinski,** Dresden **85.50**
48 **Relais Il Falconiere,** Arezzo, Italy **85.42**
49 **La Bastide de Moustiers,** Moustiers Ste.-Marie, France **85.23**
50 **Hotel Adlon Kempinski,** Berlin **85.02**

Top 5 Hotel Spas in Europe

1 **Villa d'Este,** Cernobbio, Italy **87.15**
2 **Four Seasons Hotel George V,** Paris **85.98**
3 **Brenner's Park-Hotel & Spa,** Baden-Baden, Germany **85.00**
4 **Le Sirenuse,** Positano, Italy **84.38**
5 **The Ritz,** Paris **80.95**

Fishing on the lake at Inverlochy Castle, Fort William, Scotland. Clockwise from left: The hotel's lobby; the lake, a guest room.

Kichwa Tembo, in Kenya's Masai Mara, left. Right: Lebombo Lodge, at Singita Private Game Reserve, in Sabi Sands, South Africa.

Top 25 Hotels in Africa + the Middle East

1 **Singita Private Game Reserve,** Sabi Sands, South Africa **97.56**

2 **Chief's Camp,** Moremi Game Reserve, Botswana **90.53**

3 **Mombo Camp,** Moremi Game Reserve, Botswana **90.39**

4 **MalaMala Game Reserve,** Sabi Sands, South Africa **90.00**

5 **Kichwa Tembo,** Masai Mara, Kenya **89.83**

6 **Kirawira Camp,** Serengeti National Park, Tanzania **89.74**

7 **Phinda Private Game Reserve,** KwaZulu-Natal, South Africa **89.25**

8 **Cape Grace,** Cape Town **89.01**

9 **Chobe Chilwero Lodge,** Chobe National Park, Botswana **88.54**

10 **Royal Livingstone,** Livingstone, Zambia **88.04**

11 **Sabi Sabi Private Game Reserve,** Sabi Sands, South Africa **87.00**

12 **Mount Nelson Hotel,** Cape Town **86.98**

13 **Four Seasons Hotel,** Amman, Jordan **86.87**

14 **Londolozi Private Game Reserve,** Sabi Sands, South Africa **86.86**

15 **Mount Kenya Safari Club,** Nanyuki, Kenya **86.74**

16 **Four Seasons Hotel Cairo at the First Residence 86.58**

17 **Ngorongoro Crater Lodge,** Tanzania **85.25**

18 **Grace in Rosebank,** Johannesburg **85.15**

19 **Four Seasons Hotel Cairo at Nile Plaza 84.77**

20 **Table Bay Hotel,** Cape Town **84.35**

21 **Ritz-Carlton,** Doha, Qatar **83.75**

22 **La Mamounia,** Marrakesh **83.59**

23 **Grand Hyatt,** Dubai **83.25**

24 **Mara Serena Safari Lodge,** Masai Mara, Kenya **82.73**

25 **Michelangelo Hotel,** Johannesburg **82.69**

239

WORLD'S BEST
RANKINGS

Ritz-Carlton Bali Resort & Spa, in Jimbaran.

Top 50 Hotels in Asia

1 **Four Seasons Resort Bali at Sayan** 96.11
2 **Oberoi Udaivilas,** Udaipur, India 94.28
3 **The Peninsula,** Bangkok 94.03
4 **Four Seasons Resort Bali at Jimbaran Bay** 93.59
5 **Oberoi Rajvilas,** Jaipur, India 93.50
6 **Ritz-Carlton Bali Resort & Spa** 93.18
7 **The Oriental,** Bangkok 92.40
8 **Taj Lake Palace,** Udaipur, India 91.79
9 **Four Seasons Resort,** Chiang Mai, Thailand 91.72
10 **The Peninsula,** Hong Kong 91.06
11 **Banyan Tree,** Phuket, Thailand 89.89
12 **Four Seasons Hotel,** Hong Kong 89.89
13 **Amanpuri,** Phuket, Thailand 89.67
14 **Four Seasons Hotel,** Singapore 89.04
15 **Oberoi Amarvilas,** Agra, India 88.94
16 **Raffles Hotel,** Singapore 88.62
17 **Mandarin Oriental,** Hong Kong 88.62
18 **St. Regis Hotel,** Beijing 88.39
19 **Ana Mandara Resort & Six Senses Spa,** Nha Trang, Vietnam 88.33
20 **The Sukhothai,** Bangkok 87.88
21 **InterContinental,** Hong Kong 87.47
22 **Peninsula Palace,** Beijing 86.97
23 **Four Seasons Hotel,** Shanghai 86.88
24 **Ritz-Carlton,** Osaka 86.55
25 **Ritz-Carlton, Millenia,** Singapore 86.50
26 **The Imperial,** New Delhi 86.13
27 **Shangri-La Hotel,** Bangkok 86.04
28 **Grand Hyatt,** Bali 85.83
29 **Mandarin Oriental Dhara Dhevi,** Chiang Mai, Thailand 85.71
30 **JW Marriott Phuket Resort & Spa,** Thailand 85.47
31 **The Oriental,** Singapore 85.34
32 **Mandarin Oriental,** Kuala Lumpur 85.34
33 **Raffles Grand Hotel d'Angkor,** Siem Reap, Cambodia 85.31
34 **Taj Mahal Palace & Tower,** Mumbai 84.75
35 **Shangri-La Hotel,** Singapore 84.48
36 **Royal Orchid Sheraton Hotel & Towers,** Bangkok 84.37
37 **Park Hyatt,** Tokyo 84.11
38 **Island Shangri-La,** Hong Kong 84.10
39 **Shangri-La's Far Eastern Plaza Hotel,** Taipei 83.96
40 **Sofitel Metropole,** Hanoi 83.95
41 **Raffles Hotel Le Royal,** Phnom Penh, Cambodia 83.94
42 **Grand Hyatt Erawan,** Bangkok 83.93
43 **Fullerton Hotel,** Singapore 83.87
44 **The Conrad,** Hong Kong 83.84
45 **Portman Ritz-Carlton,** Shanghai 83.82
46 **JW Marriott Hotel,** Bangkok 83.53
47 **Ritz-Carlton,** Hong Kong 83.48
48 **The Shilla,** Seoul 83.43
49 **Rambagh Palace,** Jaipur, India 83.43
50 **Ritz-Carlton,** Kuala Lumpur 83.30

Top 10 Hotel Spas in Asia

1 **Four Seasons Resort,** Chiang Mai, Thailand 95.66
2 **Four Seasons Resort Bali at Jimbaran Bay** 95.05
3 **JW Marriott Phuket Resort & Spa,** Thailand 93.75
4 **The Oriental,** Bangkok 91.49
5 **The Peninsula,** Hong Kong 88.62
6 **The Peninsula,** Bangkok 88.03
7 **Shangri-La Hotel,** Bangkok 86.56
8 **InterContinental,** Hong Kong 84.38
9 **Raffles Grand Hotel d'Angkor,** Siem Reap, Cambodia 83.41
10 **Four Seasons Hotel,** Shanghai 80.31

Oberoi Udaivilas,
in Udaipur, India.

THE
BEST
OF
2007

ASIA

WORLD'S BEST
RANKINGS

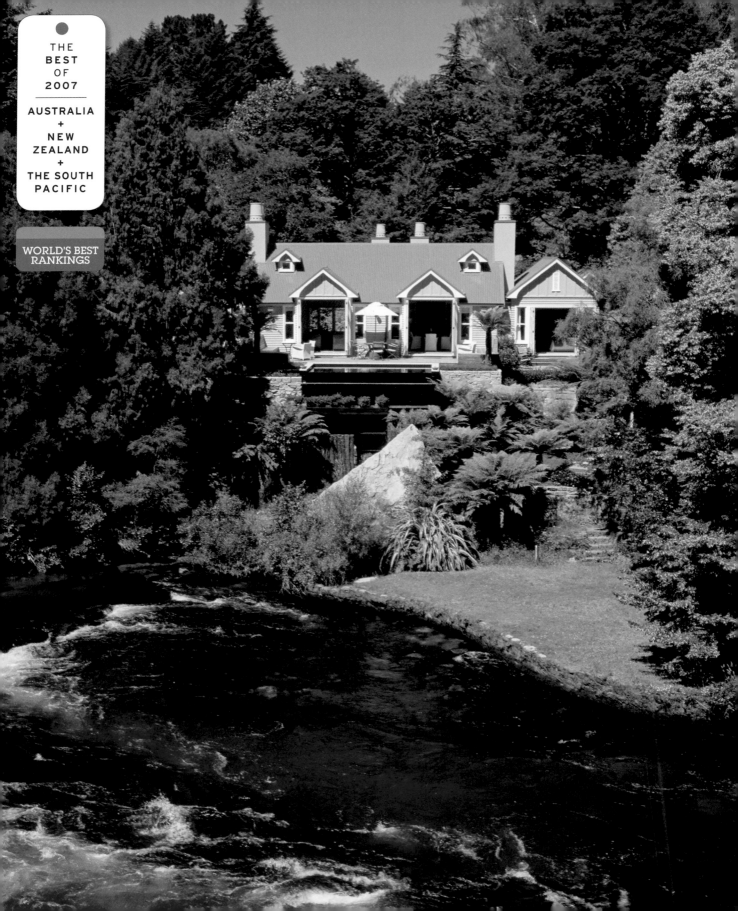

THE
BEST
OF
2007

AUSTRALIA
+
NEW
ZEALAND
+
THE SOUTH
PACIFIC

WORLD'S BEST
RANKINGS

Huka Lodge, in Taupo, New Zealand, opposite. Right: Hayman Island, on Australia's Great Barrier Reef. Below right: Voyages Dunk Island, on the Great Barrier Reef.

Top 25 Hotels in Australia + New Zealand + the South Pacific

1 **Huka Lodge,** Taupo, New Zealand **89.78**
2 **Voyages Lizard Island,** Great Barrier Reef, Australia **88.68**
3 **Bora Bora Lagoon Resort & Spa,** French Polynesia **86.61**
4 **Rydges Jamison,** Sydney **84.49**
5 **Four Seasons Hotel,** Sydney **84.35**
6 **Observatory Hotel,** Sydney **84.11**
7 **Park Hyatt,** Sydney **83.89**
8 **Hotel Bora Bora,** French Polynesia **83.16**
9 **Crown Towers,** Melbourne **83.07**
10 **Bora Bora Pearl Beach Resort & Spa,** French Polynesia **82.50**
11 **Moorea Pearl Resort & Spa,** French Polynesia **82.30**
12 **Hayman Island,** Great Barrier Reef, Australia **82.21**
13 **The Westin,** Sydney **81.21**
14 **Millbrook,** Queenstown, New Zealand **80.57**
15 **Blue,** Sydney* **80.36**
16 **InterContinental,** Sydney **80.04**
17 **Turtle Island,** Fiji **79.25**
18 **Park Hyatt,** Melbourne **79.23**
19 **Shangri-La Hotel,** Sydney **78.97**
20 **Voyages Longitude 131°,** Uluru (Ayers Rock), Australia **78.68**
21 **Voyages Cradle Mountain Lodge,** Tasmania **78.33**
22 **Sebel Reef House & Spa,** Palm Cove, Australia **78.06**
23 **Voyages Dunk Island,** Great Barrier Reef, Australia **77.73**
24 **Stamford Plaza,** Auckland **77.65**
25 **Grand Hyatt,** Melbourne **77.53**
   * **Formerly W, Sydney**

243

Chiva-Som International Health Resort, in Hua Hin, Thailand, left. Below left: The Golden Door, in Escondido, California. Opposite: Mii amo, A Destination Spa at Enchantment, in Sedona, Arizona.

Top 10 Destination Spas Worldwide

1 **Chiva-Som International Health Resort,** Hua Hin, Thailand **91.36**
2 **Grand Hyatt,** Hong Kong **86.43**
3 **Mii amo, A Destination Spa at Enchantment,** Sedona, Arizona **85.98**
4 **Wilderness Adventure Spa at Spring Creek Ranch,** Jackson Hole, Wyoming **85.56**
5 **Canyon Ranch,** Tucson, Arizona **85.21**
6 **Miraval Life in Balance,** Catalina, Arizona **84.96**
7 **Westglow Resort & Spa,** Blowing Rock, North Carolina **83.46**
8 **Golden Door,** Escondido, California **83.20**
9 **Maya Tulum Wellness Retreat & Spa,** Pueblo Tulum, Mexico **83.04**
10 **Rancho La Puerta,** Tecate, Mexico **82.91**

THE DIRECTORY

The Alvear Palace Hotel, in Buenos Aires. Clockwise from left: The St. Regis Hotel, in New York; the Mandarin Oriental, in Hong Kong; Château Les Crayères, in Reims, France.

THE
BEST
OF
2007
—
UNITED
STATES
+
CANADA

UNITED STATES

ARIZONA

CATALINA

■ **Miraval Resort & Spa** Five casita-style villages scattered around 400 Sonoran Desert acres. **STATS** 102 rooms; 3 restaurants; 1 bar. **COMPETITIVE EDGE** Top-notch spa services and unusual activities like the Quantum Leap, a jump from a 25-foot pole. **ROOMS TO BOOK** Miraval Suites, with fireplaces and Santa Catalina Mountain views. **COST** Doubles from $$$$$, all-inclusive. *800/232-3969; www.miravalresorts.com*

PHOENIX/SCOTTSDALE

■ **Boulders Resort & Golden Door Spa** Luxury adobe villas among a millennia-old rock outcrop. **STATS** 160 rooms; 55 villas; 6 restaurants; 2 bars. **COMPETITIVE EDGE** A dramatic renovation, debuting this year. **ROOMS TO BOOK** Upper-level casitas, for desert and golf-course views. **COST** Doubles from $$$. *Carefree; 866/397-6520 or 480/488-9009; www.theboulders.com*

■ **The Phoenician** 250-acre resort near Camelback Mountain with a $20 million makeover. **STATS** 647 rooms; 7 restaurants; 9 bars. **COMPETITIVE EDGE** Pure desert Hollywood, from the gilded lobby to the cabana-fringed pools. **ROOMS TO BOOK** Pool-facing rooms on the 4th floor. **COST** Doubles from $$$. *Scottsdale; 800/888-8234 or 480/941-8200; www.thephoenician.com*

SEDONA

■ **Enchantment Resort** Family friendly property inside a red-rock canyon. **STATS** 220 rooms; 3 restaurants; 1 bar. **COMPETITIVE EDGE** Extraordinary range of activities plus one of Arizona's best spas, Mii Amo. **ROOMS TO BOOK** No. 37 or 38, for unbeatable canyon views. **COST** Doubles from $$. *800/826-4180 or 928/282-2900; www.enchantmentresort.com*

TUCSON

■ **Canyon Ranch** 150-acre former dude ranch in the Catalina foothills. **STATS** 185 rooms; 2 restaurants. **COMPETITIVE EDGE** In addition to classes, guests can consult staff physicians and nutritionists. **ROOM TO BOOK** Casa Grande, a 2,700-square-foot house. **COST** Doubles from $$$$$, all-inclusive. *800/742-9000; www.canyonranch.com*

CALIFORNIA

BIG SUR

■ **Post Ranch Inn** Elegant redwood-and-stone cottages on 98 acres overlooking the Pacific. **STATS** 30 rooms; 1 restaurant; 1 bar. **COMPETITIVE EDGE** Extensive activities, including yoga and stargazing. **ROOMS TO BOOK** Romantic Tree House rooms, elevated on 9-foot stilts. **COST** Doubles from $$$. No guests under 18. *800/527-2200 or 831/667-2200; www.postranchinn.com*

■ **Ventana Inn & Spa** Cedar lodges bordering the ocean and the Ventana Wilderness area. **STATS** 62 rooms; 1 restaurant; 1 bar. **COMPETITIVE EDGE** Nature excursions and a holistic spa. **ROOMS TO BOOK** Fireplace suites with canyon or mountain views. **COST** Doubles from $$. No guests under 16. *800/628-6500 or 831/667-2331; www.ventanainn.com*

CARMEL

■ **Bernardus Lodge** Mediterranean-style resort surrounded by vineyards. **STATS** 57 rooms; 2 restaurants; 1 bar. **COMPETITIVE EDGE** Feather beds, fireplaces, and a secluded locale. **ROOMS TO BOOK** Santa Lucia rooms have the best mountain views. **COST** Doubles from $$$. *888/648-9463 or 831/658-3400; www.bernardus.com*

■ **L'Auberge** European-style inn with a brick courtyard. **STATS** 20 rooms; 1 restaurant; 1 bar. **COMPETITIVE EDGE** An unbeatable location: in the heart of the village, and just blocks from the beach. **ROOMS TO BOOK** Front rooms glimpse Carmel Bay. **COST** Doubles from $$. No guests under 18. *831/624-8578; www.laubergecarmel.com*

ESCONDIDO

■ **Golden Door** Patterned after a Japanese country inn, and surrounded by rock gardens and bonsai. **STATS** 40 rooms; 1 restaurant. **COMPETITIVE EDGE** Activities include everything from tai chi to walking meditation. **ROOM TO BOOK** Garden 6, for privacy and views. **COST** Doubles from $$$$$, all-inclusive. *800/424-0777 or 760/744-5777; www.goldendoor.com*

HALF MOON BAY

■ **Ritz-Carlton** Dramatic spa and resort on an oceanfront bluff. **STATS** 261 rooms; 2 restaurants; 2 bars. **COMPETITIVE EDGE** Two of the region's best golf courses. **ROOMS TO BOOK** One of the 38 new Patio Fireplace Rooms. **COST** Doubles from $$. *800/241-3333 or 650/712-7000; www.ritzcarlton.com*

LOS ANGELES AREA

■ **Beverly Hills Hotel & Bungalows** 1912 Mission-style hotel, minutes from Rodeo Drive. **STATS** 183 rooms; 21 bungalows; 3 restaurants; 2 bars. **COMPETITIVE EDGE** Still the most glamorous Old Hollywood poolside scene in town. **ROOMS TO BOOK** Rear rooms overlooking the gardens are quietest. **COST** Doubles from $$. *9641 Sunset Blvd., Beverly Hills; 800/283-8885 or 310/276-2251; www.beverlyhillshotel.com*

■ **Hotel Bel-Air** Pink Mission-style hideaway with gardens and a lake. **STATS** 91 rooms; 1 restaurant; 1 bar. **COMPETITIVE EDGE** Quiet, yet a short drive from Beverly Hills. **ROOMS TO BOOK** Suites in the south wing tend to be larger. **COST** Doubles from $$. *701 Stone Canyon Rd., Los Angeles; 800/648-4097 or 310/472-1211; www.hotelbelair.com*

■ **Peninsula Beverly Hills** Urbane hotel modeled after an 18th-century French country estate. **STATS** 180 rooms; 16 villas; 2 restaurants; 2 bars. **COMPETITIVE EDGE** Both tranquil (serene spa) and high wattage (glitzy bar scene). **ROOMS TO BOOK** West-wing rooms over the gardens are the most peaceful. **COST** Doubles from $$. *9882 S. Santa Monica Blvd., Beverly Hills; 800/462-7899 or 310/551-2888; www.peninsula.com*

■ **Raffles L'Ermitage Beverly Hills** Eight-story Asian-inspired hotel close to Rodeo Drive. **STATS** 119 rooms;

1 restaurant; 1 bar. **COMPETITIVE EDGE** Rooms average 675 square feet. **ROOMS TO BOOK** Those ending in -5, with views of the Hollywood Hills. **COST** Doubles from $$$. *9291 Burton Way, Beverly Hills; 800/800-2113 or 310/278-3344; www.raffleslermitagehotel.com*

■ **Regent Beverly Wilshire**
Beverly Hills legend, freshly renovated. **STATS** 395 rooms; 3 restaurants; 2 bars. **COMPETITIVE EDGE** Sits at the juncture of Rodeo Drive and Wilshire Boulevard. **ROOMS TO BOOK** Beverly Wing Deluxes have furnished balconies. **COST** Doubles from $$$. *9500 Wilshire Blvd., Beverly Hills; 800/332-3442 or 310/275-5200; www.fourseasons.com*

NAPA/SONOMA
■ **Auberge du Soleil** Napa Valley hideaway in olive groves and vineyards. **STATS** 50 rooms; 2 cottages; 1 restaurant; 1 bar. **COMPETITIVE EDGE** Private, pampering, and romantic. **ROOMS TO BOOK** Garden Views are especially secluded. **COST** Doubles from $$$. No guests under 16. *Rutherford; 800/348-5406 or 707/963-1211; www.aubergedusoleil.com*

■ **Hotel Healdsburg** Stylish modern building with a pool, on the town plaza. **STATS** 55 rooms; 1 restaurant; 2 bars. **COMPETITIVE EDGE** The surrounding shops, tasting rooms, and restaurants (including Charlie Palmer's on-site Dry Creek Kitchen). **ROOMS TO BOOK** A balcony room facing the pool. **COST** Doubles from $$. *Healdsburg; 800/889-7188 or 707/431-2800; www.hotelhealdsburg.com*

■ **Madrona Manor** 1881 estate in the hills above Dry Creek Valley. **STATS** 22 rooms; 1 restaurant; 1 bar. **COMPETITIVE EDGE** A secluded retreat packed with period details. **ROOMS TO BOOK** The 4 original bedrooms (Nos. 201-204), with fireplaces. **COST** Doubles from $$. No guests under 12. *Healdsburg; 800/258-4003 or 707/433-4231; www.madronamanor.com*

OJAI
■ **Ojai Valley Inn & Spa**
Mission-style resort in the Topa

Topa mountains, 14 miles from the Pacific Ocean. **STATS** 308 rooms; 4 restaurants; 3 bars. **COMPETITIVE EDGE** An on-site apothecary where guests can concoct their own perfumes and scented lotions. **ROOM TO BOOK** Paseo Suite No. 733, with an outdoor fireplace. **COST** Doubles from $$. *800/422-6524 or 805/646-1111; www.ojairesort.com*

ORANGE COUNTY
■ **Montage, Laguna Beach**
Craftsman-style resort near downtown Laguna. **STATS** 251 rooms; 3 restaurants; 3 bars. **COMPETITIVE EDGE** The coastal bluff location and pristine beaches. **ROOMS TO BOOK** All face the ocean; the quietest are on the southern side. **COST** Doubles from $$$$. *888/715-6700 or 949/715-6000; www.montagelagunabeach.com*

■ **Ritz-Carlton, Laguna Niguel**
Family-friendly, yet formal resort just a short drive to the beach. **STATS** 393 rooms; 2 restaurants; 1 bar. **COMPETITIVE EDGE** A recent $40 million overhaul. **ROOMS TO BOOK** Ocean Views have unobstructed Pacific vistas. **COST** Doubles from $$. *800/241-3333 or 949/240-2000; www.ritzcarlton.com*

■ **St. Regis Monarch Beach Resort & Spa** Tuscan-inspired hillside property. **STATS** 400 rooms; 5 restaurants; 6 bars. **COMPETITIVE EDGE** A seaside escape with plenty of activities for young guests. **ROOMS TO BOOK** Ones on floors 3-5 of the South Wing, for the best views of the ocean and the grounds. **COST** Doubles from $$$. *877/787-3447 or 949/234-3200; www.stregis.com*

PASADENA
■ **Ritz-Carlton, Huntington Hotel & Spa** 1907 landmark in the San Gabriel foothills. **STATS** 392 rooms; 2 restaurants; 2 bars. **COMPETITIVE EDGE** Chef Craig Strong's Dining Room—one of the country's best hotel restaurants. **ROOMS TO BOOK** First-floor rooms in the main building, with French doors leading to the garden. **COST** Doubles from $$. *1401 S. Oak Knoll Ave.; 800/241-3333 or 626/568-3900; www.ritzcarlton.com*

PEBBLE BEACH
■ **Inn at Spanish Bay**
Contemporary California-style golf resort on the Monterey Peninsula. **STATS** 269 rooms; 3 restaurants; 2 bars. **COMPETITIVE EDGE** A younger vibe than the Lodge (see below); it plays Tiger Woods to its sister property's Jack Nicklaus. **ROOMS TO BOOK** Those on the 1st fairway. **COST** Doubles from $$$. *800/654-9300 or 831/647-7500; www.pebblebeach.com*

■ **Lodge at Pebble Beach** 1919 stucco building that overlooks the ocean. **STATS** 169 rooms; 5 restaurants; 2 bars. **COMPETITIVE EDGE** A classic golf-resort hotel with a prime location on the Pebble Beach Golf Links. **ROOMS TO BOOK** One with a fireplace and a balcony facing the 18th hole. **COST** Doubles from $$$. *800/654-9300 or 831/647-7500; www.pebblebeach.com*

SAN DIEGO AREA
■ **Four Seasons Resort Aviara**
Spanish colonial-style property overlooking Batiquitos Lagoon. **STATS** 329 rooms; 4 restaurants; 2 bars. **COMPETITIVE EDGE** The area's only Arnold Palmer golf course. **ROOMS TO BOOK** Those in the South Wing with lagoon views. **COST** Doubles from $$. *800/332-3442 or 760/603-6800; www.fourseasons.com*

■ **Rancho Valencia Resort & Spa**
Mediterranean-style casitas in a private canyon. **STATS** 49 rooms; 1 hacienda; 1 restaurant; 1 bar. **COMPETITIVE EDGE** A true hideaway, with avocado body wraps in the spa and 6 world-renowned golf courses within 20 miles. **ROOMS TO BOOK** Nos. 126, 127, 130, and 131 have great canyon views. **COST** Doubles from $$. *Rancho Santa Fe; 800/548-3664 or 858/756-1123; www.ranchovalencia.com*

SAN FRANCISCO
■ **Campton Place** Business hotel with a residential feel. **STATS** 110 rooms; 1 restaurant; 1 bar. **COMPETITIVE EDGE** Serene and quiet, thanks to great soundproofing. **ROOMS TO BOOK** Those ending in 01 are largest and overlook Union

THE
BEST
OF
2007

UNITED
STATES
+
CANADA

Square. **COST** Doubles from $$. *340 Stockton St.; 866/332-1670 or 415/781-5555; www.camptonplace.com*

■ **Four Seasons Hotel** Polished tower overlooking the Yerba Buena Gardens. **STATS** 277 rooms; 1 restaurant; 1 bar. **COMPETITIVE EDGE** Has one of the city's best modern art collections. **ROOMS TO BOOK** Above the 10th floor on the Market Street side. **COST** Doubles from $$. *757 Market St.; 800/332-3442 or 415/633-3000; www.fourseasons.com*

■ **Ritz-Carlton** 1909 Neoclassical hotel near the Financial District and Union Square. **STATS** 336 rooms; 2 restaurants; 3 bars. **COMPETITIVE EDGE** Lures local society and visiting luminaries alike. **ROOMS TO BOOK** Courtyard-facing rooms are quietest. **COST** Doubles from $$. *600 Stockton St.; 800/241-3333 or 415/296-7465; www.ritzcarlton.com*

SANTA BARBARA
■ **Four Seasons Resort, The Biltmore** 1927 Spanish colonial-style estate with a new, $225 million overhaul. **STATS** 207 rooms; 1 restaurant; 1 bar. **COMPETITIVE EDGE** The location, between the Santa Ynez Mountains and the Pacific. **ROOMS TO BOOK** Those with a patio looking out on the grounds. **COST** Doubles from $$$. *800/332-3442 or 805/969-2261; www.fourseasons.com*

■ **San Ysidro Ranch** Recently renovated former citrus ranch in the Montecito foothills. **STATS** 25 rooms; 15 cottages; 2 restaurants; 1 bar. **COMPETITIVE EDGE** Every room has an outdoor shower and a hot tub. **ROOMS TO BOOK** The 4 Creekside Cottages have the most privacy. **COST** Doubles from $$$$. *800/368-6788 or 805/565-1700; www.sanysidroranch.com*

YOSEMITE AREA
■ **Château du Sureau** Stone-and-stucco castle in the foothills of the Sierra Nevadas. **STATS** 10 rooms; 1 villa; 1 restaurant; 1 bar. **COMPETITIVE EDGE** A refined hotel convenient to the national park. **ROOM TO BOOK** The Saffron Room, with its Napoleon-era bedroom set.

COST Doubles from $$. *559/683-6860; www.chateausureau.com*

COLORADO
ASPEN
■ **Little Nell** Modern ski lodge at the base of the mountain with David Easton–designed public spaces. **STATS** 92 rooms; 1 restaurant; 2 bars. **COMPETITIVE EDGE** Aspen's only ski-in, ski-out property, plus a legendary après-ski scene. **ROOMS TO BOOK** Nos. 36, 38, and 40 overlook both the inner courtyard and Aspen Mountain. **COST** Doubles from $$. *888/843-6355 or 970/920-4600; www.littlenell.com*

■ **St. Regis Resort** Red-brick buildings with an impressive art collection. **STATS** 179 rooms; 1 restaurant; 1 bar. **COMPETITIVE EDGE** A well-rounded range of services and amenities, including a Remède spa. **ROOMS TO BOOK** Aspen-facing Deluxes. **COST** Doubles from $$. *888/454-9005 or 970/920-3300; www.stregis.com*

BEAVER CREEK
■ **Ritz-Carlton Beaver Creek, Bachelor Gulch** Baronial lodge with dramatic public spaces, on the Bachelor Gulch slopes. **STATS** 237 rooms; 3 restaurants; 2 bars. **COMPETITIVE EDGE** A village unto itself, with a private chairlift and a 21,000-square-foot spa. **ROOMS TO BOOK** Mountainside Residential Suites on the 7th floor. **COST** Doubles from $$. *800/241-3333 or 970/748-6200; www.ritzcarlton.com*

COLORADO SPRINGS
■ **The Broadmoor** 3,000-acre Italianate resort in the foothills of the Rockies. **STATS** 700 rooms; 7 restaurants; 7 bars. **COMPETITIVE EDGE** Loads of activities and a laid-back vibe. **ROOMS TO BOOK** South Tower Superiors with lake and mountain views. **COST** Doubles from $$. *800/634-7711 or 719/577-5775; www.broadmoor.com*

■ **Cliff House at Pikes Peak** Turreted 19th-century inn just outside Colorado Springs, in Manitou Springs. **STATS** 55 rooms; 2 restaurants, 1 bar. **COMPETITIVE EDGE** An authentic historical air in one of Colorado's

historic towns. **ROOMS TO BOOK** West-facing 4th-floor Junior Suites have vaulted ceilings, fireplaces, and mountain views. **COST** Doubles from $. *888/212-7000 or 719/685-3000; www.thecliffhouse.com*

TELLURIDE
■ **Hotel Telluride** Elegantly rustic hotel in the historic district, 2 blocks from the slopes. **STATS** 57 rooms; 1 restaurant; 1 bar. **COMPETITIVE EDGE** Just steps from lively restaurants and shops. **ROOMS TO BOOK** Those on the 3rd floor facing the mountain. **COST** Doubles from $$. *866/468-3501 or 970/369-1188; www.thehoteltelluride.com*

DELAWARE
MONTCHANIN
■ **Inn at Montchanin Village** 19th-century hamlet with buildings dating from 1799, in the Brandywine Valley. **STATS** 28 rooms; 1 restaurant. **COMPETITIVE EDGE** The sprawling gardens with thousands of perennials. **ROOMS TO BOOK** 1-bedroom suites have sitting areas and private courtyards. **COST** Doubles from $. *800/269-2473 or 302/888-2133; www.montchanin.com*

FLORIDA
AMELIA ISLAND
■ **Ritz-Carlton** Eight-story tower set between dunes and fairways, 30 minutes from Jacksonville. **STATS** 444 rooms; 3 restaurants; 3 bars. **COMPETITIVE EDGE** A family-friendly resort with sophisticated amenities, such as the new 28,000-square-foot spa. **ROOMS TO BOOK** Ocean Views with private balconies. **COST** Doubles from $$. *800/241-3333 or 904/277-1100; www.ritzcarlton.com*

FLORIDA KEYS
■ **Little Palm Island Resort & Spa** South Seas–style idyll on a private 6-acre island. **STATS** 30 suites; 1 restaurant; 2 bars. **COMPETITIVE EDGE** Florida's most secluded retreat. **ROOMS TO BOOK** Nos. 15 and 16, which have just been refurbished. **COST** Doubles from $$$$$, including meals. No guests under 16. *800/343-8567 or 305/872-2524; www.littlepalmisland.com*

THE
BEST
OF
2007

UNITED
STATES
+
CANADA

WORLD'S BEST
DIRECTORY

■ **Marquesa Hotel** Four interconnected clapboard houses with pools and gardens in Key West's historic district. **STATS** 27 rooms; 1 restaurant; 1 bar. **COMPETITIVE EDGE** A calm oasis in the center of town. **ROOMS TO BOOK** No. 14, for cozy window seats set in dormers; No. 11, for its abundant windows and light. **COST** Doubles from $$. *800/869-4631 or 305/292-1919; www.marquesa.com*

MIAMI
■ **Mandarin Oriental** Contemporary high-rise with Asian-inspired décor on an island. **STATS** 327 rooms; 2 restaurants; 3 bars. **COMPETITIVE EDGE** A serene location plus a 15,000-square-foot spa and a private beach. **ROOMS TO BOOK** Superior Bay Views on the 9th through 16th floors, with large balconies. **COST** Doubles from $$$. *500 Brickell Key Dr.; 800/526-6566 or 305/913-8383; www.mandarinoriental.com*

NAPLES
■ **Ritz-Carlton** Mediterranean-style beachfront complex (the flagship Ritz-Carlton resort); facilities at the sister Ritz-Carlton Golf Resort available via shuttle. **STATS** 450 rooms; 5 restaurants; 4 bars. **COMPETITIVE EDGE** An outstanding spa and access to some of the state's best golf. **ROOMS TO BOOK** South-facing Coastals for views of the Gulf. **COST** Doubles from $$$. *800/241-3333 or 239/598-3300; www.ritzcarlton.com*

ORLANDO
■ **Ritz-Carlton, Grande Lakes** A 500-acre tropical complex with a Greg Norman–designed golf course. **STATS** 584 rooms; 3 restaurants; 2 bars. **COMPETITIVE EDGE** Orlando's most exclusive hotel. **ROOMS TO BOOK** West-facing lakefront Deluxes, to take in the sunset and gardens. **COST** Doubles from $$$. *800/241-3333 or 407/206-2400; www.ritzcarlton.com*

PALM BEACH
■ **Four Seasons** Stucco low-rise with a tailored South Florida look; a new, Asian-inspired spa opens this summer. **STATS** 210 rooms; 3 restaurants; 2 bars. **COMPETITIVE EDGE** A peaceful oasis, minutes from downtown Palm Beach. **ROOMS TO BOOK** Splurge on a Premiere for extra space and ocean views. **COST** Doubles from $$$. *800/332-3442 or 561/582-2800; www.fourseasons.com*

PONTE VEDRA
■ **Ponte Vedra Inn & Club** Golf-and-tennis resort spread across 300 acres. **STATS** 250 rooms; 4 restaurants; 4 bars. **COMPETITIVE EDGE** Golf, tennis, and a new 28,000-square-foot oceanfront spa. **ROOMS TO BOOK** Any in the Atlantic House; No. 292, a corner room, has pool and ocean views. **COST** Doubles from $$. *800/234-7842 or 904/285-1111; www.pvresorts.com*

SANTA ROSA BEACH
■ **WaterColor Inn** Beachfront hotel in a 499-acre oceanfront development. **STATS** 60 rooms; 2 restaurants; 2 bars. **COMPETITIVE EDGE** Access to wide-ranging amenities, from a 220-acre lake to multiple restaurants and parks. **ROOMS TO BOOK** Those on the 1st floor have private outdoor showers; Nos. 101 and 102 are especially quiet. **COST** Doubles from $$. *866/426-2656 or 850/534-5000; www.watercolorinn.com*

GEORGIA
GREENSBORO
■ **Ritz-Carlton Lodge, Reynolds Plantation** Shingle-style lodge and cottages on 10,000 acres, an hour east of Atlanta. **STATS** 251 rooms; 7 houses; 3 restaurants; 3 bars. **COMPETITIVE EDGE** A traditional lakeside retreat with all the amenities of a Ritz-Carlton. **ROOMS TO BOOK** One of the lodge's lake-view rooms on the ground floor ($50 extra), for easy access to the water. **COST** Doubles from $$. *800/241-3333 or 706/467-0600; www.ritzcarlton.com*

SEA ISLAND
■ **The Cloister at Sea Island** Family-friendly resort with a main building and oceanfront houses, on a private barrier island. **STATS** 156 rooms; 6 restaurants; 3 bars. **COMPETITIVE EDGE** A refreshed classic; the Addison Mizner–designed inn just received a stunning renovation. **ROOMS TO BOOK** Those in the wings of the main inn are large and face the river. **COST** Doubles from $$$. *800/732-4752 or 912/638-3611; www.seaisland.com*

HAWAII
BIG ISLAND
■ **The Fairmont Orchid** Two oceanfront towers on 32 acres, including a 36-hole golf course and tennis academy. **STATS** 540 rooms; 5 restaurants; 3 bars. **COMPETITIVE EDGE** The outdoor spa. **ROOMS TO BOOK** One of 45 Gold Floor rooms atop the North Tower. **COST** Doubles from $$$. *800/257-7544 or 808/885-2000; www.fairmont.com*

■ **Four Seasons Resort Hualalai** Bungalow-style beachfront resort with 5 pools on the Kona coast. **STATS** 243 rooms; 3 restaurants; 2 bars. **COMPETITIVE EDGE** The Big Island's only hotel with ocean views from every room. **ROOMS TO BOOK** For seclusion, those in the Palm Grove Crescent. **COST** Doubles from $$$. *888/340-5662 or 808/325-8000; www.fourseasons.com*

■ **Hapuna Beach Prince** Series of low-slung buildings on a bluff overlooking Hapuna Beach. **STATS** 350 rooms; 5 restaurants; 3 bars. **COMPETITIVE EDGE** On a tranquil bay on of the island's best beaches. **ROOMS TO BOOK** Those in Tower 3 have great views and are a short walk from the water. **COST** Doubles from $$. *866/774-6236 or 808/880-1111; www.princeresortshawaii.com*

■ **Hilton Waikoloa Village** Splashy, fun-filled resort with a $7 million art collection. **STATS** 1,240 rooms; 9 restaurants; 9 bars. **COMPETITIVE EDGE** The 62 lush acres are so expansive that guests use Swiss-made trams and mahogany canal boats to get around. **ROOMS TO BOOK** For a peaceful respite, Ocean Tower rooms have Pacific views; for families, those in Lagoon Tower overlook the dolphin lagoon. **COST** Doubles from $$$. *800/445-8667 or 808/866-1234; www.hiltonwaikoloavillage.com*

■ **Kona Village Resort** An ancient Hawaiian fishing village of

THE
BEST
OF
2007

UNITED
STATES
+
CANADA

WORLD'S BEST
DIRECTORY

thatched-roof bungalows converted into a luxurious resort on Kahuwai Bay. **STATS** 125 rooms; 2 restaurants; 4 bars. **COMPETITIVE EDGE** Relaxed Pacific Island-style getaway with a unique past as an authentic village. **ROOM TO BOOK** Lava Tahitian No. 10, at the extreme north end of the resort on dramatic black lava cliffs. **COST** Doubles from $$$, including meals. *800/367-5290 or 808/825-5124; www.konavillage.com*

■ **Mauna Lani Bay Hotel & Bungalows** Low-rise hotel bungalows between 2 beaches on the Kohala Coast. **STATS** 343 rooms; 5 bungalows; 6 restaurants; 6 bars. **COMPETITIVE EDGE** A high glamour quotient and the island's most comprehensive spa. **ROOMS TO BOOK** Deluxe Ocean Views, for brilliant sunsets. **COST** Doubles from $$. *800/367-2323 or 808/885-6622; www.maunalani.com*

KAUAI
■ **Grand Hyatt Resort & Spa** Plantation-style resort with a saltwater swimming lagoon, above Shipwreck Beach. **STATS** 602 rooms; 5 restaurants; 6 bars. **COMPETITIVE EDGE** Kauai's best spa: 25,000 square feet, with a 20,000-square-foot garden treatment area in the works. **ROOMS TO BOOK** Poipu Wing rooms are especially peaceful. **COST** Doubles from $$. *800/742-2353 or 808/742-1234; www.grandhyattkauai.com*

■ **Marriott Resort & Beach Club** Contemporary resort flanked by mountains on Kalapaki Bay. **STATS** 356 rooms; 5 restaurants; 3 bars. **COMPETITIVE EDGE** A convenient beachfront location near Lihue Airport—the perfect starting point for a Hawaiian vacation. **ROOMS TO BOOK** Pool View rooms (you can still see the ocean from the balcony, but for about $100 less than an Ocean View). **COST** Doubles from $$. *800/220-2925 or 808/245-5050; www.marriott.com*

■ **Princeville Resort** Three terraced buildings with great vistas, overlooking a Hanalei Bay beach. **STATS** 252 rooms; 4 restaurants; 2 bars. **COMPETITIVE EDGE** A secluded hideaway with the amenities (golf course, spa, tennis) of a top resort. **ROOMS TO BOOK** Suites (an additional $150) have 50 percent more space and look out on Bali Hai. **COST** Doubles from $$$. *800/325-3589 or 808/826-9644; www.princeville.com*

LANAI
■ **Four Seasons Resort, Lodge at Koele** Country manor (formerly Lodge at Koele), reopened after an extensive renovation, 20 minutes from the beach. **STATS** 102 rooms; 3 restaurants, 1 bar. **COMPETITIVE EDGE** Unique up-country experience with hunting, horseback riding, and a Greg Norman-designed golf course. **ROOMS TO BOOK** Koele Deluxes, with large lanais. **COST** Doubles from $$. *800/321-4666 or 808/565-4000; www.fourseasons.com*

■ **Four Seasons Resort at Manele Bay** Asian-influenced hotel, fresh from a $50 million renovation, on red-lava cliffs overlooking Hulopo'e Bay. **STATS** 236 rooms; 4 restaurants, 2 bars. **COMPETITIVE EDGE** The only beachfront hotel on this quiet island. **ROOMS TO BOOK** Oceanfronts in the Plumeria or Lotus wings, for panoramic views. **COST** Doubles from $$. *800/321-4666 or 808/565-2000; www.fourseasons.com*

MAUI
■ **Fairmont Kea Lani** White 7-story landmark with 3 pools, set on Polo Beach. **STATS** 413 suites; 37 villas; 4 restaurants; 4 bars. **COMPETITIVE EDGE** The island's only all-suite resort. **ROOMS TO BOOK** For tranquillity and ocean views, even-numbered rooms in buildings H5 and H6. **COST** Doubles from $$. *800/659-4100 or 808/875-4100; www.fairmont.com*

■ **Four Seasons Resort at Wailea** Tropical resort and gardens on a bluff above one of Maui's best beaches. **STATS** 380 rooms; 3 restaurants; 2 bars. **COMPETITIVE EDGE** A host of free activities (snorkeling, scuba clinics, yoga classes) on an island where most resorts charge extra. **ROOMS TO BOOK** Couples should upgrade to Lokelani Suites, with whirlpools and gardens. **COST** Doubles from $$. *800/334-6284 or 808/874-8000; www.fourseasons.com*

■ **Grand Wailea Resort Hotel & Spa** Family-friendly property set on 40 acres fronting Maui's Wailea Beach. **STATS** 780 rooms; 6 restaurants; 6 bars. **COMPETITIVE EDGE** A supersize resort with Hawaii's biggest spa (50,000 square feet) and a 9-pool water park. **ROOMS TO BOOK** Napua Tower rooms have been renovated and include a dedicated concierge, a buffet breakfast, and afternoon cocktails. **COST** Doubles from $$$. *800/888-6100 or 808/875-1234; www.grandwailea.com*

■ **Hotel Hana-Maui & Honua Spa** Secluded plantation house and cottages near Hamoa Beach on the eastern coast. **STATS** 69 cottages; 1 house; 2 restaurants; 1 bar. **COMPETITIVE EDGE** Pure escapism: no televisions, radios, or even alarm clocks in the rooms. **ROOMS TO BOOK** Deluxe Ocean Views with Spas, for private decks with hot tubs. **COST** Doubles from $$. *800/321-4262 or 808/248-8211; www.hotelhanamaui.com*

■ **Hyatt Regency Resort & Spa** Contemporary resort along Kaanapali Beach. **STATS** 806 rooms; 4 restaurants; 4 bars. **COMPETITIVE EDGE** The island's largest self-contained resort is a 40-acre tropical paradise (half-acre pool, waterfall, exotic birds). **ROOMS TO BOOK** Deluxe Ocean Views on the 14th floor, for large lanais. **COST** Doubles from $$. *800/233-1234 or 808/661-1234; www.hyatt.com*

■ **Ritz-Carlton, Kapalua** Secluded plantation-style resort with extensive cultural programs, only steps from the beach. **STATS** 548 rooms; 3 restaurants; 3 bars. **COMPETITIVE EDGE** A golfer's paradise with three 18-hole championship courses. **ROOMS TO BOOK** An Oceanfront, with views of D. T. Fleming Beach. **COST** Doubles from $$$. *800/241-3333 or 808/669-6200; www.ritzcarlton.com*

■ **Westin Resort & Spa** Activity-filled getaway on Kaanapali beach. **STATS** 758 rooms; 3 restaurants; 3 bars. **COMPETITIVE EDGE** An 87,000-square-foot aquatic playground, a spa, scuba diving and snorkeling, and lei-making classes. **ROOMS TO BOOK** Ocean View rooms, with lanais. **COST** Doubles from $$$. *800/228-3000 or 808/667-2525; www.starwoodhotels.com*

OAHU

■ **Halekulani** Five interconnected buildings with unfettered views of Diamond Head. **STATS** 455 rooms; 3 restaurants; 3 bars. **COMPETITIVE EDGE** Exceptional service: attentive staff and knowledgeable concierges. **ROOMS TO BOOK** Diamond Head Suites on floors 9 and above, for ocean and volcano vistas. **COST** Doubles from $$. *800/367-2343 or 808/923-2311; www.halekulani.com*

■ **Hilton Hawaiian Village Beach Resort & Spa** Self-contained property with 6 separate towers on 22 oceanfront acres. **STATS** 3,386 rooms; 16 restaurants; 5 bars. **COMPETITIVE EDGE** An abundance of dining options, 90 boutiques, 5 pools, and the Mandara Spa. **ROOMS TO BOOK** Alii Tower rooms have a separate pool area, terrace and whirlpool. **COST** Doubles from $$. *800/445-8667 or 808/949-4321; www.hiltonhawaiianvillage.com*

■ **Hyatt Regency Waikiki Resort & Spa** Twin 40-story towers across the street from Waikiki Beach. **STATS** 1,230 rooms; 4 restaurants; 3 bars. **COMPETITIVE EDGE** The first spa in Waikiki, specializing in lomilomi (an ancient Hawaiian style of massage). **ROOMS TO BOOK** Deluxe Ocean rooms, for unobstructed views and a glimpse of Diamond Head Crater. **COST** Doubles from $$. *800/233-1234 or 808/923-1234; www.waikiki.hyatt.com*

■ **JW Marriott Ihilani Resort & Spa** High-rise resort with 4 man-made lagoons, on the beach in Ko Olina. **STATS** 387 rooms; 4 restaurants; 3 bars. **COMPETITIVE EDGE** A remote Leeward Coast location and countless activities. **ROOMS TO BOOK** West-facing Ocean Views and Deluxe Ocean Views, for spectacular vistas of the Waianae Mountains. **COST** Doubles from $$. *800/626-4446 or 808/679-0079; www.ihilani.com*

■ **Kahala Hotel & Resort** 10-story oceanfront resort (formerly Kahala Mandarin Oriental) in a posh neighborhood close to Waikiki. **STATS** 345 rooms; 4 restaurants; 2 bars. **COMPETITIVE EDGE** The feel of an outer-island property, on a secluded beach and lagoon. **ROOMS TO BOOK** Stylish Prime Ocean View Lanais with teak floors, Tibetan rugs, and balconies. **COST** Doubles from $$. *800/367-2525 or 808/739-8888; www.kahalaresort.com*

■ **Royal Hawaiian** Landmark 1920's pink palazzo-style hotel (the site of Hawaiian Queen Kaahumanu's former summer home). **STATS** 528 rooms; 1 restaurant; 1 bar. **COMPETITIVE EDGE** A tranquil atmosphere in bustling Waikiki. **ROOMS TO BOOK** Historic Wing rooms with ocean views and sitting areas. **COST** Doubles from $$. *888/488-3535 or 808/923-7311; www.royal-hawaiian.com*

■ **Sheraton Moana Surfrider** Legendary Oahu landmark built in 1901, with the addition of a modern tower. **STATS** 793 rooms; 2 restaurants; 1 bar. **COMPETITIVE EDGE** A property with a storied past and a private marine park. **ROOMS TO BOOK** Banyan Ocean rooms in the original building. **COST** Doubles from $$. *800/716-8140 or 808/922-3111; www.starwood hotels.com*

ILLINOIS
CHICAGO

■ **Four Seasons Hotel** Floors 31–46 of a tower above an upscale mall; rooms are undergoing renovation in phases. **STATS** 343 rooms; 2 restaurants; 1 bar. **COMPETITIVE EDGE** Chicago's tallest hotel, with dramatic city views from every room. **ROOMS TO BOOK** Those ending in -25 are more spacious. **COST** Doubles from $$. *120 E. Delaware Pl.; 800/332-3442 or 312/280-8800; www.fourseasons.com*

■ **The Peninsula** Sleek tower with stylish interiors and a rooftop spa, near Michigan Avenue shops. **STATS** 339 rooms; 4 restaurants; 1 bar. **COMPETITIVE EDGE** A local favorite, with 2 of the city's best restaurants, Shanghai Terrace and Avenues. **ROOMS TO BOOK** Northeast Corners are larger and take in Michigan Avenue and the lake beyond. **COST** Doubles from $$$. *108 E. Superior St.; 866/288-8889 or 312/337-2888; www.peninsula.com*

■ **Ritz-Carlton** Lavishly decorated hotel occupying 21 floors of a high-rise next to the historic water tower. **STATS** 435 rooms; 3 restaurants; 2 bars. **COMPETITIVE EDGE** Traditional style and exceptional service. **ROOMS TO BOOK** Deluxes on the southeast side, with great views of the lake and Navy Pier. **COST** Doubles from $$. *160 E. Pearson St.; 800/332-3442 or 312/266-1000; www.ritzcarlton.com*

LOUISIANA
NEW ORLEANS

■ **Windsor Court Hotel** 23-story business-district building. **STATS** 324 rooms; 1 restaurant; 2 bars. **COMPETITIVE EDGE** Original paintings by Gainsborough and Reynolds. **ROOMS TO BOOK** Riversides above the 12th floor, for best Mississippi views. **COST** Doubles from $$. *300 Gravier St.; 800/262-2662 or 504/523-6000; www.windsorcourthotel.com*

MASSACHUSETTS
BOSTON

■ **XV Beacon** Turn-of-the-century Beaux-Arts building on a secluded Beacon Hill street. **STATS** 60 rooms; 1 restaurant; 1 bar. **COMPETITIVE EDGE** One of the city's most stylish hotels, in a peaceful location. **ROOMS TO BOOK** Corner Studios on floors 8-10, for Boston Common views and a lot of natural light. **COST** Doubles from $$. *15 Beacon St.; 877/982-3226 or 617/670-1500; www.xvbeacon.com*

LENOX

■ **Blantyre** Tudor-style 1902 manor with a pretty all-wood spa and impressive antique collection

THE
BEST
OF
2007

UNITED
STATES
+
CANADA

WORLD'S BEST
DIRECTORY

on 117 acres in the Berkshires. **STATS** 25 rooms; 1 restaurant. **COMPETITIVE EDGE** A peaceful setting with history and charm to spare. **ROOMS TO BOOK** Wyndhurst, with a bamboo canopy bed, and Dorr, with a private terrace. **COST** Doubles from $$$. *413/637-3556; www.blantyre.com*

■ **Wheatleigh** 1893 Italianate villa with museum-quality contemporary art and a renowned restaurant, minutes from Tanglewood. **STATS** 19 rooms; 2 restaurants; 1 bar. **COMPETITIVE EDGE** A refreshingly stylish and sophisticated country-house hotel. **ROOMS TO BOOK** No. 1A, for a fireplace; No. 2R, for a sitting nook and view of the herb garden. **COST** Doubles from $$$$. *413/637-0610; www.wheatleigh.com*

MARTHA'S VINEYARD
■ **Charlotte Inn** 19th-century whaling merchant's house with English-style interiors, on a tree-lined street. **STATS** 25 rooms; 1 restaurant. **COMPETITIVE EDGE** An extremely high level of refinement even for this cultivated island. **ROOMS TO BOOK** For a lovely private terrace, No. 21 in the Garden House, or cozy No. 12 in the Main Building, for a fireplace. **COST** Doubles from $$. *Edgartown; 508/627-4151; www.relaischateaux.com*

NANTUCKET
■ **The Wauwinet** Shingled inn and cottages next to a wildlife sanctuary. **STATS** 33 rooms; 1 restaurant; 1 bar. **COMPETITIVE EDGE** An oceanfront setting that feels wild and remote. **ROOM TO BOOK** No. 207, for its sitting room and bay views. **COST** Doubles from $$. *800/426-8718 or 508/228-0145; www.wauwinet.com*

MICHIGAN
BIRMINGHAM
■ **Townsend Hotel** Stately brick hotel with European-style interiors, in a tony Detroit suburb. **STATS** 150 rooms; 1 restaurant; 1 bar. **COMPETITIVE EDGE** A sophisticated hotel that's convenient to the city. **ROOMS TO BOOK** Suites, for their

balconies. **COST** Doubles from $$. *100 Townsend St.; 800/548-4172 or 248/642-7900; www.townsendhotel.com*

MISSISSIPPI
NATCHEZ
■ **Monmouth Plantation** 1818 Greek Revival plantation on 26 acres about a mile from the Mississippi. **STATS** 30 rooms; 1 restaurant; 1 bar. **COMPETITIVE EDGE** An atmospheric hotel on a gorgeous estate with centuries-old oak trees. **ROOMS TO BOOK** Those in the main house, for an authentic antebellum feel. **COST** Doubles from $. *800/828-4531 or 601/442-5852; www.monmouthplantation.com*

NEVADA
LAS VEGAS
■ **Bellagio** Italian-themed extravaganza on a manmade lake in the middle of the Strip. **STATS** 3,933 rooms; 14 restaurants; 8 bars. **COMPETITIVE EDGE** Quintessential Vegas, complete with a palatial spa, top-notch dining, and a dancing fountain. **ROOMS TO BOOK** Those in the newer Spa Tower. **COST** Doubles from $. *3600 Las Vegas Blvd. S.; 888/987-6667 or 702/693-7111; www.bellagio.com*

■ **Four Seasons Hotel** Floors 35-39 of a tower adjacent to Mandalay Bay, on the Strip's south end. **STATS** 424 rooms; 2 restaurants; 2 bars. **COMPETITIVE EDGE** The city's most exclusive and understated hotel, with nary a slot machine in sight. **ROOMS TO BOOK** 2,225-square-foot Strip View suites. **COST** Doubles from $$. *3960 Las Vegas Blvd. S.; 800/332-3442 or 702/632-5000; www.fourseasons.com*

NEW HAMPSHIRE
JACKSON VILLAGE
■ **Inn at Thorn Hill & Spa** Recently refurbished inn and spa in the White Mountains. **STATS** 22 rooms; 3 cottages; 2 restaurants; 1 bar. **COMPETITIVE EDGE** A country getaway for adults only. **ROOM TO BOOK** The octagonal Mount Washington room, for stunning views. **COST** Doubles from $, including breakfast, tea, and dinner.

800/289-8990 or 603/383-4242; *www.innatthornhill.com*

NEW MEXICO
SANTA ANA PUEBLO
■ **Hyatt Regency Tamaya Resort & Spa** A pueblo-style building located on a reservation, with horseback riding, golf, and spa. **STATS** 350 rooms; 5 restaurants; 1 bar. **COMPETITIVE EDGE** Guests can learn to make traditional Pueblo-oven bread and pottery. **ROOMS TO BOOK** Mountain Views, for Sandia Mountain vistas. **COST** Doubles from $. *800/554-9288 or 505/867-1234; www.hyatt.com*

SANTA FE
■ **Inn of the Anasazi** Pueblo-style hotel filled with local art. **STATS** 57 rooms; 1 restaurant; 1 bar. **COMPETITIVE EDGE** Some of the city's most authentic regional design. **ROOMS TO BOOK** Nos. 306 and 320–the sunniest Standards. **COST** Doubles from $$. *13 Washington Ave.; 800/688-8100 or 505/988-3030; www.innoftheanasazi.com*

NEW YORK
ADIRONDACKS
■ **Lake Placid Lodge** Sophisticated resort overlooking Lake Placid; the 1882 main lodge was destroyed by fire and will reopen next January. **STATS** 11 cabins; 1 restaurant; 1 bar. **COMPETITIVE EDGE** Plush cabins done in Adirondack style at its finest. **ROOM TO BOOK** The Owl's Head cabin for a sauna and steam room. **COST** Doubles from $$. No guests under 14. *877/523-2700 or 518/523-2700; www.lakeplacidlodge.com*

■ **The Point** 1930's Great Camp on a Saranac Lake peninsula. **STATS** 11 rooms; 1 restaurant. **COMPETITIVE EDGE** Rustic but elegant escape that has as much–or as little–as you'd like to do. **ROOM TO BOOK** Weatherwatch has lake-facing picture windows and a historic bathroom. **COST** Doubles from $$$$$, all-inclusive. No guests under 18. *800/255-3530 or 518/891-5674; www.thepointresort.com*

NEW YORK CITY
■ **Four Seasons Hotel** Sleek,

I. M. Pei-designed 52-story tower in Midtown. **STATS** 368 rooms; 2 restaurants; 2 bars. **COMPETITIVE EDGE** The luxury of space (rooms average 600 square feet) in a central location. **ROOMS TO BOOK** Corners in the lower tower have 2 windows and a lot of natural light. **COST** Doubles from $$$$. *57 E. 57th St.; 800/487-3769 or 212/758-5700; www.fourseasons.com*

■ **The Lowell** Upper East Side mainstay (a 2-year renovation is nearly complete) on a tree-lined block near Madison Avenue. **STATS** 70 rooms; 2 restaurants; 1 bar. **COMPETITIVE EDGE** The most intimate of the city's top hotels, with a hushed, residential atmosphere. **ROOM TO BOOK** 10C—the only junior suite with a terrace and fireplace. **COST** Doubles from $$$. *28 E. 63rd St.; 800/221-4444 or 212/838-1400; www.lowellhotel.com*

■ **Mandarin Oriental** Asian-influenced hotel with sweeping Central Park views, in the Time Warner Center. **STATS** 248 rooms; 1 restaurant; 2 bars. **COMPETITIVE EDGE** State-of-the-art facilities, including an exceptional spa and a pool with views of the Hudson River. **ROOMS TO BOOK** Standards overlooking Central Park on floors 38–39. **COST** Doubles from $$$. *80 Columbus Circle; 866/801-8880 or 212/805-8800; www.mandarinoriental.com*

■ **Ritz-Carlton Central Park** 22-floor hotel with a town house feel at the southern edge of Central Park. **STATS** 261 rooms; 1 restaurant; 1 bar. **COMPETITIVE EDGE** Polished service, comfortable rooms, and all of Central Park at your doorstep. **ROOMS TO BOOK** Park Views are worth the extra $250; No. 2214 is the highest corner room. **COST** Doubles from $$$$. *50 Central Park S.; 800/241-3333 or 212/308-9100; www.ritzcarlton.com*

■ **St. Regis** 1904 Beaux-Arts landmark near Central Park, Carnegie Hall, and Fifth Avenue. **STATS** 227 rooms; 1 restaurant; 1 bar. **COMPETITIVE EDGE** A classic with newly refreshed public spaces and spa. **ROOMS TO BOOK** Deluxes ending in -28 (an extra $50)

are large and quiet. **COST** Doubles from $$$$. *2 E. 55th St.; 800/759-7550 or 212/753-4500; www.stregis.com*

■ **Trump International Hotel & Tower** Luxurious hotel occupying 14 floors of a tower on Columbus Circle. **STATS** 167 rooms; 2 restaurants; 1 bar. **COMPETITIVE EDGE** A Central Park address with room service by Jean-Georges Vongerichten. **ROOMS TO BOOK** Those on the higher floors ending in -04 have great light and park views; No. 1704 is the best. **COST** Doubles from $$$. *1 Central Park W.; 888/448-7867 or 212/299-1000; www.trumpintl.com*

NORTH CAROLINA
ASHEVILLE
■ **Grove Park Inn Resort & Spa** The oldest hotel in the area, with views of the Blue Ridge Mountains. **STATS** 510 rooms; 4 restaurants; 4 bars. **COMPETITIVE EDGE** A 40,000-square-foot, state-of-the-art spa. **ROOMS TO BOOK** Mountain View rooms in the Historic Main Inn, built in 1913. **COST** Doubles from $$. *800/438-5800 or 828/252-2711; www.groveparkinn.com*

■ **Inn on Biltmore Estate** Manor house on 8,000 acres adjacent to the Biltmore House, George Vanderbilt's 19th-century château. **STATS** 510 rooms; 4 restaurants; 4 bars. **COMPETITIVE EDGE** Sophisticated rooms in the gorgeous Blue Ridge Mountains. **ROOM TO BOOK** The third-floor Palm Court room, which overlooks the city of Asheville. **COST** Doubles from $$. *800/624-1575 or 828/225-1600; www.biltmore.com*

BLOWING ROCK
■ **Westglow Resort & Spa** Intimate Greek-revival mansion with new spa treatment rooms. **STATS** 11 rooms; 1 restaurant. **COMPETITIVE EDGE** Claw-foot tubs and crystal chandeliers in a renovated National Register of Historic Places building in the Blue Ridge Mountains. **ROOM TO BOOK** No. 14, the largest suite in the house, with a picture window that captures the morning sunlight. **COST** Doubles from $$$$$, all-inclusive. *800/562-0807; www.westglow.com*

PINEHURST
■ **Pinehurst Resort** A century-old resort with 3 historic hotel buildings in the rolling Sand Hills. **STATS** 475 rooms; 10 restaurants; 4 bars. **COMPETITIVE EDGE** The 31,000-square-foot spa with lap pool and 28 treatment rooms. **ROOMS TO BOOK** Traditional Rooms in the Manor Inn, for a luxe lodge feel. **COST** Doubles from $$$. *800/487-4653 or 910/295-6811; www.pinehurst.com*

PITTSBORO
■ **Fearrington House Country Inn** Pastoral inn with trellised English gardens near Raleigh-Durham and Chapel Hill. **STATS** 33 rooms; 1 restaurant; 1 bar. **COMPETITIVE EDGE** An idyllic rural retreat on a historic dairy farm. **ROOM TO BOOK** No. 6, with views of the fragrant White Garden. **COST** Doubles from $. *800/277-0130 or 919/542-2121; www.fearringtonhouse.com*

OREGON
GOLD BEACH
■ **Tu Tu' Tun Lodge** Mission-style lodge on the Rogue River's banks. **STATS** 18 rooms; 2 houses; 1 restaurant; 1 bar. **COMPETITIVE EDGE** Outdoor activities (hiking, kayaking) and plenty of creature comforts (wine tastings, high-speed Internet). **ROOM TO BOOK** The 3-bedroom house has a fireplace and outdoor tub. **COST** Doubles from $. *800/864-6357 or 541/247-6664; www.tututun.com*

PENNSYLVANIA
PHILADELPHIA
■ **Four Seasons Hotel** Eight-story granite hotel with newly renovated rooms, on Logan Square. **STATS** 364 rooms; 2 restaurants; 1 bar. **COMPETITIVE EDGE** A central location in the city's cultural heart, and the best spa in town. **ROOMS TO BOOK** Those on the 7th floor with private balconies. **COST** Doubles from $$. *1 Logan Square; 866/516-1100 or 215/963-1500; www.fourseasons.com*

■ **Rittenhouse Hotel** Nine floors of a 33-story Rittenhouse Square building. **STATS** 98 rooms; 3 restaurants; 2 bars. **COMPETITIVE EDGE** An intimately scaled hotel in a revitalized downtown

THE
BEST
OF
2007

UNITED
STATES
+
CANADA

neighborhood. **ROOM TO BOOK** No. 508 looks onto the historic square. **COST** Doubles from $$. *210 W. Rittenhouse Square; 800/635-1042 or 215/546-9000; www.rittenhousehotel.com*

SOUTH CAROLINA
CHARLESTON
■ **Charleston Place** Grand hotel in the Historic District. **STATS** 440 rooms; 2 restaurants; 2 bars. **COMPETITIVE EDGE** The city's most complete luxury hotel, with great service, a rooftop pool, and excellent dining. **ROOMS TO BOOK** For views of City Market, southeast-facing rooms above the 2nd floor. **COST** Doubles from $$. *205 Meeting St.; 800/611-5545 or 843/722-4900; www.charlestonplace.com*

■ **Wentworth Mansion** Restored 1886 residence with original Tiffany windows and marble fireplaces. **STATS** 21 rooms; 1 restaurant; 1 bar. **COMPETITIVE EDGE** A refined property that has perfected Southern hospitality. **ROOM TO BOOK** No. 6 has a porch and an elevated bathroom. **COST** Doubles from $$. *149 Wentworth St.; 888/466-1886 or 843/853-1886; www.wentworthmansion.com*

KIAWAH ISLAND
■ **Sanctuary at Kiawah Island Golf Resort** Oceanside estate with world-class golf and tennis facilities. **STATS** 255 rooms; 3 restaurants; 2 bars. **COMPETITIVE EDGE** Top-notch golf and a lovely beach, on a barrier island just 30 minutes south of Charleston. **ROOM TO BOOK** No. 578, a corner room with three balconies. **COST** Doubles from $$. *877/683-1234 or 843/768-6000; www.thesanctuary.com*

TENNESSEE
WALLAND
■ **Blackberry Farm** Country manor in the Great Smoky Mountain foothills outside Knoxville. **STATS** 51 rooms; 1 restaurant; 2 bars. **COMPETITIVE EDGE** Plush quarters in a gorgeous Appalachian setting. **ROOMS TO BOOK** Main house Estates, for communal fireplaces. **COST** Doubles from $$$, including meals. *800/273-6004 or 865/984-8166; www.blackberryfarm.com*

TEXAS
DALLAS
■ **Mansion on Turtle Creek** Glamorous, restored 1920's residence and modern tower, near downtown. **STATS** 143 rooms; 2 restaurants; 1 bar. **COMPETITIVE EDGE** All the amenities of a grand hotel, with a residential feel. **ROOMS TO BOOK** Odd-numbered rooms on the south side, overlooking the pool. **COST** Doubles from $$. *2821 Turtle Creek Blvd.; 800/527-5432 or 214/559-2100; www.rosewoodhotels.com*

HOUSTON
■ **The Houstonian Hotel, Club & Spa** 18-acre forested oasis 15 minutes from the heart of downtown. **STATS** 284 rooms; 3 restaurants; 1 bar. **COMPETITIVE EDGE** The 2-story gym, outfitted with a rock-climbing wall, basketball court, and 3 pools. **ROOMS TO BOOK** Spacious Corner Kings. **COST** Doubles from $$. *111 North Post Oak Lane; 800/231-2759 or 713/680-2626; www.houstonian.com*

■ **The Lancaster** Regal 12-story hotel in the business district; currently undergoing renovation. **STATS** 93 rooms; 1 restaurant; 1 bar. **COMPETITIVE EDGE** Ideal for business travelers, with town-car service and a 24-hour concierge. **ROOMS TO BOOK** One of the -07 corner Kings—the same price as Standards, but larger and sunnier. **COST** Doubles from $$. *701 Texas Ave.; 800/231-0336 or 713/228-9500; www.thelancasterhouston.com*

SAN ANTONIO
■ **Watermark Hotel & Spa** Contemporary hotel with Western influences, on the River Walk. **STATS** 99 rooms; 1 restaurant; 1 bar. **COMPETITIVE EDGE** An oasis in the heart of town, with a world-class 17,000-square-foot spa. **ROOMS TO BOOK** River Views with balconies. **COST** Doubles from $$. *212 W. Crockett; 866/605-1212 or 210/396-5800; www.watermarkhotel.com*

UTAH
PARK CITY
■ **Stein Eriksen Lodge** Norwegian-style ski chalet at Deer Valley Resort, newly polished, thanks to an $8 million renovation. **STATS** 175 rooms; 1 restaurant; 1 bar. **COMPETITIVE EDGE** A ski-in, ski-out setting and impeccable service (expect warmed boots in the morning). **ROOMS TO BOOK** West Wings have the best views of the Rockies. **COST** Doubles from $$$$. *800/453-1302 or 435/649-3700; www.steinlodge.com*

VERMONT
SHELBURNE
■ **The Inn at Shelburne Farms** Queen Anne–style estate on Lake Champlain near the Adirondacks. **STATS** 24 rooms; 2 cottages; 1 restaurant; 1 bar. **COMPETITIVE EDGE** A perfect rural escape, with miles of walking trails on a 1,400-acre farm. **ROOM TO BOOK** Overlook, the bedroom of former owner Lila Vanderbilt Webb. **COST** Doubles from $. *802/985-8498; www.shelburnefarms.org*

VIRGINIA
WASHINGTON
■ **The Inn at Little Washington** Early-20th-century house—a theatrical riot of fabrics and wallpapers—with a cottage down the road, near the Shenandoah Valley. **STATS** 16 rooms; 1 restaurant; 1 bar. **COMPETITIVE EDGE** Chef Patrick O'Connell's legendary eclectic American cuisine. **ROOM TO BOOK** No. 16, for a soaking tub, a garden, and country views. **COST** Doubles from $$$. *540/675-3800; www.theinnatlittlewashington.com*

WASHINGTON
BELLEVUE
■ **Bellevue Club Hotel** Sophisticated property in central Bellevue. **STATS** 67 rooms; 3 restaurants; 1 bar. **COMPETITIVE EDGE** A pampered and personalized experience in a charming city. **ROOMS TO BOOK** Club rooms, which have 12-foot ceilings and private patios. **COST** Doubles from $$. *11200 S.E. 6th St.; 800/579-1110 or 425/454-4424; www.bellevueclub.com*

SEATTLE
■ **Inn at the Market** Eight-story

brick building at the entrance to the Pike Place Market. **STATS** 70 rooms; 3 restaurants; 2 bars. **COMPETITIVE EDGE** An intimate refuge in the city's most vibrant shopping area. **ROOM TO BOOK** No. 708, for views of Elliott Bay from your bed. **COST** Doubles from $. *86 Pine St.; 800/446-4484 or 206/443-3600; www.innatthemarket.com*

WEST VIRGINIA
WHITE SULPHUR SPRINGS
■ **The Greenbrier** Georgian-style retreat in the Allegheny Mountains; recently renovated. **STATS** 802 rooms; 4 restaurants; 4 bars. **COMPETITIVE EDGE** A classic American resort (golf courses, spa) with an adult feel. **ROOMS TO BOOK** Spring Row cottages, for large tubs and porches. **COST** Doubles from $$. *800/624-6070 or 304/536-1110; www.greenbrier.com*

WISCONSIN
KOHLER
■ **American Club at Destination Kohler** Tudor-style resort (with Kohler fixtures) north of Milwaukee. **STATS** 240 rooms; 3 restaurants; 3 bars. **COMPETITIVE EDGE** World-class golf and a 21,000-square-foot spa. **ROOMS TO BOOK** Carriage House rooms, which are closest to the spa. **COST** Doubles from $$. *800/344-2838 or 920/457-8000; www.destinationkohler.com*

WYOMING
JACKSON HOLE
■ **Four Seasons Resort** Alpine-lodge-inspired hotel at the base of the Tetons. **STATS** 124 rooms; 2 restaurants; 3 bars. **COMPETITIVE EDGE** An ideal getaway, with ski-in, ski-out access and outdoor concierge service. **ROOMS TO BOOK** Premium Kings, for fireplaces, terraces, and mountain or valley views. **COST** Doubles from $$$. *800/332-3442 or 307/732-5000; www.fourseasons.com*

■ **Spring Creek Ranch** Sprawling resort on 1,000 acres of the Gros Ventre Butte. **STATS** 87 rooms; 39 houses and condos; 1 restaurant; 1 bar. **COMPETITIVE EDGE** A 7,000-foot elevation with unparalleled views and an equally spectacular spa. **ROOMS**

TO BOOK Choate units, on the butte overlooking Grand Teton. **COST** Doubles from $$. *800/443-6139 or 307/733-8833; www.springcreekranch.com*

CANADA

ALBERTA
BANFF
■ **Fairmont Banff Springs** Scottish-style manor a short drive from town. **STATS** 770 rooms; 12 restaurants; 3 bars. **COMPETITIVE EDGE** Banff's most historic property, with a private golf course and easy access to skiing. **ROOMS TO BOOK** Avoid tiny Fairmonts; east-facing Valley Views (an extra $40) look onto Bow River. **COST** Doubles from $$. *800/441-1414 or 403/762-2211; www.fairmont.com*

■ **Rimrock Resort Hotel** Modern lodge built into the hillside, 750 feet up Sulphur Mountain. **STATS** 346 rooms; 2 restaurants; 2 bars. **COMPETITIVE EDGE** Extraordinary views of Banff National Park and close to the Upper Hot Springs. **ROOMS TO BOOK** Deluxes have unobstructed views of Mount Rundle. **COST** Doubles from $$. *888/746-7625 or 403/762-3356; www.rimrockresort.com*

LAKE LOUISE
■ **Fairmont Chateau** Imposing 1890's resort on the lake. **STATS** 550 rooms; 8 restaurants; 2 bars. **COMPETITIVE EDGE** Surrounded by snowcapped peaks above a glacial blue lake. **ROOMS TO BOOK** Rooms in the new Mount Temple Wing are 30 to 50 percent larger than the others. **COST** Doubles from $$. *800/441-1414 or 403/522-3511; www.fairmont.com*

■ **Post Hotel & Spa** Alpine resort with a 1942 lodge on the Pipestone River, 5 minutes from Lake Louise. **STATS** 92 rooms; 5 cabins; 1 restaurant; 1 bar. **COMPETITIVE EDGE** Feels more intimate than the region's other properties. **ROOMS TO BOOK** Those in the original lodge, with wood-burning fireplaces, 2-person Jacuzzis, and king-size beds. **COST** Doubles from $. *800/661-1586 or 403/522-3989; www.posthotel.com*

BRITISH COLUMBIA
VANCOUVER
■ **Wedgewood Hotel & Spa** Intimate downtown hotel, across from the courthouse and Robson Square. **STATS** 83 rooms; 1 restaurant; 1 bar. **COMPETITIVE EDGE** Vancouver's most genteel property, popular with politicos and Hollywood North types. **ROOMS TO BOOK** Front-facing Deluxe Executives have pretty views of the museum and courts. **COST** Doubles from $$. *845 Hornby St.; 800/663-0666 or 604/689-7777; www.wedgewood hotel.com*

VANCOUVER ISLAND
■ **The Aerie** Mediterranean-style resort high in the Malahat Mountains. **STATS** 35 rooms; 1 restaurant; 1 bar. **COMPETITIVE EDGE** Pampering service and 180-degree views of the Cascades, the Olympic range, and the pine-covered San Juan Islands. **ROOMS TO BOOK** Nos. 5 and 6 have private balconies and vistas stretching all the way to Saanich Inlet. **COST** Doubles from $$. *Malahat; 800/518-1933 or 250/743-7115; www.aerie.bc.ca*

■ **Sooke Harbour House** Sprawling, art-filled clapboard overlooking Pacific beach and the Olympic Mountains, 45 minutes from Victoria. **STATS** 28 rooms; 1 restaurant. **COMPETITIVE EDGE** Chef Edward Tuson's legendary and inventive regional cuisine. **ROOM TO BOOK** Edible Blossom, with a private garden and outdoor tub. **COST** Doubles from $$, including breakfast and lunch. *Sooke; 800/889-9688 or 250/642-3421; www.sookeharbourhouse.com*

■ **Wickaninnish Inn** Cedar inn on a remote, rocky promontory on the island's rugged western coast. **STATS** 75 rooms; 1 restaurant; 1 bar. **COMPETITIVE EDGE** Picturesquely located between a temperate rain forest and the ocean. **ROOMS TO BOOK** Any in the original building, for unobstructed Pacific views. **COST** Doubles from $$. *Tofino; 800/333-4604 or 250/725-3100; www.wickinn.com*

ONTARIO
OTTAWA
■ **Fairmont Château Laurier**

THE
BEST
OF
2007

UNITED
STATES
+
CANADA

Magnificent 1912 limestone mansion, built in the style of a French château. **STATS** 429 rooms; 2 restaurants; 1 bar. **COMPETITIVE EDGE** Near Parliament and the National Gallery. **ROOMS TO BOOK** Fairmont Views overlook the Rideau Canal. **COST** Doubles from $. *1 Rideau St.; 800/441-1414 or 613/241-1414; www.fairmont.com*

TORONTO
■ **Park Hyatt** Modern glass-and-marble tower in the heart of Yorkville. **STATS** 346 rooms; 1 restaurant; 1 bar. **COMPETITIVE EDGE** The 10,000-square-foot spa and 18th-floor roof lounge. **ROOMS TO BOOK** Luxury rooms in the new North Tower. **COST** Doubles from $. *4 Avenue Rd.; 800/233-1234 or 416/925-1234; www.parkhyatttoronto.com*

QUEBEC
MONTEBELLO
■ **Fairmont Le Château** 1930 country château between Ottawa and Montreal. **STATS** 211 rooms; 2 restaurants; 2 bars. **COMPETITIVE EDGE** A rambling estate adjacent to an enormous private nature reserve. **ROOMS TO BOOK** Alcove rooms, for their Ottawa River views. **COST** Doubles from $. *800/441-1414 or 819/423-6341; www.fairmont.com*

MONTREAL
■ **Hôtel Le Germain** Sleek downtown hotel with modern wood interiors. **STATS** 101 rooms; 1 restaurant; 1 bar. **COMPETITIVE EDGE** Stylish, loft-like rooms that are equally appealing for business or pleasure. **ROOMS TO BOOK** Those facing President Kennedy Street for glittering city views. **COST** Doubles from $$. *2050 Rue Mansfield; 877/333-2050 or 514/849-2050; www.hotelgermain.com*

■ **Hôtel Le St.-James** Discreet art-filled hotel in a former bank building. **STATS** 60 rooms; 1 restaurant; 1 bar. **COMPETITIVE EDGE** A hip but classic vibe. **ROOMS TO BOOK** East-facing rooms above the 8th floor, for sunlight. **COST** Doubles from $$. *355 Rue St.-Jacques; 866/841-3111 or 514/841-3111; www.hotellestjames.com*

MEXICO + CENTRAL + SOUTH AMERICA

ARGENTINA
BARILOCHE
■ **Llao Llao Hotel & Resort, Golf-Spa** 1940 mountain lodge overlooking Lake Moreno. **STATS** 158 rooms; 1 cabin; 2 restaurants; 1 bar. **COMPETITIVE EDGE** Majestic architecture in harmony with the landscape. **ROOMS TO BOOK** One of 56 Lake Rooms. **COST** Doubles from $$. *54-29/4444-8530; www.llaollao.com*

BUENOS AIRES
■ **Alvear Palace Hotel** Landmark 1932 palace; a La Prairie spa is due to open early this year. **STATS** 210 rooms; 2 restaurants; 2 bars. **COMPETITIVE EDGE** The grand dame of South American luxury hotels. **ROOMS TO BOOK** Premiers above the 8th floor, for best city views. **COST** Doubles from $$$. *1891 Avda. Alvear; 800/223-6800 or 54-11/4808-2100; www.alvearpalace.com*

■ **Caesar Park** Newly renovated high-rise on a quiet Recoleta side street. **STATS** 172 rooms; 1 restaurant; 2 bars. **COMPETITIVE EDGE** The posh Patio Bullrich Shopping Center is across the street. **ROOMS TO BOOK** Garden Views on floors 2–5. **COST** Doubles from $$. *1232 Posadas; 877/223-7272 or 54-11/4819-1100; www.caesar-park.com*

■ **Four Seasons Hotel** 1916 Belle-Époque mansion and contemporary tower. **STATS** 165 rooms; 1 restaurant; 1 bar. **COMPETITIVE EDGE** An outdoor heated pool and a great restaurant. **ROOMS TO BOOK** For views of the Obelisk and Avda. 9 de Julio, Premiers ending in -01 and -09 and Deluxe Premiers ending in -03, -11, and -15. **COST** Doubles from $$. *1086-1088 Posadas; 800/332-3442 or 54-11/4321-1200; www.fourseasons.com*

■ **Park Tower** Sleek downtown high-rise near Puerto Madero, soon to become South America's first

St. Regis. **STATS** 181 rooms; 1 restaurant; 1 bar. **COMPETITIVE EDGE** The largest standard rooms in town, starting at 624 square feet and up. **ROOMS TO BOOK** The 15th floor and above, for views over the Río de la Plata. **COST** Doubles from $$. *1193 Avda. Leandro N. Alem; 800/325-3589 or 54-11/4318-9100; www.starwood.com*

MENDOZA
■ **Park Hyatt** Seven-story building with restored 19th-century Spanish-colonial façade on downtown's Plaza Independencia. **STATS** 186 rooms; 2 restaurants; 2 bars. **COMPETITIVE EDGE** The most luxurious rooms in the city. **ROOMS TO BOOK** An Andes Room on the top floor is only $20 extra. **COST** Doubles from $$. *1124 Chile; 800/223-1234 or 54-261/441-1234; www.hyatt.com*

BELIZE
SAN IGNACIO
■ **Blancaneaux Lodge** Francis Ford Coppola's jungle resort near the Mayan ruins of Caracol. **STATS** 17 cottages; 1 restaurant; 1 bar. **COMPETITIVE EDGE** A host of luxe amenities in a remote forest-reserve setting. **ROOM TO BOOK** Cabana No. 6 is the most private. **COST** Doubles from $$, including breakfast. *800/746-3743 or 011-501/824-3878; www.blancaneaux.com*

CHILE
SANTIAGO
■ **Ritz-Carlton** 15-story building in the city's exclusive El Golf neighborhood. **STATS** 205 rooms; 1 restaurant; 1 bar. **COMPETITIVE EDGE** Classic Ritz refinement—unrivaled in the city. **ROOMS TO BOOK** Deluxes above the 7th floor, for dazzling views. **COST** Doubles from $$. *15 Calle el Alcade; 800/241-3333 or 56-2/470-8500; www.ritzcarlton.com*

COSTA RICA
LA FORTUNA DE SAN CARLOS
■ **Tabacón Grand Spa Thermal Resort** Known for its thermal mineral water spa on 940 untouched acres in northern Costa Rica's rain forests. **STATS** 114 rooms; 2 restaurants; 3 bars. **COMPETITIVE EDGE** Unobstructed views of the Arenal Volcano from your

private balcony. **ROOMS TO BOOK** A newly renovated Deluxe room with bed crafted by local artisans. **COST** Doubles from $. *877/277-8291; www.tabacon.com*

PENINSULA PAPAGAYO
■ **Four Seasons Resort** Tico-style resort flanked by 2 beaches. **STATS** 163 rooms; 4 restaurants; 1 bar. **COMPETITIVE EDGE** Authentic local design meets Four Seasons luxury and services. **ROOMS TO BOOK** The 2000 series on upper floors, for the most privacy. **COST** Doubles from $$$. *800/332-3442 or 011-506/696-0098; www.fourseasons.com*

GUATEMALA
ANTIGUA
■ **Casa Santo Domingo** Restored 16th-century convent with museum near downtown. **STATS** 125 rooms; 1 restaurant; 1 bar. **COMPETITIVE EDGE** A historic jewel, full of local artifacts. **ROOMS TO BOOK** Nos. 240 and 241 are the quietest and have spectacular volcano views. **COST** Doubles from $. *28A 3A Calle Oriente; 502/7820-1220; www.casasantodomingo.com.gt*

MEXICO
ACAPULCO
■ **Las Brisas** Bungalows with private pools overlooking the water. **STATS** 263 rooms; 2 restaurants; 2 bars. **COMPETITIVE EDGE** An isolated retreat near a renowned party town. **ROOMS TO BOOK** Fourth-level Beach Club rooms have the best views. **COST** Doubles from $$. *525 Carr. Escénica; 800/223-6800 or 52-744/469-6900; www.brisas.com.mx*

BAJA
■ **Esperanza** Sprawling resort on a rocky bluff over the Sea of Cortés. **STATS** 56 suites; 3 restaurants; 1 bar. **COMPETITIVE EDGE** The most intimate of Cabo's high-end properties. **ROOMS TO BOOK** Palapa Casitas have infinity hot tubs. **COST** Doubles from $$$. *Cabo San Lucas; 866/311-2226 or 52-624/145-6400; www.esperanzaresort.com*

■ **One & Only Palmilla** Legendary 1956 Spanish revival-style retreat on one of Cabo's few swimmable beaches. **STATS** 172 rooms; 3 restaurants; 2 bars.

COMPETITIVE EDGE Mega-resort in a boutique setting. **ROOM TO BOOK** Oceanfront Deluxe. **COST** Doubles from $$$. *San José del Cabo; 866/829-2977 or 52-624/146-7000; www.oneandonlyresorts.com*

■ **Las Ventanas al Paraíso, A Rosewood Resort** Sophisticated resort along a pristine white beach. **STATS** 71 suites; 2 restaurants; 2 bars. **COMPETITIVE EDGE** The largest standard rooms in Cabo. **ROOMS TO BOOK** Oceanview Rooftop Terrace Junior Suites, with outdoor whirlpools. **COST** Doubles from $$$. *San José del Cabo; 888/767-3966 or 52-624/144-2800; www.rosewoodhotels.com*

CANCÚN
■ **JW Marriott Resort and Spa** Beachfront tower renovated head-to-toe after Hurricane Wilma. **STATS** 448 rooms; 3 restaurants; 1 bar. **COMPETITIVE EDGE** An intimate feel, even after its $60 million restoration. **ROOMS TO BOOK** Odd-numbered rooms on the 12th floor have idyllic Caribbean views. **COST** Doubles from $$. *888/813-2776 or 52-998/848-9600; www.jwmarriottcancun.com*

■ **Ritz-Carlton** Hacienda-style resort in the hotel zone; recent $15 million renovation introduced a tennis club and beachside restaurant. **STATS** 365 rooms; 6 restaurants; 3 bars. **COMPETITIVE EDGE** A refreshingly adult atmosphere. **ROOMS TO BOOK** Ocean Fronts for panoramic vistas. **COST** Doubles from $$$. *800/241-3333 or 52-998/881-0808; www.ritzcarlton.com*

CUERNAVACA
■ **Las Mañanitas** Landmark 1955 estate in downtown Cuernavaca. **STATS** 32 suites; 1 restaurant; 1 bar. **COMPETITIVE EDGE** Renowned art and formal gardens. **ROOMS TO BOOK** Mañanitas Residence suites with a private pool. **COST** Doubles from $. *888/413-9199 or 52-777/362-0000; www.lasmananitas.com.mx*

MAYA RIVIERA
■ **Royal Hideaway Playacar** Colonial-style villas near downtown

Playa del Carmen. **STATS** 200 rooms; 6 restaurants; 2 bars. **COMPETITIVE EDGE** No need to have your wallet during your stay. **ROOMS TO BOOK** Second-floor rooms in villas 27 and 31 have beach and pool views. **COST** Doubles from $$$, all-inclusive. *800/999-9182 or 52-984/873-4500; www.royalhideaway.com*

MEXICO CITY
■ **Four Seasons Hotel** Eight-story hacienda-style hotel on the most prestigious avenue. **STATS** 240 rooms; 1 restaurant; 1 bar. **COMPETITIVE EDGE** Location and luxury; the city's most coveted property. **ROOMS TO BOOK** Deluxe Kings above the tranquil courtyard. **COST** Doubles from $$. *500 Paseo de la Reforma; 800/332-3442 or 52-55/5230-1818; www.fourseasons.com*

PUEBLO TULUM
■ **Maya Tulum Wellness Retreat & Spa** Thatched-roof casitas along a deserted strip of white sand. **STATS** 45 rooms; 1 restaurant; 1 bar. **COMPETITIVE EDGE** Spa treatments with indigenous ingredients. **ROOM TO BOOK** Villa A, on a rocky point over lapping waves. **COST** Doubles from $. *888/515-4580; www.mayatulum.com*

PUNTA MITA
■ **Four Seasons Resort** Tiled-roof casitas on a pristine isthmus outside Puerto Vallarta. **STATS** 150 rooms; 8 villas; 4 restaurants; 6 bars. **COMPETITIVE EDGE** Serenity—it's the only resort in sight. **ROOMS TO BOOK** Casita Beachfronts. **COST** Doubles from $$$. *800/332-3442 or 52-329/291-6000; www.fourseasons.com*

SAN MIGUEL DE ALLENDE
■ **Casa de Sierra Nevada** Spanish 16th- to 18th-century mansions. **STATS** 33 rooms; 2 restaurants; 2 bars. **COMPETITIVE EDGE** Old-world charm in one of Mexico's most historic towns. **ROOM TO BOOK** No. 3 in the Parque House, for its serene garden and patio. **COST** Doubles from $$. *35 Hospicio; 800/701-1561 or 52-415/152-7040; www.casadesierranevada.com*

TECATE
■ **Rancho La Puerta** Folk art-

THE
BEST
OF
2007

MEXICO
+
CENTRAL
+
SOUTH
AMERICA

WORLD'S BEST
DIRECTORY

filled casitas on a 3,000-acre nature preserve. **STATS** 87 rooms; 1 restaurant **COMPETITIVE EDGE** Over 40 miles of hiking trails and 50 daily fitness classes. **ROOMS TO BOOK** Rooms in the Villa Sol, with its own pool and hot tub. **COST** Doubles from $$$$, all-inclusive. (One week minimum stay.) *877/440-7778 or 858/764-5500; www.rancholapuerta.com*

ZIHUATANEJO
■ **La Casa Que Canta** Cliff-hugging adobe resort above Zihuatanejo Bay. **STATS** 25 suites; 2 villas; 1 restaurant; 1 bar. **COMPETITIVE EDGE** Romantic hideaway with brand-new spa. **ROOMS TO BOOK** No. 9, for spectacular ocean views, or No. 15, which has 869 square feet. **COST** Doubles from $$. *888/523-5050 or 52-755/555-7030; www. lacasaquecanta.com*

PERU
CUZCO
■ **Hotel Monasterio** Converted 16th-century monastery; 32 more rooms and a spa opening midyear. **STATS** 127 rooms; 2 restaurants; 1 bar. **COMPETITIVE EDGE** The most luxurious hotel in Cuzco. **ROOMS TO BOOK** Deluxes are oxygen-enriched to keep altitude sickness at bay. **COST** Doubles from $$. *136 Calle Palacios; 800/237-1236 or 51-84/241-777; www.monasteriohotel.com*

MACHU PICCHU
■ **Machu Picchu Sanctuary Lodge** Eco-friendly lodge on the Inca Trail. **STATS** 31 rooms; 2 restaurants; 1 bar. **COMPETITIVE EDGE** The only hotel within the Incan citadel. **ROOM TO BOOK** No. 21, with Huayna Picchu outside its window. **COST** Doubles from $$$, including meals. *800/237-1236 or 51-84/211-039; www.orient-express.com*

URUGUAY
CARMELO
■ **Four Seasons Resort** Golf-and-spa retreat in a eucalyptus forest along the River Plate. **STATS** 44 suites; 2 restaurants; 1 bar. **COMPETITIVE EDGE** A fraction of the usual Four Seasons cost. **ROOMS TO BOOK** Riverfront Bungalows with carved beds and private gardens. **COST** Doubles from $$. *800/332-3442 or 598/542-9000; www.fourseasons.com*

THE CARIBBEAN + BERMUDA + THE BAHAMAS

ANGUILLA
■ **Cap Juluca** Whitewashed resort with an emphasis on privacy. **STATS** 98 rooms; 3 restaurants; 2 bars. **COMPETITIVE EDGE** Every room has a prime spot on the mile-long crescent of alabaster sand. **ROOMS TO BOOK** Junior Suites with indoor–outdoor showers and secluded solariums. **COST** Doubles from $$$$. *888/858-5822 or 264/497-6666; www.capjuluca.com*

■ **CuisinArt Resort & Spa** Mediterranean-style buildings clustered around a dramatic infinity pool that leads to the beach. **STATS** 93 rooms; 2 restaurants; 2 bars. **COMPETITIVE EDGE** The hydroponic farm provides produce and herbs for the restaurants and spa treatments. **ROOMS TO BOOK** An upgrade to a suite with an ocean view is worth it. **COST** Doubles from $$$. *800/943-3210 or 264/498-2000; www.cuisinartresort.com*

■ **Malliouhana Hotel & Spa** A family-friendly beachfront property partially atop a rocky promontory jutting into Meads Bay. **STATS** 55 rooms; 2 restaurants; 1 bar. **COMPETITIVE EDGE** The biggest spa on the island, at 15,000 square feet. **ROOMS TO BOOK** Corner rooms with wraparound balconies. **COST** Doubles from $$$. *800/835-0796 or 264/497-6111; www.malliouhana.com*

ANTIGUA
■ **Curtain Bluff Resort** Eco-friendly resort set between 2 beaches. **STATS** 72 rooms; 2 restaurants; 2 bars. **COMPETITIVE EDGE** A grown-up take on all-inclusive: everything from yoga to scuba to a customized mini-bar. **ROOMS TO BOOK** The Morris and Grace Bay Suites, with modern décor. **COST** Doubles from $$$$, all-inclusive. *888/289-9898 or 268/462-8400; www.curtainbluff.com*

■ **Jumby Bay, A Rosewood Resort** Secluded colonial- style property on a 300-acre island accessible only by boat. **STATS** 40 suites; 11 villas; 2 restaurants; 3 bars. **COMPETITIVE EDGE** So intimate that the rooms don't have keys and staff knows your name. **ROOMS TO BOOK** Rondavels, with wraparound terraces and outdoor showers. **COST** Doubles from $$$$$, all-inclusive. *888/767-3966 or 268/ 462-6000; www.rosewoodhotels.com*

BAHAMAS
■ **Four Seasons Resort Great Exuma at Emerald Bay** 225-acre resort on a quiet island, rimmed with perfect white-sand beaches. **STATS** 183 rooms; 3 restaurants; 2 bars. **COMPETITIVE EDGE** The oceanside Greg Norman golf course—one of the region's most challenging (and rewarding). **ROOMS TO BOOK** For privacy, reserve a Beachfront at either end of the resort. **COST** Doubles from $$. *800/332-3442 or 242/336-6800; www.fourseasons.com*

■ **One & Only Ocean Club at Paradise Island** 1939 Huntington beachside estate with a genteel feel. **STATS** 101 rooms; 3 villas; 2 cottages; 4 restaurants; 2 bars. **COMPETITIVE EDGE** Polished amenities (a Jean Georges restaurant, designed by Christian Liaigre). Also, access to a range of activities (water parks and casinos) at nearby Atlantis. **ROOMS TO BOOK** Those in the Crescent Wing are newer. **COST** Doubles from $$$$. *800/321-3000 or 242/363-2501; www.oneandonlyresorts.com*

■ **Pink Sands** Chris Blackwell's Moroccan-, Indian-, and Balinese-inspired village on a 3-mile beach. **STATS** 25 cottages; 1 restaurant; 1 bar. **COMPETITIVE EDGE** Tropical grounds that double as a bird sanctuary. **ROOMS TO BOOK** Oceanview Cottages look onto the Atlantic and have private paths to the water. **COST** Doubles from $$$$, including breakfast and dinner. *800/688-7678 or 242/333-2030; www.islandoutpost.com*

BARBADOS
■ **Sandy Lane** High-end (yet family-friendly) Palladian-style beachfront resort, with one of the largest spas in

the Caribbean. **STATS** 112 rooms; 1 villa; 4 restaurants; 5 bars. **COMPETITIVE EDGE** Over-the-top glamour combined with high-tech rooms. **ROOMS TO BOOK** From May through October, Ocean Rooms are $100 more and worth the splurge. **COST** Doubles from $$$$$.
866/444-4080 or 246/444-2000; www.sandylane.com

BERMUDA

■ **The Reefs** Intimate cliffside hideaway of pink stucco cottages. **STATS** 65 rooms; 3 restaurants; 2 bars. **COMPETITIVE EDGE** Tranquil setting featuring a private, umbrella-flecked beach. **ROOMS TO BOOK** Premiers and Deluxes in Building H, for views down the South coastline. **COST** Doubles from $$$, including breakfast, afternoon tea, and dinner. *800/742-2008 or 441/238-0222; www.thereefs.com*

■ **Waterloo House** Harbor-front manor house in downtown Hamilton, near shopping and dining. **STATS** 30 rooms; 1 restaurant. **COMPETITIVE EDGE** A relaxed but business-friendly retreat in the center of town. **ROOMS TO BOOK** Those with terraces overlooking the harbor. **COST** Doubles from $$, including breakfast. *800/468-4100 or 441/295-4480; www.waterloohouse.com*

BRITISH VIRGIN ISLANDS

PETER ISLAND

■ **Peter Island Resort** Two-story bungalows on an 1,800-acre private island with 5 beaches, miles of hiking and biking trails, and prime diving. **STATS** 52 rooms; 3 villas; 2 restaurants; 2 bars. **COMPETITIVE EDGE** The exclusivity of an island accessible only by helicopter or boat. **ROOMS TO BOOK** One of the renovated beachfront Junior Suites, with knockout views. **COST** Doubles from $$$. *800/346-4451 or 284/495-2000; www.peterisland.com*

VIRGIN GORDA

■ **Biras Creek** Pastel cottages on a secluded 140-acre peninsula with panoramic ocean views and a pretty beach. **STATS** 31 rooms; 2 restaurants; 3 bars. **COMPETITIVE EDGE** The most relaxed of the secluded island

properties. **ROOMS TO BOOK** Ocean Suites 11A or 11B are steps from the pool and have ocean views. **COST** Doubles from $$$$, including meals. *800/223-1108 or 284/494-3555; www.biras.com*

■ **Little Dix Bay, A Rosewood Resort** Light and airy cedar-shingled beachside villas with an updated yet simple style. **STATS** 100 rooms; 3 restaurants; 3 bars. **COMPETITIVE EDGE** The spa, with a couples treatment room and an infinity-pool relaxation area. **ROOMS TO BOOK** The 12 Tree House Cottages have outdoor decks and patios with hammocks beneath. **COST** Doubles from $$$. *888/767-3966 or 284/495-5555; www.littledixbay.com*

JAMAICA

■ **Couples Sans Souci** A 35-acre resort set on a hillside above 2 beaches. **STATS** 148 rooms; 5 restaurants; 5 bars. **COMPETITIVE EDGE** The smallest of the Couples resorts: the benefits of an all-inclusive on a more intimate scale. **ROOMS TO BOOK** Halfway up the hill, the D-block suites are centrally located, large, and quiet. **COST** Doubles from $$$, all-inclusive. *800/268-7537 or 876/994-1206; www.couples.com*

■ **Couples Swept Away** Recently expanded all-suite property on Negril's pristine Seven Mile Beach. **STATS** 312 rooms; 6 restaurants; 7 bars. **COMPETITIVE EDGE** Extensive fitness facilities: open-air gym; 82-foot lap pool; jogging track. **ROOMS TO BOOK** The older ones, for their large balconies with hammocks. **COST** Doubles from $$$, all-inclusive. *800/268-7537 or 876/957-4061; www.couples.com*

■ **Half Moon** Classic 53-year-old colonial style estate on 400 acres with a 2-mile private beach. **STATS** 398 rooms; 6 restaurants; 8 bars. **COMPETITIVE EDGE** Polished, attentive service; endless activity options. **ROOMS TO BOOK** Spa Suites have bubble-jet chromatherapy soaking tubs and steam showers. **COST** Doubles from $$. *866/648-6951 or 876/953-2211; www.halfmoon.com*

■ **Jamaica Inn Hotel** Genteel low-rise retreat on one of the island's best beaches. **STATS** 47 suites; 4 cottages; 1 restaurant; 2 bars. **COMPETITIVE EDGE** One of Jamaica's most romantic spots. **ROOMS TO BOOK** Those in the Beach Wing, right on the sand. **COST** Doubles from $$$. *800/837-4608 or 876/974-2514; www.jamaicainn.com*

NEVIS

■ **Four Seasons Resort** Colonial-style resort along pretty Pinney's Beach. **STATS** 196 rooms; 4 restaurants; 4 bars. **COMPETITIVE EDGE** Terrific golf course and spa, coupled with family-friendly activities, make this an unusually well-rounded resort. **ROOMS TO BOOK** The affordable Mountain Views have lovely vistas. **COST** Doubles from $$$. *800/332-3442 or 869/469-1111; www.fourseasons.com*

ST. BART'S

■ **Eden Rock Hotel** Historic house-hotel (undergoing expansion) on a rocky promontory surrounded by Baie de St.-Jean. **STATS** 28 rooms; 2 restaurants; 2 bars. **COMPETITIVE EDGE** The place to see and be seen—with the island's liveliest beach. **ROOMS TO BOOK** The Harbour House and De Haenen, for panoramic views. **COST** Doubles from $$$$, including breakfast. *877/563-7105 or 590-590/297-999; www.edenrockhotel.com*

■ **Hôtel Saint-Barth Isle de France** French plantation–style resort with an Asian twist, on the Baie des Flamands. **STATS** 33 rooms; 1 restaurant; 1 bar. **COMPETITIVE EDGE** A familial atmosphere, thanks to gracious staff and return guests. **ROOMS TO BOOK** Those on the 2nd floor of the main building, for ocean views. **COST** Doubles from $$$$, including breakfast. *800/810-4691 or 590-590/275-666; www.isle-de-france.com*

ST. LUCIA

■ **Anse Chastanet Resort** Cluster of colorful villas scattered in the foothills of the Piton mountains and along a small beach. **STATS** 49 rooms; 2 restaurants; 2 bars. **COMPETITIVE EDGE** Fewer than 50 rooms on 600

THE
BEST
OF
2007
—
THE
CARIBBEAN
+
BERMUDA
+
THE
BAHAMAS

acres ensure maximum privacy. **ROOMS TO BOOK** Premium Hillsides, with an open fourth wall. **COST** Doubles from $$. *800/223-1108 or 758/459-7000; www.ansechastanet.com*

■ **Ladera** Stylish eco-lodge in a rain forest; beaches are a shuttle ride away. **STATS** 21 suites; 6 villas; 1 restaurant; 1 bar. **COMPETITIVE EDGE** Every activity under the sun—astrology sessions, fashion shows, mixology classes. **ROOMS TO BOOK** Gros Piton Suites have a plunge pool, waterfall, and spectacular views. **COST** Doubles from $$$, including breakfast. *866/290-0978 or 758/459-7323; www.ladera.com*

ST. MARTIN
■ **La Samanna** Whitewashed Moorish-inspired resort on 55 acres on Baie Longue. **STATS** 81 rooms; 1 villa; 2 restaurants; 2 bars. **COMPETITIVE EDGE** Set along the island's most beautiful white-sand beach. **ROOMS TO BOOK** The new Premium Suites, with private rooftop gazebos and pools. **COST** Doubles from $$$$. *800/854-2252 or 590-590/876-400; www.lasamanna.com*

TURKS AND CAICOS
■ **Grace Bay Club** Relaxed Spanish-style resort of villas and an adults-only main hotel on a superb beach; just added a spa and gym. **STATS** 60 suites; 3 restaurants; 2 bars. **COMPETITIVE EDGE** Appeals to couples and families alike and has impeccable service; the resort runs a hotel training school. **ROOMS TO BOOK** Those in the main building, which are quieter than the villas. **COST** Doubles from $$$$. *800/946-5757 or 649/946-5757; www.gracebayclub.com*

■ **Parrot Cay** Trendsetting private island with a 3-mile stretch of sand. **STATS** 65 rooms; 2 restaurants; 2 bars. **COMPETITIVE EDGE** A serene Asian aesthetic and quiet setting. **ROOM TO BOOK** No. 703 has Technicolor sunsets from its terrace. **COST** Doubles from $$$. *877/754-0726 or 649/946-7788; www.parrotcay.como.bz*

EUROPE

AUSTRIA
SALZBURG
■ **Hotel Goldener Hirsch** 15th-century Old Town hotel with an intimate lodge feel and antique pine furnishings. **STATS** 69 rooms; 2 restaurants; 1 bar. **COMPETITIVE EDGE** A Salzburg institution, especially among Austria's elite. **ROOMS TO BOOK** For a king-size bed, book an Exclusive or larger. **COST** Doubles from $$. *37 Getreidegasse; 800/325-3589 or 43-662/80840; www.luxurycollection.com*

CZECH REPUBLIC
PRAGUE
■ **Four Seasons Hotel** Adjoining historic and contemporary buildings on the Vltava River. **STATS** 161 rooms; 1 restaurant; 1 bar. **COMPETITIVE EDGE** Spotless service and luxurious rooms. **ROOMS TO BOOK** Seventh-floor Superiors, with vaulted ceilings. **COST** Doubles from $$. *2A/1098 Veleslavinova; 800/332-3442 or 420-2/2142-7000; www.fourseasons.com*

ENGLAND
GLOUCESTERSHIRE
■ **Buckland Manor Country House Hotel** Stone manor with antiques and original oil paintings, in the Cotswolds. **STATS** 13 rooms; 1 restaurant; 1 bar. **COMPETITIVE EDGE** A bucolic setting on 10 acres of gardens, streams, and waterfalls; impeccable service. **ROOM TO BOOK** The Blue Room, for its lovely garden view. **COST** Doubles from $$. *Buckland; 800/735-2478 or 44-1386/852-626; www.bucklandmanor.com*

LONDON
■ **The Goring** Edwardian-era hotel with classic interiors, in Belgravia, just behind Buckingham Palace. **STATS** 71 rooms; 1 restaurant; 1 bar. **COMPETITIVE EDGE** A bastion of old-school English hospitality, run by the same family for 4 generations. **ROOMS TO BOOK** Any with a view of the surprisingly large garden. **COST** Doubles from $$$. *Beeston Place, Grosvenor Gardens;* 800/525-4800 or 44-20/7396-9000; *www.goringhotel.co.uk*

■ **The Lanesborough** Regency-style building on Hyde Park Corner, restored to its 19th-century grandeur. **STATS** 97 rooms; 1 restaurant; 1 bar. **COMPETITIVE EDGE** Exceptionally attentive service: guests get personal butlers, who are at their beck and call. **ROOMS TO BOOK** Those on the 1st and 2nd floors have the highest ceilings; insist on a Hyde Park view. **COST** Doubles from $$$$. *Hyde Park Corner; 877/787-3447 or 44-20/7259-5599; www.lanesborough.com*

FINLAND
HELSINKI
■ **Hotel Kämp** Belle Époque landmark with traditional décor. **STATS** 179 rooms; 2 restaurants; 2 bars. **COMPETITIVE EDGE** Prime location opposite Esplanade Park, near Helsinki's best shopping. **ROOMS TO BOOK** For views of the city, opt for an Executive. **COST** Doubles from $520. *29 Pohjoisesplanadi; 800/325-3589 or 358-9/576-111; www.hotelkamp.fi*

FRANCE
CÔTE D'AZUR
■ **Château de la Chèvre d'Or** Cliffside complex of historic stone buildings, in the medieval village of Èze. **STATS** 32 rooms; 4 restaurants; 1 bar. **COMPETITIVE EDGE** A secluded and spectacular setting (terraced gardens; narrow alleyways; panoramic Riviera views). **ROOMS TO BOOK** Each is unique; the Presidential Suite has a private lap pool. **COST** Doubles from $$. *Èze; 800/735-2478 or 33-4/92-10-66-66; www.chevredor.com*

■ **La Colombe d'Or** Atmospheric family-run villa surrounded by cypress trees, 12 miles from Nice. **STATS** 26 rooms; 1 restaurant; 1 bar. **COMPETITIVE EDGE** An extensive collection of artwork left by former guests (Picasso, Matisse, Klee, Calder). **ROOM TO BOOK** No. 12, for its Renaissance-style fresco. **COST** Doubles from $$. *St.-Paul-de-Vence; 33-4/93-32-80-02; www.la-colombe-dor.com*

■ **Grand-Hôtel du Cap-Ferrat** White Belle Époque palace, among 17 acres of gardens and forest. **STATS** 53 rooms; 1 villa; 2 restaurants; 1 bar. **COMPETITIVE EDGE** Exclusive location at the tip of the Cap-Ferrat peninsula, between Nice and Monaco. **ROOMS TO BOOK** No. 402, for great views; the Villa Rose-Pierre is like having your own private Riviera château. **COST** Doubles from $$$. *St.-Jean-Cap-Ferrat; 800/525-4800 or 33-4/93-76-50-50; www.grand-hotel-cap-ferrat.com*

■ **Hôtel Château Eza** Elegant 400-year-old château (former residence of Prince William of Sweden) built into the medieval walls of Èze. **STATS** 10 rooms; 1 restaurant; 1 bar. **COMPETITIVE EDGE** Romantic retreat with exceptional views from its 1,300-foot-high perch. **ROOMS TO BOOK** Nos. 312 or 313, for a balcony overlooking the sea; No. 316, which has 2 stone fireplaces. **COST** Doubles from $$. *Èze; 800/525-4800 or 33-4/93-41-12-24; www.chateaueza.com*

■ **La Réserve de Beaulieu** 1880 Renaissance-style villa, in one of the Riviera's most attractive villages. **STATS** 39 rooms; 2 restaurants; 2 bars. **COMPETITIVE EDGE** A recent $17 million renovation, extensive spa, and Michelin 2-starred restaurant keep this landmark at the head of the class. **ROOMS TO BOOK** 3rd-floor rooms, for Old Port views. **COST** Doubles from $$$$$. *Beaulieu-sur-Mer; 800/223-6800 or 33-4/93-01-00-01; www.reservebeaulieu.com*

DORDOGNE-PÉRIGORD
■ **Le Vieux Logis** 17th-century former priory with gardens and a yellow-limestone pool, in the Périgord Noir. **STATS** 26 rooms; 2 restaurants; 1 bar. **COMPETITIVE EDGE** Affordable French country style that feels as inviting as a grandmother's house. **ROOMS TO BOOK** No. 5 is large and light-filled; No. 8, under the eaves, is perfect for couples looking for privacy. **COST** Doubles from $. *Trémolat; 800/735-2478 or 33-5/53-22-80-06; www.vieux-logis.com*

LOIRE VALLEY
■ **Domaine des Hauts de Loire** Ivy-covered 19th-century former hunting manor in a 185-acre wooded park, between Blois and Amboise. **STATS** 34 rooms; 1 restaurant. **COMPETITIVE EDGE** A central base for exploring château country, plus one of the region's best restaurants. **ROOMS TO BOOK** No. 27 has a small balcony; Nos. 2, 3, and 12 have views of the pond; No. 35 has floor-to-ceiling windows. **COST** Doubles from $. *Onzain; 800/735-2478 or 33-2/54-20-72-57; www.domainehautsloire.com*

PARIS
■ **Four Seasons Hotel George V** Ornate 1928 landmark with superb service and amenities (top-notch spa and gym; Michelin 3-starred restaurant). **STATS** 245 rooms; 2 restaurants; 1 bar. **COMPETITIVE EDGE** A location near the Champs-Élysées, and unbeatable views of the Eiffel Tower. **ROOMS TO BOOK** All are big (minimum is 430 square feet); Duplex Suites are worth the upgrade for skyline views. **COST** Doubles from $$$$. *31 Ave. George V; 800/332-3442 or 33-1/49-52-70-00; www.fourseasons.com*

■ **Hôtel de Crillon** Gilded 18th-century Louis XV-style palace, in a central location, just steps from the Tuileries and the Seine. **STATS** 147 rooms; 2 restaurants; 2 bars. **COMPETITIVE EDGE** The most impressive architecture among the city's top hotels. **ROOMS TO BOOK** Nos. 409 and 511 have balconies and Eiffel Tower views. **COST** Doubles from $$$$. *10 Place de la Concorde; 800/223-6800 or 33-1/44-71-15-00; www.crillon.com*

■ **Le Meurice** 1835 palace with Louis XVI-style décor, facing the Tuileries. **STATS** 160 rooms; 2 restaurants; 1 bar. **COMPETITIVE EDGE** Historical ambience meets modern comfort, thanks to ongoing multimillion-dollar renovations. **ROOMS TO BOOK** The Belle Étoile suite, for the best Tuileries views; Nos. 524 and 528, for vistas stretching to Sacré Cœur. **COST** Doubles from $$$$. *228 Rue de Rivoli; 800/650-1842 or 33-1/44-58-10-09; www.meuricehotel.com*

■ **The Ritz** César Ritz's legendary turn-of-the-20th-century hotel, within walking distance of the Louvre and the Opéra. **STATS** 162 rooms; 2 restaurants; 2 bars. **COMPETITIVE EDGE** The most venerable, iconic address in the city—Coco Chanel called it home for 37 years. **ROOMS TO BOOK** Suites overlooking Place Vendôme; Deluxes and Superior Executives that have views of the garden and Ministry of Justice. **COST** Doubles from $$$$. *15 Place Vendôme; 800/223-6800 or 33-1/43-16-30-30; www.ritzparis.com*

PROVENCE
■ **La Bastide de Moustiers** Chef Alain Ducasse's 17th-century auberge, on 10 pastoral acres in the foothills of the French Alps. **STATS** 12 rooms; 1 restaurant; 1 bar. **COMPETITIVE EDGE** The master chef's signature cuisine, sourced straight from the kitchen garden. **ROOMS TO BOOK** Volière, for a four-poster bed and claw-foot tub; Olive, for a fireplace and terrace. **COST** Doubles from $. *Moustiers-Ste.-Marie; 33-4/92-70-47-47; www.bastide-moustiers.com*

■ **Hôtel Crillon le Brave** Seven restored stone houses linked by cobblestoned alleys and gardens, in a village 30 minutes from Avignon. **STATS** 32 rooms; 2 restaurants; 1 bar. **COMPETITIVE EDGE** A secluded getaway that offers a real taste of French village life. **ROOMS TO BOOK** Nos. 29 and 31, in the Maison Philibert, for views of both Mont Ventoux and the Rhône Valley. **COST** Doubles from $$. *Crillon le Brave; 800/735-2478 or 33-4/90-65-61-61; www.crillonlebrave.com*

■ **Oustau de Baumanière** 15th-century farmhouse, with gardens and a Michelin 2-starred restaurant, near Les Baux-de-Provence. **STATS** 30 rooms; 1 restaurant. **COMPETITIVE EDGE** An ideal base for visiting the area's UNESCO World Heritage sites. **ROOMS TO BOOK** Nos. 61, 62, and 63 are contemporary in style. **COST** Doubles from $$. *Les Baux-de-Provence; 800/735-2478 or 33-4/90-54-33-07; www.oustaudebaumaniere.com*

■ **Villa Gallici** Traditional 18th-century residence, decorated in elegant period style, a short walk from downtown Aix-en-Provence. **STATS** 22 rooms; 1 restaurant; 1 bar. **COMPETITIVE**

THE
BEST
OF
2007
___
EUROPE

WORLD'S BEST
DIRECTORY

EDGE Sumptuous Italianate décor and rich details—a nice change from the region's typical rustic look. **ROOMS TO BOOK** Nos. 5 and 15–18 have private gardens. **COST** Doubles from $$. *Aix-en-Provence; 800/735-2478 or 33-4/42-23-29-23; www.villagallici.com*

REIMS
■ **Château Les Crayères** Turn-of-the-20th-century château on a private 17-acre park, in the heart of the Champagne region. **STATS** 20 rooms; 1 restaurant; 1 bar. **COMPETITIVE EDGE** The exceptional Michelin 2-starred restaurant, headed up by chef Didier Elena. **ROOM TO BOOK** All have been recently redone by designer Pierre-Yves Rochon; opt for the Comtesse suite, for its sitting area. **COST** Doubles from $$. *800/735-2478 or 33-3/26-82-80-80; www.gerardboyer.com*

GERMANY
BADEN-BADEN
■ **Brenner's Park-Hotel & Spa** Legendary 130-year-old resort overlooking Lichtentaler Allee near the Black Forest. **STATS** 100 rooms; 2 restaurants; 2 bars. **COMPETITIVE EDGE** A traditional European spa experience: equal parts medicinal and pampering. **ROOMS TO BOOK** Superiors and Deluxes, for balconies with the best Allee views. **COST** Doubles from $$. *800/628-8929 or 49-7221/9000; www.brenners.com*

BERLIN
■ **Hotel Adlon Kempinski** Faithful yet contemporary re-creation of Berlin's most historic hotel, right beside the Brandenburg Gate. **STATS** 384 rooms; 3 restaurants; 1 bar. **COMPETITIVE EDGE** An unbeatable central location. **ROOMS TO BOOK** One of the 15 new Luxury Suites, fresh from a $15 million renovation. **COST** Doubles from $$. *77 Unter den Linden; 800/426-3135 or 49-30/22610; www.h......on.de*

DRESDEN
■ **Hotel Taschenberg Kempinski** Former palac...... in the war and rebuilt in 19... Baroque and modern int... the Semper Opera. **STATS**...... 3 restaurants; 1 bar. **COMPE**...

An aristocratic meeting place for opera devotees and high society. **ROOMS TO BOOK** Second-floor Kurfuerstens, with high ceilings and views of the city's monuments. **COST** Doubles from $$. *3 Taschenberg; 800/426-3135 or 49-351/491-20; www.kempinski.com*

HUNGARY
BUDAPEST
■ **Four Seasons Hotel Gresham Palace** Three-year-old hotel housed in a 1905 building, on the Danube facing Old Buda and Castle Hill. **STATS** 179 rooms; 2 restaurants; 1 bar. **COMPETITIVE EDGE** Breathtaking architecture, including a glass-domed lobby. **ROOMS TO BOOK** Danube Superiors, for views of the Chain Bridge. **COST** Doubles from $$. *5-6 Roosevelt Tér; 800/332-3442 or 36-1/268-6000; www.fourseasons.com*

IRELAND
CO. CLARE
■ **Dromoland Castle** Baronial castle dating from the 16th century, set on 410 forested acres. **STATS** 100 rooms; 2 restaurants; 2 bars. **COMPETITIVE EDGE** One of Ireland's most storied castles—with a fairy-tale setting to boot. **ROOMS TO BOOK** East Wing rooms have high ceilings and oversize windows. **COST** Doubles from $$$. *800/346-7007 or 353-61/368-144; www.dromoland.ie*

CO. KERRY
■ **Sheen Falls Lodge** 18th-century riverside lodge with contemporary interiors. **STATS** 66 rooms; 3 cottages; 2 restaurants; 1 bar. **COMPETITIVE EDGE** An extensive range of outdoor pursuits, from fishing, to horseback riding, to clay shooting. **ROOMS TO BOOK** Those with windows overlooking Sheen Falls, which is illuminated at night. **COST** Doubles from $$$. *Kenmare; 800/735-2478 or 353-64/41600; www.sheenfallslodge.ie*

CO. LIMERICK
■ **Adare Manor Hotel & Golf Resort** 19th-century Tudor-revival manor with ornate embellishments, beside the River Maigue. **STATS** 72 rooms; 23 houses; 46 villas; 2 restaurants; 3 bars. **COMPETITIVE EDGE** The Robert Trent Jones, Sr.-designed

golf course—one of Ireland's finest. **ROOMS TO BOOK** Those in the manor house are the most sumptuous. **COST** Doubles from $$. *Adare; 800/462-3273 or 353-61/396-566; www.adaremanor.ie*

CO. MAYO
■ **Ashford Castle** 700-year-old castle with 19th-century additions on a 350-acre lakeside estate. **STATS** 83 rooms; 2 restaurants; 2 bars. **COMPETITIVE EDGE** All the romance of the Irish countryside, from a dramatic setting to activities such as falconry lessons and horseback riding. **ROOMS TO BOOK** Staterooms in the original castle are more atmospheric; affordable Lake Views are just as plush. **COST** Doubles from $$$. *800/346-7007 or 353-94/954-6003; www.ashford.ie*

CO. WATERFORD
■ **Waterford Castle Hotel & Golf Club** 17th-century castle with Victorian interiors on a 310-acre island in the River Suir. **STATS** 19 rooms; 1 restaurant; 2 bars. **COMPETITIVE EDGE** Seclusion: the castle is accessible only by boat. **ROOM TO BOOK** The Ormonde, with a four-poster bed, fireplace, and sweeping views of the gardens and golf course. **COST** Doubles from $$. *353-51/878-203; www.waterfordcastle.com*

ITALY
AMALFI COAST
■ **Il San Pietro** Serene family-owned property (an architectural wonder), above a quiet cove outside Positano. **STATS** 62 rooms; 1 restaurant; 1 bar. **COMPETITIVE EDGE** Discreet out-of-town refuge with sweeping views. **ROOMS TO BOOK** No. 23, for a stunning panorama; Deluxes are an excellent value. **COST** Doubles from $$$. No guests under 10. *Positano; 800/735-2478 or 39-089/875-455; www.ilsanpietro.it*

■ **Le Sirenuse** 18th-century family-run villa turned stylish retreat, overlooking the sea and Positano. **STATS** 63 rooms; 1 restaurant; 2 bars. **COMPETITIVE EDGE** Impeccable service and some of the most glamorous public spaces on the coast. **ROOMS TO BOOK** Upgrade to a Sea View for a private

THE
BEST
OF
2007
—
EUROPE

WORLD'S BEST
DIRECTORY

balcony. **COST** Doubles from $$$. No guests under 8 in high season. *Positano; 800/745-8883 or 39-089/875-066; www.sirenuse.it*

■ **Palazzo Sasso** Pink palazzo dating from the 12th century, in the mountain village of Ravello. **STATS** 43 rooms; 2 restaurants; 1 bar. **COMPETITIVE EDGE** A particularly peaceful–and romantic–setting high above the sea. **ROOMS TO BOOK** King Double Sea Views have spectacular views. **COST** Doubles from $$. *Ravello; 39-089/818-181; www.palazzosasso.com*

ASOLO

■ **Hotel Villa Cipriani** Intimate 16th-century villa (once home to Robert Browning), in a quiet medieval hill town an hour from Venice. **STATS** 31 rooms; 1 restaurant; 1 bar. **COMPETITIVE EDGE** Ideal for exploring the Palladian villas and nearby towns of Treviso, Vicenza, and Padua. **ROOMS TO BOOK** Nos. 101 and 102, for their terraces; large corners with lovely garden views. **COST** Doubles from $$. *800/325-3535 or 39-0423/523-411; www.sheraton.com*

CORTONA

■ **Relais Il Falconiere** Collection of 17th-century buildings on a working wine estate. **STATS** 19 rooms; 1 restaurant; 1 bar. **COMPETITIVE EDGE** An informal, country atmosphere that's within easy reach of Tuscany and Umbria. **ROOMS TO BOOK** Those adjacent to the chapel, for privacy. **COST** Doubles from $$. *800/735-2478 or 39-0575/612-679; www.ilfalconiere.it*

FLORENCE AREA

■ **Villa San Michele** 15th-century monastery (façade attributed to Michelangelo) in the hills of Fiesole. **STATS** 46 rooms; 1 restaurant; 3 bars. **COMPETITIVE EDGE** An entrancing location only a short distance from Florence. **ROOMS TO BOOK** Superior Junior Suites, each with a private garden. **COST** Doubles from $$$$$. *Fiesole; 800/237-1236 or 39-055/567-8200; www.villasanmichele.com*

LAKE COMO

■ **Villa d'Este** Renaissance-era lakeside estate surrounded by a 25-acre park. **STATS** 158 rooms; 2 villas; 3 restaurants; 2 bars. **COMPETITIVE EDGE** The most prestigious of the lake's hotels, with a jet-set atmosphere. **ROOMS TO BOOK** Queen's Pavilion rooms are the most romantic. **COST** Doubles from $$$$. *Cernobbio; 800/745-8883 or 39-031/3481; www.villadeste.it*

LAKE GARDA

■ **Grand Hotel a Villa Feltrinelli** Opulent 19th-century villa at the lake's western end. **STATS** 21 rooms; 1 restaurant; 1 bar. **COMPETITIVE EDGE** So intimate and cosseting, it feels like your own private country manor. **ROOMS TO BOOK** One of the 7 in the main villa with original frescoed ceilings. **COST** Doubles from $$$$$. No guests under 12. *Gargnano; 39-0365/798-000; www.villafeltrinelli.com*

MILAN

■ **Four Seasons Hotel** Converted 15th-century convent with courtyard in the city's fashion district. **STATS** 118 rooms; 2 restaurants; 1 bar. **COMPETITIVE EDGE** A trendy location and highly personalized service. **ROOMS TO BOOK** 2nd- and 3rd-floor Deluxes facing the courtyard–a good value for their size. **COST** Doubles from $$$$. *6/8 Via Gesù; 800/332-3442 or 39-02/77088; www.fourseasons.com*

PORTOFINO

■ **Grand Hotel Miramare** Turn-of-the-20th-century hotel with landscaped grounds, outside Portofino. **STATS** 84 rooms; 1 restaurant; 2 bars. **COMPETITIVE EDGE** Grand style and adult amenities, yet surprisingly family-friendly. **ROOMS TO BOOK** Sea views are worth the $25-$50 upgrade; rooms on upper floors have private terraces. **COST** Doubles from $$. *800/745-8883 or 39-0185/287-013; www.grandhotelmiramare.it*

VENICE

■ **Bauer Il Palazzo** Quiet 18th-century property with its own Grand Canal berth, adjacent to the modern Bauer Hotel. **STATS** 82 rooms; 1 restaurant; 2 bars. **COMPETITIVE EDGE** Discreet, personalized service in a historic setting. **ROOMS TO BOOK** Light-filled upper-floor rooms for their Venetian décor; No. 618 has a romantic mansard roof. **COST** Doubles from $$$$. *1413/D San Marco; 800/745-8883 or 39-041/520-7022; www.bauerhotels.com*

■ **Hotel Gritti Palace** Renaissance palazzo with old-world atmosphere on the Grand Canal. **STATS** 91 rooms; 1 restaurant; 1 bar. **COMPETITIVE EDGE** An opulent palace that lets you play doge for the day. **ROOMS TO BOOK** Request a canal-view room with 2 windows. **COST** Doubles from $$$$$. *Campo Santa Maria del Giglio; 800/325-3589 or 39-041/794-611; www.luxurycollection.com*

MONACO

MONTE CARLO

■ **Hôtel Hermitage** Belle Époque palace on a cliff overlooking the harbor. **STATS** 280 rooms; 1 restaurant; 2 bars. **COMPETITIVE EDGE** Near boutiques and the casino, but sheltered from the frenzied center. **ROOMS TO BOOK** Those on the top 2 floors of the Prince and Midi wings with sea-view balconies. **COST** Doubles from $$$. *Square Beaumarchais; 800/223-6800 or 377/98-06-48-12; www.montecarloresort.com*

■ **Hôtel de Paris** Celebrated Beaux Arts landmark, with Alain Ducasse's Michelin 3-starred Louis XV, in Place du Casino. **STATS** 187 rooms; 3 restaurants; 1 bar. **COMPETITIVE EDGE** Less an address than a legend, adjacent to the equally famed casino. **ROOMS TO BOOK** For a sea view, Nos. 320, 420, and 520. **COST** Doubles from $$$. *Place du Casino; 800/223-6800 or 377/98-06-30-16; www.montecarloresort.com*

SCOTLAND

FORT WILLIAM

■ **Inverlochy Castle Hotel** Turreted 1863 castle with antiques-filled interiors, in the shadow of Ben Nevis, the United Kingdom's highest mountain. **STATS** 18 rooms; 1 restaurant. **COMPETITIVE EDGE** Pure romance amid the Highlands' steep glens and lochs. **ROOM TO BOOK** ... gis room has particularly ... **COST** Doubles from $$$$.

THE
BEST
OF
2007
———
EUROPE

WORLD'S BEST
DIRECTORY

888/424-0106 or 44-1397/702-177;
www.inverlochycastlehotel.com

SWITZERLAND

LAUSANNE

■ **Beau-Rivage Palace** 1861 Beaux Arts hotel on 10 manicured lakeside acres. **STATS** 169 rooms; 2 restaurants; 2 bars. **COMPETITIVE EDGE** Discreet ambience and pitch-perfect service draw A-list guests. **ROOMS TO BOOK** Nos. 155, 355, and 455 in the Palace wing have large lakefront balconies. **COST** Doubles from $$. *800/223-6800 or 41-21/613-3333; www.brp.ch*

LUCERNE

■ **Palace Luzern** Belle Époque hotel with a grand lobby on the shores of Lake Lucerne, 5 minutes from town. **STATS** 136 rooms; 3 restaurants; 1 bar. **COMPETITIVE EDGE** The setting is spectacular—bucolic but convenient. **ROOMS TO BOOK** A Deluxe or Junior Suite with a balcony and lake view. **COST** Doubles from $$. *10 Haldenstrasse; 800/223-6800 or 41-41/416-1616; www.palace-luzern.com*

ZURICH

■ **Baur au Lac** 162-year-old family-owned hotel overlooking Lake Zurich and the mountains. **STATS** 124 rooms; 2 restaurants; 1 bar. **COMPETITIVE EDGE** Both historic and up-to-date: $79 million worth of improvements in the past decade, including a relaunch of the hotel's restaurant Rive Gauche. **ROOMS TO BOOK** One of the 15 new Art Deco rooms. **COST** Doubles from $$$. *1 Talstrasse; 800/223-6800 or 41-1/220-5020; www.bauraulac.ch*

TURKEY

ISTANBUL

■ **Four Seasons Hotel** Historic property with Turkish-inspired interiors and a courtyard, next to Hagia Sophia and the Topkapi Palace. **STATS** 65 rooms; 1 restaurant; 1 bar. **COMPETITIVE EDGE** An unparalleled Old City location. **ROOMS TO BOOK** Request one with a partial Blue Mosque view, or splurge on a 4th-floor Deluxe with a large balcony. **COST** Doubles from $$. *1 Tevkifhane Sokak; 800/332-3442 or 90-212/638-8200; www.fourseasons.com*

AFRICA + THE MIDDLE EAST

BOTSWANA

CHOBE NATIONAL PARK

■ **Chobe Chilwero Lodge** Collection of bungalows built to resemble a village, overlooking the Chobe River. **STATS** 15 bungalows; 1 restaurant; 1 bar. **COMPETITIVE EDGE** A location high above the floodplain. **ROOMS TO BOOK** Nos. 6 and 9, for the best riverside perch. **COST** Doubles from $$$$, including meals, drinks, and activities. *800/554-7094 or 27-11/438-4650; www.sanctuarylodges.com*

MOREMI GAME RESERVE

■ **Chief's Camp** Contemporary-meets-classic bush lodge above a game-rich plain. **STATS** 12 pavilions; 1 restaurant; 1 bar. **COMPETITIVE EDGE** Evening water safaris, plus architecture so integrated into the landscape that guests can spot animals without leaving the camp. **ROOM TO BOOK** No. 1 is the most secluded of the Luxury Bush Pavilions. **COST** Doubles from $$$$, including meals, drinks, and activities. *800/554-7094 or 27-11/438-4650; www.sanctuarylodges.com*

■ **Mombo Camp** Intimate camp of lavish tents (plush leather chairs; Afro-chic tapestries), linked by raised walkways. **STATS** 9 tents; 1 restaurant; 1 bar. **COMPETITIVE EDGE** Sheer luxury on an island that nearly guarantees leopard, lion, and cheetah sightings. **ROOM TO BOOK** For privacy, No. 1, the tent farthest from the outdoor dining area. **COST** Doubles from $$$$, including meals, drinks, and activities. *27-11/807-1800; www.wilderness-safaris.com*

EGYPT

CAIRO

■ **Four Seasons Hotel at the First Residence** Glass tower with Egyptian and Neoclassical design influences, overlooking the pyramids and Botanical Gardens. **STATS** 269 rooms; 2 restaurants; 1 bar. **COMPETITIVE EDGE** A location on the

Nile's west bank in the heart of the ultrachic First Residence shopping complex. **ROOMS TO BOOK** Any facing west with a balcony. **COST** Doubles from $$. *35 Giza St.; 800/332-3442 or 20-2/573-1212; www.fourseasons.com*

■ **Four Seasons Hotel at Nile Plaza** Elegant 30-story hotel outside Garden City, on the Nile's east bank. **STATS** 365 rooms; 8 restaurants; 1 bar. **COMPETITIVE EDGE** Great business amenities just a stone's throw from the financial district. **ROOMS TO BOOK** Terraces with sweeping river views. **COST** Doubles from $$. *1089 Corniche el Nil; 800/332-3442 or 20-2/791-7000; www.fourseasons.com*

JORDAN

AMMAN

■ **Four Seasons Hotel** 15-story hilltop retreat ideally set between the financial district and a quiet residential neighborhood. **STATS** 192 rooms; 4 restaurants; 1 bar. **COMPETITIVE EDGE** Hands down, the best rooms and service in the city. **ROOMS TO BOOK** Top-floor balcony suites for a refuge high above the city. **COST** Doubles from $. *5th Circle, Al-Kindi St., Jabal Amman; 800/332-3442 or 962-6/550-5555; www.fourseasons.com*

KENYA

MASAI MARA

■ **Kichwa Tembo** Pair of tented camps, both well-appointed, in the heart of the Mara. **STATS** 49 tents; 2 restaurants; 2 bars. **COMPETITIVE EDGE** Tranquil location in one of Africa's most cinematic landscapes. **ROOMS TO BOOK** One of the tented suites—No. 7 is the most remote—at the Bateleur Camp. **COST** Doubles from $$$, including meals and activities. *888/882-3742 or 27-11/809-4300; www.ccafrica.com*

■ **Mara Serena Safari Lodge** Collection of domed huts modeled after a Masai village and set above a migratory path. **STATS** 74 rooms; 1 restaurant; 1 bar. **COMPETITIVE EDGE** Local design influences, and a front-row seat for the annual migration. **ROOMS TO BOOK** Nos. 1-26 and 55-78, which overlook the river. **COST** Doubles

THE
BEST
OF
2007

AFRICA
+
THE
MIDDLE
EAST

WORLD'S BEST
DIRECTORY

from $$, including meals. *27-11/465-0808; www.serenahotels.com*

NANYUKI
■ **Mount Kenya Safari Club** Colonial-style cottages on 100 acres in the Mount Kenya foothills. **STATS** 116 rooms; 2 restaurants; 4 bars. **COMPETITIVE EDGE** Refined English atmosphere in the lush African countryside. **ROOMS TO BOOK** Upgrade to a Riverside Suite with a veranda facing the mountain. **COST** Doubles from $$, including meals. *800/441-1414 or 254-20/216-940; www.fairmont.com*

MOROCCO
MARRAKESH
■ **La Mamounia** Opulent 80-year-old palace with 18th-century gardens. (Note: Hotel is closed until summer while undergoing a major overhaul by French designer Jacques Garcia.) **STATS** 231 rooms; 5 restaurants; 6 bars. *Ave. Bab Jdid; 800/223-6800 or 212-24/388-643; www.mamounia.com*

QATAR
DOHA
■ **Ritz-Carlton** Service-driven Arabian Gulf resort with a private 235-slip marina and extravagant pool. **STATS** 374 rooms; 4 restaurants; 4 bars. **COMPETITIVE EDGE** All the luxury and amenities of a Ritz-Carlton resort in a gorgeous coastal location. **ROOMS TO BOOK** Sea View suites, overlooking the marina. **COST** Doubles from $$. *800/241-3333 or 974-484/8000; www.ritzcarlton.com*

SOUTH AFRICA
CAPE TOWN
■ **Cape Grace** Refined property on its own quay right on the Victoria & Alfred Waterfront. **STATS** 122 rooms; 1 restaurant; 1 bar. **COMPETITIVE EDGE** A successful marriage of old (traditional décor) and new (innovative restaurant and spa). **ROOMS TO BOOK** Superiors with marina views. **COST** Doubles from $$$, including breakfast. *West Quay Rd.; 800/223-6800 or 27-21/410-7100; www.capegrace.com*

■ **Mount Nelson Hotel** Colonial-style property in a leafy residential neighborhood beneath Table Mountain. **STATS** 201 rooms; 2 restaurants; 1 bar. **COMPETITIVE EDGE** An atmospheric property dripping with history. **ROOMS TO BOOK** 4th-floor mountain-view Superiors with balconies. **COST** Doubles from $$$. *76 Orange St.; 800/237-1236 or 27-21/483-1000; www.mountnelson.co.za*

■ **Table Bay Hotel** Polished Victorian-style building on the Victoria & Alfred Waterfront. **STATS** 329 rooms; 2 restaurants; 2 bars. **COMPETITIVE EDGE** The saltwater pool and harborside setting adjacent to the main quay and close to upscale shops. **ROOMS TO BOOK** Top-floor rooms for views of Table Mountain beyond the harbor. **COST** Doubles from $$$. *Quay 6, Victoria & Alfred Waterfront; 800/223-6800 or 27-21/406-5000; www.suninternational.com*

JOHANNESBURG
■ **Grace in Rosebank** Discreet hotel set in the tony suburb of Rosebank. **STATS** 73 rooms; 1 restaurant; 1 bar. **COMPETITIVE EDGE** Refined residential feel thanks to a doting staff and a glitzy Rosebank address. **ROOMS TO BOOK** Those with views of the 4th-floor garden. **COST** Doubles from $$. *54 Bank Ave., Rosebank; 27-11/280-7200; www.thegrace.co.za*

■ **The Michelangelo** Italian Renaissance-style hotel on Sandton's restaurant-laden Nelson Mandela Square. **STATS** 242 rooms; 2 restaurants; 2 bars. **COMPETITIVE EDGE** First-class dining and conference facilities make this prime power-player territory. **ROOMS TO BOOK** Superiors overlooking the alfresco dining scene on the Square. **COST** Doubles from $$. *Nelson Mandela Square, Sandton; 27-11/282-7000; www.legacyhotels.co.za*

KRUGER NATIONAL PARK AREA
■ **Londolozi Private Game Reserve** Exclusive camp of thatched-roof bush suites, in the Sabi Sands Game Reserve. **STATS** 30 rooms; 4 restaurants; 4 bars. **COMPETITIVE EDGE** A model camp with excellent game viewing and progressive conservation practices. **ROOMS TO BOOK** Varty Camp suites along the Sand River for a central location. **COST** Doubles from $$$$$, including meals and drinks. *888/882-3742 or 27-11/280-6655; www.londolozi.co.za*

■ **MalaMala Game Reserve** Trio of renowned bush camps on 33,000 acres along the Sand River. **STATS** 33 rooms; 6 dining areas; 3 bars. **COMPETITIVE EDGE** Some of the best guides in the business. **ROOMS TO BOOK** Those in the Rattray's camp for private plunge pools and river views. **COST** Doubles from $$$$$, including meals. *888/882-3742 or 27-11/442-2267; www.malamala.com*

■ **Sabi Sabi Private Game Reserve** Four diverse lodges, including the new 6-room Little Bush Camp, next to Kruger. **STATS** 52 rooms; 4 restaurants; 4 bars. **COMPETITIVE EDGE** Classic bush experience with a lodge to suit any mood. **ROOMS TO BOOK** Little Bush Camp, for thatched roofs and polished wood-and-stone finishes. **COST** Doubles from $$$$, including meals and drinks. *27-11/483-3939; www.sabisabi.com*

■ **Singita** Quartet of chic lodges ranging in style from mod-colonial (Boulders) to ultramodern (Lebombo). **STATS** 45 rooms; 4 restaurants; 4 bars. **COMPETITIVE EDGE** It's Hollywood in the bush: modern architecture, winning service, and luxe amenities. **ROOMS TO BOOK** Airy glass-and-timber cabins at Lebombo Camp. **COST** Doubles from $$$$$, including meals and drinks. *800/735-2478 or 27-21/683-3424; www.singita.com*

KWAZULU NATAL
■ **Phinda Game Reserve** Seven high-design lodges set in a 52,000-acre private game reserve. **STATS** 60 rooms; 6 restaurants; 6 bars. **COMPETITIVE EDGE** Unrivaled natural surroundings: 7 distinct habitats home to hundreds of bird species and the Big Five. **ROOM TO BOOK** Getty Lodge: a 4-room house with butler, chef, and infinity pool. **COST** Doubles from $$$$$, including meals. *888/882-3742 or 27-11/809-4300; www.phinda.com*

THE
BEST
OF
2007
———
AFRICA
+
THE
MIDDLE
EAST

WORLD'S BEST
DIRECTORY

TANZANIA

NGORONGORO CRATER

■ **Ngorongoro Crater Lodge**
Spectacularly designed property of huts set on stilts overlooking the 3-million-year-old crater. **STATS** 30 suites; 3 restaurants; 3 bars. **COMPETITIVE EDGE** Architecture and design that nearly rival the extraordinary natural surroundings. **ROOM TO BOOK** The highest, No. 22, for the most dramatic view of the crater. **COST** Doubles from $$$$$, including meals and drinks. *888/882-3742 or 27-11/809-4300; www.ccafrica.com*

SERENGETI

■ **Kirawira Camp** Edwardian-style camp in the Western Serengeti. **STATS** 25 tents; 1 restaurant; 1 bar. **COMPETITIVE EDGE** Exhaustively sourced décor (vintage chairs; phonographs) transport you to another era. **ROOM TO BOOK** No. 11 is the most private tent. **COST** Doubles from $$$$, including meals and drinks. *800/525-4800 or 255-028/262-1518; www.serenahotels.com*

UNITED ARAB EMIRATES

DUBAI

■ **Grand Hyatt** Conference and resort hotel on 37 acres with views of Dubai Creek. **STATS** 674 rooms; 186 apartments; 7 restaurants; 4 bars. **COMPETITIVE EDGE** Outstanding amenities—from a jogging track to the popular nightclub Mix. **ROOMS TO BOOK** Affordable Creekside Twins with marble soaking tubs. **COST** Doubles from $$$. *800/233-1234 or 971-4/317-1234; www.grand.hyatt.com*

ZAMBIA

LIVINGSTONE

■ **Royal Livingstone** Graceful property with large colonial-style verandas on the banks of the Zambezi River. **STATS** 173 rooms; 1 restaurant; 1 bar. **COMPETITIVE EDGE** Unbeatable location on Victoria Falls. **ROOMS TO BOOK** North-facing Standards are affordable and have river views. **COST** Doubles from $$$. *260-3/321-122; www.suninternational.com*

ASIA

CAMBODIA

PHNOM PENH

■ **Raffles Hotel Le Royal** French colonial-era mansion surrounded by gardens in the city center. **STATS** 170 rooms; 2 restaurants; 2 bars. **COMPETITIVE EDGE** The city's best amenities. **ROOMS TO BOOK** Those in the original building, for Art Deco touches. **COST** Doubles from $$. *92 Rukhak Vithei Daun Penh; 800/768-9009 or 855-23/981-888; www.raffles.com*

SIEM REAP

■ **Raffles Grand Hotel d'Angkor** Stylishly restored 1930's hotel with extensive grounds near Angkor Wat. **STATS** 131 rooms; 3 restaurants; 2 bars. **COMPETITIVE EDGE** Historic ambience in a tradition-rich location. **ROOMS TO BOOK** Upgrade to a colonial-style Landmark room. **COST** Doubles from $$, including breakfast and dinner; *800/768-9009 or 855-63/963-888; www.raffles.com*

CHINA

BEIJING

■ **The Peninsula** Opulent hotel (formerly the Peninsula Palace) with Chinese influences, a short walk from the Forbidden City and shopping. **STATS** 525 rooms; 2 restaurants; 1 bar. **COMPETITIVE EDGE** State-of-the-art rooms, thanks to a recent $35 million face-lift. **ROOMS TO BOOK** Grand Deluxes facing the pool. **COST** Doubles from $$. *8 Goldfish Lane; 866/382-8388 or 86-10/8516-2888; www.peninsula.com*

■ **St. Regis Hotel** High-rise with refined modern décor in the Jian Guo Men Wai business district. **STATS** 273 rooms; 5 restaurants; 4 bars. **COMPETITIVE EDGE** A high staff-to-guest ratio ensures pampering. **ROOMS TO BOOK** Rooms on the north side, with views of the diplomatic district. **COST** Doubles from $$. *21 Jian Guo Men Wai Rd.; 877/787-3447 or 86-10/6460-6688; www.stregis.com*

HONG KONG

■ **The Conrad** Modern rooms on floors 40 through 61 of a tower, above the Pacific Place mall. **STATS** 513 rooms; 4 restaurants; 2 bars. **COMPETITIVE EDGE** Comprehensive business facilities and some of the city's largest standard rooms. **ROOMS TO BOOK** Those on the Executive floor, for private lounge access. **COST** Doubles from $$. *88 Queensway; 800/445-8667 or 852/2521-3838; www.conradhotels.com*

■ **Four Seasons Hotel** Sleek hotel occupying 2 towers of the centrally located IFC complex. **STATS** 399 rooms; 3 restaurants; 1 bar. **COMPETITIVE EDGE** Some of the city's freshest rooms plus a 22,000-square-foot spa and the gorgeous Caprice restaurant. **ROOMS TO BOOK** We prefer the understated Western rooms to the somewhat fussy lacquer-and-gold leaf Oriental ones. **COST** Doubles from $$. *8 Finance St.; 800/819-5053 or 852/3196-8888; www.fourseasons.com*

■ **Grand Hyatt** Lavish waterfront hotel with Art Deco lobby, by the convention center. **STATS** 549 rooms; 5 restaurants; 3 bars. **COMPETITIVE EDGE** The fitness center, including outdoor pool, driving range, and tennis courts. **ROOMS TO BOOK** Grand Harbours, with floor-to-ceiling windows. **COST** Doubles from $$$. *1 Harbour Rd.; 888/591-1234 or 852/2588-1234; www.hyatt.com*

■ **The InterContinental** Modern hotel on the Kowloon waterfront. **STATS** 495 rooms; 5 restaurants; 3 bars. **COMPETITIVE EDGE** High-tech rooms (Bose sound systems, air purification, flat-screen TV's) built on feng shui principles. **ROOMS TO BOOK** Go for a harbor view ($130 extra). **COST** Doubles from $$$. *18 Salisbury Rd.; 800/327-0200 or 852/2721-1211; www.intercontinental.com*

■ **Island Shangri-La** Elliptical tower (connected to the Pacific Place mall) with a dramatic atrium lobby. **STATS** 565 rooms; 7 restaurants; 2 bars. **COMPETITIVE EDGE** A local feel and a prime business location. **ROOMS TO BOOK** Those ending in -01 through -16 on floors 48-55 have harbor views.

COST Doubles from $$$. *Supreme Court Rd.; 866/565-5050 or 852/2877-3838; www.shangri-la.com*

■ **Mandarin Oriental** Hong Kong institution decorated with Asian antiques, in the business district; recently reopened after a $140 million overhaul. **STATS** 502 rooms; 5 restaurants; 3 bars. **COMPETITIVE EDGE** A classic hotel, now updated with enlarged rooms and a 3-level spa. **ROOMS TO BOOK** Ask for a room with a view of the harbor and vibrant Statue Square. **COST** Doubles from $$. *5 Connaught Rd.; 800/526-6566 or 852/2522-0111;www.mandarinoriental.com*

■ **The Peninsula** 78-year-old grande dame, a favorite of dignitaries and celebrities, on the harbor in Kowloon. **STATS** 300 rooms; 7 restaurants; 1 bar. **COMPETITIVE EDGE** Old-world atmosphere (white-glove service, lobby orchestra) and modern additions (new spa). **ROOMS TO BOOK** The colonial-style rooms in the original building. **COST** Doubles from $$. *Salisbury Rd.; 866/382-8388 or 852/2920-2888; www.peninsula.com*

■ **Ritz-Carlton** European-style hotel in the financial district, blocks from the waterfront. **STATS** 216 rooms; 6 restaurants; 1 bar. **COMPETITIVE EDGE** Clubby feel and great attention to detail (guest-room flowers are refreshed daily). **ROOMS TO BOOK** Peak Views, which look at Victoria Peak. **COST** Doubles from $$. *3 Connaught Rd.; 800/241-3333 or 852/2877-6666; www.ritzcarlton.com*

SHANGHAI
■ **Four Seasons Hotel** Contemporary 37-story tower, a short walk from Nanjing Road shopping and People's Square. **STATS** 439 rooms; 4 restaurants; 2 bars. **COMPETITIVE EDGE** A well-rounded hotel: terrific service, residential-style rooms, and a central location that's hard to beat. **ROOMS TO BOOK** Deluxes on floors 30 or above for value and views. **COST** Doubles from $$. *500 Weihai Rd.; 800/332-3442 or 86-21-6256-8888; www.fourseasons.com*

■ **Portman Ritz-Carlton** 45-story tower with Asian-accented interiors, in the Shanghai Center shopping and office complex. **STATS** 578 rooms; 4 restaurants; 1 bar. **COMPETITIVE EDGE** Exceptional business amenities and a convenient address. **ROOMS TO BOOK** Renovated Shanghais with large baths. **COST** Doubles from $$. *1376 Nanjing Xi Rd.; 800/241-3333 or 86-21-6279-8888; www.ritzcarlton.com*

INDIA
AGRA
■ **Oberoi Amarvilas** Moghul-style palace (built in 2001) with fountained courtyards, gardens, and a spa, steps from the Taj Mahal. **STATS** 102 rooms; 2 restaurants; 1 bar. **COMPETITIVE EDGE** Every room offers a bird's-eye view of one of the world's greatest monuments. **ROOMS TO BOOK** Premiers with private terraces ($50 extra) overlooking the Taj Mahal. **COST** Doubles from $$$. *800/562-3764 or 91-562/223-1515; www.oberoiamarvilas.com*

JAIPUR
■ **Oberoi Rajvilas** Maharajah fantasy of lotus-filled ponds, blooming gardens, and lavish architecture, on 32 acres outside of Jaipur. **STATS** 71 rooms; 1 restaurant; 1 bar. **COMPETITIVE EDGE** A hotel that raises the bar for both service and design. **ROOMS TO BOOK** Royal Tents with Burmese-teak floors and claw-foot bathtubs. **COST** Doubles from $600. *800/562-3764 or 91-141/268-0101; www.oberoirajvilas.com*

■ **Rambagh Palace** Elaborate 19th-century hunting lodge turned palace, on 47 acres. **STATS** 85 rooms; 3 restaurants; 2 bars. **COMPETITIVE EDGE** The luxury of staying in the King of Jaipur's former hunting lodge. **ROOMS TO BOOK** Those in the Garden Wing for green vistas. **COST** Doubles from $$. *866/969-1825 or 91-141/221-1919; www.tajhotels.com*

MUMBAI
■ **Taj Mahal Palace & Tower** 1903 building and modern tower overlooking the city's famous landmark Gateway of India. **STATS** 565 rooms; 6 restaurants; 2 bars. **COMPETITIVE EDGE** Historic grandeur in a prime location. **ROOMS TO BOOK** Colonial-style Sea Views. **COST** Doubles from $$. *Apollo Bunder; 800/223-6800 or 91-22/6665-3366; www.tajhotels.com*

NEW DELHI
■ **The Imperial** Art Deco landmark (dating from the Raj), steps from Connaught Place. **STATS** 231 rooms; 6 restaurants; 2 bars. **COMPETITIVE EDGE** Old-world charm (a backdrop for dazzling parties) and a fantastic art collection. **ROOMS TO BOOK** Imperials, for colonial furnishings; Nos. 22, 23, 40, and 41 overlook the lawns. **COST** Doubles from $$. *Janpath; 800/323-7500 or 91-11/2334-1234; www.theimperialindia.com*

UDAIPUR
■ **Oberoi Udaivilas** Exceptionally well-run Mewari palace–style hotel (hand-painted murals, fountains, verdant gardens) on 30 acres overlooking Lake Pichola. **STATS** 87 rooms; 2 restaurants; 1 bar. **COMPETITIVE EDGE** Architecture so luxe, the hotel itself has become a destination. **ROOMS TO BOOK** Premier Lake Views with access to a semiprivate pool. **COST** Doubles from $$$. *800/562-3764 or 91-294/243-3300; www.oberoiudaivilas.com*

■ **Taj Lake Palace** Restored 18th-century marble palace, in the middle of Lake Pichola. **STATS** 83 rooms; 2 restaurants; 1 bar. **COMPETITIVE EDGE** All the ambience of staying in a 260-year-old palace. **ROOMS TO BOOK** Consider spending an extra $100 for a Luxury with a claw-foot tub and captivating views of the lake. **COST** Doubles from $$$. *800/223-6800 or 91-294/252-8800; www.tajhotels.com*

INDONESIA
BALI
■ **Four Seasons Resort at Jimbaran Bay** Collection of thatched-roof villas with private plunge pools, built into a hillside above a beach. **STATS** 147 villas; 4 restaurants; 2 bars. **COMPETITIVE EDGE** An intimate, pampering property, with the amenities of a larger resort. **ROOMS TO BOOK**

KEY TO THE PRICE ICONS **$** UNDER $250 **$$** $250-$499 **$$$** $500-$749 **$$$$** $750-$999 **$$$$$** $1,000 AND UP

THE
BEST
OF
2007

ASIA

WORLD'S BEST
DIRECTORY

Villas 101–109 are closest to the beach. **COST** Doubles from $$$. *Jimbaran; 800/332-3442 or 62-361/701-010; www.fourseasons.com*

■ **Four Seasons Resort at Sayan** Thatched-roof villas with modern indoor-outdoor interiors and lotus pools, overlooking the Ayung River Valley. **STATS** 18 rooms; 42 villas; 2 restaurants; 1 bar. **COMPETITIVE EDGE** Pure romance: a private jungle hideaway with exquisite architecture and views. **ROOM TO BOOK** A 1-bedroom villa with a plunge pool. **COST** Doubles from $$. *Ubud; 800/332-3442 or 62-361/977-577; www.fourseasons.com*

■ **Grand Hyatt Resort** A 40-acre resort with pools inspired by Balinese water palaces and colorful gardens, at Nusa Dua. **STATS** 648 rooms; 2 villas; 5 restaurants; 3 bars. **COMPETITIVE EDGE** Freshly renovated rooms (thanks to an ongoing redo) at an unbeatable price. **ROOMS TO BOOK** Ground-floor rooms that open onto the gardens. **COST** Doubles from $. *Nusa Dua; 800/233-1234 or 62-361/771-234; www.grand.hyatt.com*

■ **Ritz-Carlton Resort & Spa** Cliffside villa resort (with a new infinity pool and Thalasso spa), on a private jetty with views over the sea at Jimbaran Bay. **STATS** 290 rooms; 84 villas; 8 restaurants; 4 bars. **COMPETITIVE EDGE** The luxury of a Ritz-Carlton resort, at wallet-friendly rates. **ROOMS TO BOOK** Club rooms (an extra $80) for great views and all-day snacks and drinks. **COST** Doubles from $$. *Jimbaran; 800/241-3333 or 62-361/702-222; www.ritzcarlton.com*

JAPAN
OSAKA

■ **Ritz-Carlton** Cozy hotel with classic interiors, close to the railway station in the Nishi-umeda district. **STATS** 292 rooms; 4 restaurants; 3 bars. **COMPETITIVE EDGE** Residential style and atmosphere. **ROOMS TO BOOK** Deluxes have panoramic views and are worth the extra $51. **COST** Doubles from $$$. *2-5-25 Umeda, Kita-ku; 800/241-3333 or 81-6/6343-7000; www.ritzcarlton.com*

TOKYO

■ **Park Hyatt** Iconic hotel on the top 14 floors of Kenzo Tange's Shinjuku Park Tower. **STATS** 177 rooms; 3 restaurants; 3 bars. **COMPETITIVE EDGE** Staggering views from the gym, bars, and some guest-room baths. **ROOMS TO BOOK** Those ending with -12 on floors 42–52 look out on Mount Fuji. **COST** Doubles from $$. *3-7-1-2 Nishi-Shinjuku, Shinjuku-ku; 800/223-1234 or 81-3/5322-1234; www.hyatt.com*

MALAYSIA
KUALA LUMPUR

■ **Mandarin Oriental** Modern 30-story high-rise next to the Petronas Twin Towers. **STATS** 643 rooms; 6 restaurants; 2 bars. **COMPETITIVE EDGE** Every amenity for business travelers, plus a prime location in the Kuala Lumpur City Centre complex. **ROOMS TO BOOK** Those facing the 50-acre park. **COST** Doubles from $. *Kuala Lumpur City Centre; 800/526-6566 or 60-3/2380-8888; www.mandarinoriental.com*

■ **Ritz-Carlton** European-style hotel 5 minutes from Bintang Walk. **STATS** 248 rooms; 2 restaurants; 1 bar. **COMPETITIVE EDGE** Personalized service (dedicated butlers on each floor) and the city's largest standard rooms. **ROOMS TO BOOK** Those with views of the Petronas Towers. **COST** Doubles from $$. *168 Jalan Imbi; 800/241-3333 or 60-3/2142-8000; www.ritzcarlton.com*

SINGAPORE
SINGAPORE

■ **Four Seasons Hotel** 20-story building with an art collection and gardens, a short walk from Orchard Road. **STATS** 254 rooms; 2 restaurants; 1 bar. **COMPETITIVE EDGE** Residential atmosphere, minutes from the city center. **ROOMS TO BOOK** A large corner Premier with skyline views–only $40 extra. **COST** Doubles from $$. *190 Orchard Blvd.; 800/332-3442 or 65/6734-1110; www.fourseasons.com*

■ **The Fullerton** 1928 Neoclassical former post office, adjacent to Raffles Place. **STATS** 400 rooms; 4 restaurants; 1 bar. **COMPETITIVE EDGE** A beautifully restored historic landmark. **ROOMS TO BOOK** Quays with views of Marina Bay. **COST** Doubles from $$. *1 Fullerton Square; 800/323-7500 or 65/6733-8388; www.fullertonhotel.com*

■ **The Oriental** Fan-shaped tower with contemporary interiors, on Marina Bay. **STATS** 527 rooms; 5 restaurants; 2 bars. **COMPETITIVE EDGE** Feels new after a redesign of the atrium and a refurb of all the rooms. **ROOMS TO BOOK** Premier Harbours for floor-to-ceiling water views. **COST** Doubles from $$. *5 Raffles Ave.; 866/526-6567 or 65/6338-0066; www.mandarinoriental.com*

■ **Raffles Hotel** Landmark 1887 building with tropical gardens in the business district. **STATS** 103 rooms; 13 restaurants; 5 bars. **COMPETITIVE EDGE** The city's most iconic hotel, filled with period furniture and a colonial ambience. **ROOMS TO BOOK** Request one away from the shopping arcade; Palm Court Suites facing south are particularly peaceful. **COST** Doubles from $$. *1 Beach Rd.; 800/768-9009 or 65/6337-1886; www.raffles.com*

■ **Ritz-Carlton, Millenia** 32-story tower on a 7-acre garden in Marina Centre. **STATS** 608 rooms; 3 restaurants; 1 bar. **COMPETITIVE EDGE** The city's largest standard rooms (an average of 549 square feet), all with views. **ROOMS TO BOOK** It's worth the $95 upgrade for Club Lounge access, which includes all-day snacks. **COST** Doubles from $$. *7 Raffles Ave.; 800/241-3333 or 65/6337-8888; www.ritzcarlton.com*

■ **Shangri-La Hotel** Collection of towers comprising Shangri-La's flagship hotel and residential complex, a 5-minute walk from Orchard Road. **STATS** 750 rooms; 5 restaurants; 1 bar. **COMPETITIVE EDGE** A lush, resort-style environment in the city. **ROOMS TO BOOK** Valley Wings have a separate entrance and complimentary breakfast. **COST** Doubles from $$. *22 Orange Grove Rd.; 800/565-5750 or 65/6737-3644; www.shangri-la.com*

SOUTH KOREA

SEOUL

■ **The Shilla** High-rise hotel in a 23-acre private park in central Seoul. **STATS** 465 rooms; 5 restaurants; 1 bar. **COMPETITIVE EDGE** Some of the city's largest standard rooms, combined with a peaceful setting. **ROOMS TO BOOK** Opt for those at the rear that have mountain views. **COST** Doubles from $$. *202 Jangchung-Dong 2-Ga, Jung-Gu; 800/745-8883 or 82-2/2230-3310; www.shilla.net*

TAIWAN

TAIPEI

■ **Shangri-La's Far Eastern Plaza Hotel** 43-story hotel with an atrium lobby, right next to the Mall and on top of the Taipei metro. **STATS** 420 rooms; 6 restaurants; 2 bars. **COMPETITIVE EDGE** A perfect location in the city's commercial center. **ROOMS TO BOOK** Those that look toward the Taipei 101 tower. **COST** Doubles from $$. *201 Tun Hwa South Rd.; 866/565-5050 or 886-2/2378-8888; www.shangri-la.com*

THAILAND

BANGKOK

■ **Grand Hyatt Erawan** Contemporary tower near the Erawan Shrine in the shopping district. **STATS** 386 rooms; 9 restaurants; 2 bars. **COMPETITIVE EDGE** Attached to the Erawan Plaza. **ROOMS TO BOOK** Grand Deluxes for views of the city and adjacent golf club. **COST** Doubles from $. *494 Rajadamri Rd.; 800/233-1234 or 66-2/254-1234; www.grand.hyatt.com*

■ **JW Marriott Hotel** Business-friendly high-rise, steps from the sky-train on Sukhumvit Road, the city's restaurant and nightlife district. **STATS** 441 rooms; 7 restaurants; 3 bars. **COMPETITIVE EDGE** Convenience, comfort, and style—at a great price. **ROOMS TO BOOK** Get one of the newly renovated Rooms of the Future with technology that supports all the latest gadgets. **COST** Doubles from $. *2 Sukhumvit Soi; 800/228-9290 or 66-2/656-7700; www.marriott.com*

■ **The Oriental** Legendary 130-year-old hotel and new tower on the banks of the Chao Phraya River. **STATS** 393 rooms; 9 restaurants; 2 bars. **COMPETITIVE EDGE** A landmark property with friendly, down-to-earth staff. **ROOMS TO BOOK** Split-level Gardens are high-tech and traditional. **COST** Doubles from $$. *48 Oriental Ave.; 800/526-6566 or 66-2/659-9000; www.mandarinoriental.com*

■ **The Peninsula** A 39-story tower with sleek Asian-influenced interiors and a new 19,000-foot Espa spa. **STATS** 370 rooms; 5 restaurants; 1 bar. **COMPETITIVE EDGE** Refined service and sophistication—and now, the city's most dazzling spa. **ROOMS TO BOOK** Deluxe Rooms ending in -02 or -10 for soaring views over the city. **COST** Doubles from $. *333 Charoennakorn Rd.; 866/382-8388 or 66-2/861-2888; www.peninsula.com*

■ **Royal Orchid Sheraton Hotel & Towers** 28-story high-rise on the banks of the Chao Phraya River, close to the River City shopping complex. **STATS** 740 rooms; 4 restaurants; 2 bars. **COMPETITIVE EDGE** Top-notch amenities for international business travelers. **ROOMS TO BOOK** Tower Deluxes for access to club lounge (snacks; evening cocktails). **COST** Doubles from $. *2 Charoen Krung Rd.; 800/325-3535 or 66-2/266-0123; www.sheraton.com*

■ **Shangri-La Hotel** Sprawling 2-tower complex with palm-fringed terraces and gardens on the banks of Chao Phraya River. **STATS** 799 rooms; 24 apartments; 6 restaurants; 3 bars. **COMPETITIVE EDGE** Relaxed pool area and great range of facilities give it a beach-resort-in-the-city feel. **ROOMS TO BOOK** Krung Thep-wing rooms are larger and have balconies. **COST** Doubles from $. *89 Wat Suan Plu Soi; 866/565-5050 or 66-2/236-7777; www.shangri-la.com*

■ **The Sukhothai** Sophisticated low-rise surrounded by lotus pools and gardens in the city's financial district. **STATS** 210 rooms; 4 restaurants; 1 bar. **COMPETITIVE EDGE** Ed Tuttle's striking Thai design, combined with a more intimate scale than most city hotels. **ROOMS TO BOOK** Deluxe Terrace Suites with balconies and sun beds. **COST** Doubles from $$. *13/3 South Sathorn Rd.; 800/223-6800 or 66-2/344-8888; www.sukhothai.com*

CHIANG MAI

■ **Four Seasons Resort** Cluster of Thai pavilions surrounded by rice paddies and tropical gardens in the idyllic Mae Rim Valley. **STATS** 80 rooms; 2 restaurants; 1 bar. **COMPETITIVE EDGE** World-class design that delivers an authentic Siamese up-country atmosphere. **ROOMS TO BOOK** Rice Terrace Pavilions, with cozy *salas* overlooking the paddies and resident water buffalo. **COST** Doubles from $$. *800/332-3442 or 66-53/298-181; www.fourseasons.com*

■ **Mandarin Oriental Dhara Dhevi** Sprawling 60-acre resort on the outskirts of Chiang Mai. **STATS** 54 rooms; 69 villas; 4 restaurants; 1 bar. **COMPETITIVE EDGE** Filled with leisure and cultural activities, it's one part resort and one part Epcot Center. **ROOMS TO BOOK** Deluxe Villas, with whirlpool bathtubs and rice-paddy views. **COST** Doubles from $$. *800/526-6566 or 66-53/888-888; www.mandarinoriental.com*

HUA HIN

■ **Chiva-Som International Health Resort** Eastern architecture meets ultramodern Western spa facilities at this 7-acre beachside resort set amid banyan-tree-filled gardens. **STATS** 57 rooms; 3 restaurants; 1 lounge. (Note: no alcohol is served.) **COMPETITIVE EDGE** 150 available treatments delivered by a world-class staff. **ROOM TO BOOK** The Golden Bo suite, with Gulf of Thailand views from every window. **COST** Doubles from $$$$, including all meals, classes, and daily spa treatments. *66-3/253-6536; www.chivasom.com*

PHUKET

■ **Amanpuri** Teak pavilions on 77 acres of jungle headlands above secluded Pansea beach. **STATS** 40 rooms; 30 villas; 2 restaurants; 1 bar. **COMPETITIVE EDGE** The

THE
BEST
OF
2007
——
ASIA

WORLD'S BEST
DIRECTORY

original Aman is still a standard bearer for luxe minimalism. **ROOMS TO BOOK** Nos. 103 and 105 have stunning ocean views. **COST** Doubles from $$$. *800/477-9180 or 66-76/324-333; www.amanpuri.com*

■ **Banyan Tree** Lavish Thai-style villas among the lagoons of Bang Tao Bay. **STATS** 127 villas; 4 restaurants; 2 bars. **COMPETITIVE EDGE** Some of the island's best accommodations; 22 new villas have their own infinity pools. **ROOMS TO BOOK** Lagoon villas with outdoor sunken baths. **COST** Doubles from $$$. *800/745-8883 or 66-76/324-374; www.banyantree.com*

■ **JW Marriott Resort & Spa** Family-friendly resort with 27 acres of tropical gardens, on the Andaman Sea. **STATS** 265 rooms; 5 restaurants; 4 bars. **COMPETITIVE EDGE** Sits on Phuket's quietest beach. **ROOMS TO BOOK** Standards with garden terraces. **COST** Doubles from $$. *800/228-9290 or 66-76/338-000; www.marriott.com*

VIETNAM
HANOI
■ **Sofitel Metropole** White 1901 French-colonial hotel, between Hoan Kiem Lake and the Opera House. **STATS** 232 rooms; 2 restaurants; 3 bars. **COMPETITIVE EDGE** Still the city's best hotel. **ROOMS TO BOOK** Nos. 117, 217, 317, 119, and 219 have large windows that look out to the garden. **COST** Doubles from $$. *15 Ngo Quyen St.; 800/763-4835 or 84-4/826-6919; www.sofitel.com*

NHA TRANG
■ **Evason Hideaway & Six Senses Spa at Ana Mandara** Traditional village with a stylish feel, on a quiet southern beach. **STATS** 74 rooms; 2 restaurants; 3 bars. **COMPETITIVE EDGE** Sound environmental principles that don't compromise comfort. **ROOMS TO BOOK** Ana Mandara suites with direct beach access. **COST** Doubles from $$. *800/525-4800 or 84-58/524-268; www.sixsenses.com*

AUSTRALIA + NEW ZEALAND + THE SOUTH PACIFIC

AUSTRALIA
GREAT BARRIER REEF
■ **Hayman** Pristine private-island resort on the Coral Sea. **STATS** 234 rooms; 4 restaurants; 2 bars. **COMPETITIVE EDGE** An extensive activities program. **ROOMS TO BOOK** The Beach Fronts, with private terraces. **COST** Doubles from $$. *800/223-6800 or 61-7/4940-1234; www.hayman.com.au*

■ **Voyages Dunk Island** Cabana-style rooms on a private rain-forest island. **STATS** 160 rooms; 5 restaurants; 3 bars. **COMPETITIVE EDGE** The Great Barrier Reef is a short cruise away. **ROOMS TO BOOK** Beachfront Suites, with split-level interiors and direct beach access. **COST** Doubles from $$. *61-2/8296-8010 or 61-7/4068-8199; www.voyages.com.au*

■ **Voyages Lizard Island** 2,500-acre retreat with clapboard bungalows surrounded by forest and 24 beaches. **STATS** 40 rooms; 1 restaurant; 1 bar. **COMPETITIVE EDGE** Ultra-secluded, with great snorkeling and diving. **ROOMS TO BOOK** The Sunset Point Villas. **COST** Doubles from $$$, including meals. *800/225-9849 or 61-2/8296-8010; www.lizardisland.com.au*

MELBOURNE
■ **Crown Towers** High-rise on the southern bank of the Yarra River near the business district. **STATS** 482 rooms; 7 restaurants; 2 bars. **COMPETITIVE EDGE** All-in-one location attached to the Crown Entertainment Complex. **ROOMS TO BOOK** Crystal Clubs, for access to the 24-hour lounge. **COST** Doubles from $$$. *8 Whiteman St., Southbank; 61-3/9292-6868; www.crowntowers.com.au*

■ **Park Hyatt** Discreet low-rise hotel with marble lobby, next to the Fitzroy Gardens. **STATS** 240 rooms; 1 restaurant; 1 bar. **COMPETITIVE EDGE** The most residential feeling of the city's top hotels. **ROOMS TO BOOK** Terrace Suites in the Cathedral Tower overlook St. Patrick's. **COST** Doubles from $$. *1 Parliament Square; 800/233-1234 or 61-3/9224-1234; www.park.hyatt.com*

■ **Grand Hyatt** Curving 33-story tower with Art Deco-inspired interiors. **STATS** 548 rooms; 1 restaurant; 3 bars. **COMPETITIVE EDGE** The location, on prestigious Collins Street. **ROOMS TO BOOK** Those ending in -07 above the 25th floor, for 180-degree views of the Yarra River. **COST** Doubles from $. *123 Collins St.; 800/633-7313 or 61-3/9657-1234; www.hyatt.com*

PALM COVE
■ **Sebel Reef House & Spa** Intimate colonial-style hotel in an oceanside village. **STATS** 69 rooms; 2 restaurants; 1 bar. **COMPETITIVE EDGE** Sophisticated but low-key ambience on the beach. **ROOMS TO BOOK** Brigadier Beachfront Spa Rooms, for ocean views. **COST** Doubles from $. *61-7/4055-3633; www.reefhouse.com.au*

SYDNEY
■ **Amora Hotel Jamison** Modern tower in the business district. **STATS** 415 rooms; 2 restaurants; 2 bars. **COMPETITIVE EDGE** Stylish, urban vibe. **ROOMS TO BOOK** Amora Clubs, for views and lounge access. **COST** Doubles from $$. *11 Jamison St.; 61-2/9696-2500; www.amorahotels.com*

■ **Blue** Refurbished wharf building with views of downtown Sydney. **STATS** 100 rooms; 1 restaurant; 1 bar. **COMPETITIVE EDGE** A blend of historic charm and contemporary chic on the waterfront. **ROOMS TO BOOK** Loft Suites, split-level rooms with views of the pier or marina. **COST** Doubles from $$. *6 Cowper Wharf Rd.; 866/969-1825 or 61-21/9331-9000; www.tajhotels.com*

■ **Four Seasons Hotel** Modern skyscraper in the Rocks district. **STATS** 531 rooms; 2 restaurants; 1 bar. **COMPETITIVE EDGE** General polish with top-notch service. **ROOMS TO BOOK** Full Harbour Views above the 15th floor. **COST** Doubles from $$. *199 George St.;*

THE
BEST
OF
2007
—
AUSTRALIA
+
NEW
ZEALAND
+
THE SOUTH
PACIFIC

WORLD'S BEST
DIRECTORY

800/819-5053 or 61-2/9238-0000;
www.fourseasons.com

■ **The InterContinental**
Neoclassical building near the Circular Quay. **STATS** 509 rooms; 3 restaurants; 3 bars. **COMPETITIVE EDGE** Its location between the business district and the botanical gardens. **ROOMS TO BOOK** Governor Suites, for harbor views. **COST** Doubles from $$. *Bridge St. at Phillip St.; 888/424-6835 or 61-2/9253-9000; www.sydney.intercontinental.com*

■ **Observatory Hotel** Sophisticated property modeled after a 19th-century manor. **STATS** 100 rooms; 2 restaurants; 1 bar. **COMPETITIVE EDGE** Comfortable and refined—more private residence than hotel. **ROOMS TO BOOK** Nos. 322, 324, 326, or 328—the only Suites and Deluxes with terraces. **COST** Doubles from $$$. *89-113 Kent St.; 61-2/9256-2222; www.observatoryhotel.com.au*

■ **Park Hyatt** Art-filled low-rise on its own jetty, across from the Opera House. **STATS** 158 rooms; 1 restaurant; 2 bars. **COMPETITIVE EDGE** The harborside location. **ROOMS TO BOOK** Opera Kings, for uninterrupted views. **COST** Doubles from $$. *7 Hickson Rd., The Rocks; 800/223-1234 or 61-2/9241-1234; www.park.hyatt.com*

■ **Shangri-La Hotel** High-rise in the central business district, redone in 2005. **STATS** 563 rooms; 3 restaurants; 3 bars. **COMPETITIVE EDGE** Spacious rooms, some with Sydney Harbour views. **ROOMS TO BOOK** Deluxe Grand Harbour Views. **COST** Doubles from $$. *176 Cumberland St.; 866/565-5050 or 61-2/9250-6000; www.shangri-la.com*

■ **The Westin** Former post office and skyscraper. **STATS** 416 rooms; 1 restaurant; 1 bar. **COMPETITIVE EDGE** The best for location for business travelers. **ROOMS TO BOOK** Those in the Heritage wing, for historic style. **COST** Doubles from $$. *1 Martin Place; 800/937-8461 or 61-2/8223-1111; www.westin.com.au*

TASMANIA
■ **Voyages Cradle Mountain Lodge** Timber cabins in the Tasmanian

wilderness at the edge of Lake St. Clair National Park. **STATS** 86 rooms; 2 restaurants; 1 bar. **COMPETITIVE EDGE** The park, with lakes and rugged peaks, is 100 yards away. **ROOMS TO BOOK** Spa Suites, with private verandas, fireplaces, and spa tubs. **COST** Doubles from $. *61-2/8296-8010 or 613/6492-1303; www.voyages.com.au*

ULURU (AYERS ROCK)
■ **Voyages Longitude 131°** Palatial tents on an isolated sand dune in the outback. **STATS** 15 rooms; 1 restaurant; 1 bar. **COMPETITIVE EDGE** Desert setting with uninterrupted views of Ayers Rock. **ROOMS TO BOOK** Tents 12 through 15, for privacy. **COST** Doubles from $$$$$, including meals. *800/525-4800 or 61-8/8296-8010; www.voyages.com.au*

FIJI
TURTLE ISLAND
■ **Turtle Island** Thatched cottages and 14 beaches on a private South Pacific island. **STATS** 14 rooms; 1 restaurant; 1 bar. **COMPETITIVE EDGE** A hideaway with superb service. **ROOM TO BOOK** The most private, Vonu Point. **COST** Doubles from $$$$$, including meals and drinks. *800/255-4347 or 679/666-3889; www.turtlefiji.com*

FRENCH POLYNESIA
BORA-BORA
■ **Bora Bora Lagoon Resort & Spa** Cluster of thatched-roof bungalows with elegant interiors. **STATS** 76 bungalows; 2 restaurants; 2 bars. **COMPETITIVE EDGE** The excellent Marù Spa. **ROOMS TO BOOK** Overwater rooms at the end of pontoons. **COST** Doubles from $$$. *800/860-4095 or 689/604-000; www.boraboralagoon.com*

■ **Bora Bora Pearl Beach Resort & Spa** Traditional bungalows on 46 waterfront acres. **STATS** 30 suites; 50 bungalows; 3 restaurants; 2 bars. **COMPETITIVE EDGE** Unbeatable diving facilities. **ROOMS TO BOOK** Premium overwater bungalows with Mount Otemanu views. **COST** Doubles from $$$. *Vaitape; 800/657-3275 or 689/508-453; www.pearlresorts.com*

■ **Hotel Bora Bora** Rattan and bamboo suites surrounded by gardens

along the beach. **STATS** 54 rooms; 1 restaurant; 2 bars. **COMPETITIVE EDGE** Polynesian culture (pandanus roofs, overwater suites) gets the Aman treatment. **ROOMS TO BOOK** Pool Farés, with pools and sundecks. **COST** Doubles from $$$. *Point Raititi; 800/421-1490 or 689/604-411; www.amanresorts.com*

MOOREA
■ **Moorea Pearl Resort & Spa** Private bungalows along white-sand beaches. **STATS** 30 rooms; 65 bungalows; 2 restaurants; 1 bar. **COMPETITIVE EDGE** Great access to nature, from mountain hikes to reef dives. **ROOMS TO BOOK** Deluxe Garden Bungalows with pools. **COST** Doubles from $$. *800/657-3275 or 686-50/8452; www.pearlresorts.com*

NEW ZEALAND
AUCKLAND
■ **Stamford Plaza** Modern business hotel, polished by a $10 million face-lift. **STATS** 282 rooms; 2 restaurants; 1 bar. **COMPETITIVE EDGE** It's a three-minute walk from Auckland Harbor. **ROOMS TO BOOK** Spacious Deluxe rooms on the ninth and tenth floors. **COST** Doubles from $. *22 Lower Albert St.; 64-9/309-8888; www.stamford.com.au*

QUEENSTOWN
■ **Millbrook** French provincial-style retreat in an alpine amphitheater. **STATS** 170 rooms; 3 restaurants; 1 bar. **COMPETITIVE EDGE** Majestic scenery, yet only a 20-minute drive to Queenstown. **ROOMS TO BOOK** One of the north-facing Hotel Villas; you'll wake up to morning light on snowcapped peaks. **COST** Doubles from $$. *64-3/441-7000; www.millbrook.co.nz*

TAUPO
■ **Huka Lodge** North Island fishing lodge on 17 acres, along the banks of the Waikato River. **STATS** 24 rooms; 1 restaurant; 1 bar. **COMPETITIVE EDGE** An ultra-luxe experience in the rustic countryside. **ROOMS TO BOOK** Those with their own fireplaces (4, 13, 16, and 19). **COST** Doubles from $$$$$, including breakfast, dinner, and drinks. *800/525-4800 or 64-7/378-5791; www.hukalodge.com*

Singita Private
Game Reserve,
Sabi Sands,
South Africa.

Hotel Index

Geographic Index

Contributors

Gini Alhadeff

Richard Alleman

Tom Austin

Luke Barr

Raul Barreneche

Rich Beattie

Laura Begley

Alan Brown

Jay Cheshes

Christopher R. Cox

Gillian Cullinan

Meghan Daum

Josh Dean

Simon Elegant

Mark Ellwood

Amy Farley

Andrew Ferren

Charles Gandee

Jaime Gross

Michael Gross

Michael Hannwacker

Darrell Hartman

James Patrick Herman

Tina Isaac

Karrie Jacobs

George Kalogerakis

Xander Kaplan

David Kaufman

David A. Keeps

Karen Keller

Peter Jon Lindberg

Nathan Lump

Bruno Maddox

Alexandra Marshall

Rob McKeown

Daphne Merkin

William Middleton

Clark Mitchell

Heidi Sherman Mitchell

Shane Mitchell

Bob Morris

Celeste Moure

Mitchell Owens

Attila Pelit

Christopher Petkanas

Sarah Maud Powell

Kevin Raub

Douglas Rogers

David Samuels

Maria Shollenbarger

Horacio Silva

Emma Sloley

Meline Toumani

Guy Trebay

Tom Vanderbilt

Valerie Waterhouse

Sally Webb

Amy Wilentz

Elizabeth Woodson

Photographers

Travel + Leisure is the premier chronicler of the way we travel now. The magazine explores the places, the ideas, and the trends that define modern global culture while delivering clear, comprehensive service journalism. Intelligent writing, evocative photography, and accessible design inform every article. Whether covering hotels, restaurants, the arts, and shopping, or politics, security, and industry innovations, T+L is the authority for the discerning traveler. Visit us at travelandleisure.com.